THE TERRORIST WATCH

THE
TERRORIST
WATCH

INSIDE THE DESPERATE RACE
TO STOP THE NEXT ATTACK

RONALD KESSLER

THREE RIVERS PRESS
NEW YORK

Three Rivers Press and the Tugboat design are
registered trademarks of Random House, Inc.

Originally published in hardcover in the United States by
Crown Forum, an imprint of the Crown Publishing Group,
a division of Random House, Inc., New York, in 2007.

Library of Congress Cataloging-in-Publication Data

Kessler, Ronald.
    The terrorist watch : inside the desperate race to stop the next attack / Ronald
Kessler. — 1st ed.
        p. cm.
    Includes index.
    1. Terrorism—Prevention.   2. Terrorism—Government policy—United States.
3. Intelligence service—United States.   4. War on Terrorism, 2001–   I. Title.
HV6431.K424 2007
363.325'170973—dc22

                                                                    2007031641

                            978-0-307-38214-6

                   Printed in the United States of America

                        Design by Leonard Henderson

                        10 9 8 7 6 5 4 3 2 1

                        First Paperback Edition

For Pam, Rachel, and Greg Kessler

CONTENTS

THE TERRORIST WATCH

PROLOGUE

FBI SPECIAL AGENT Arthur M. (Art) Cummings jumped into his Chrysler 300 with tinted windows and turned on the flashing blue and red lights. Pulling out of the parking garage under the Washington Field Office, he raced through the downtown traffic out to the National Counterterrorism Center (NCTC) in McLean, Virginia.

It was August 3, 2006, and Willie T. Hulon, who heads the FBI's National Security Branch, had just told Cummings that British authorities were poised to take down a plot to explode nine American airliners in flight from London.

Since December 2005, the FBI, CIA, and National Counterterrorism Center (NCTC) had been monitoring the plot. The CIA had been helping the British Security Service, known as MI5, with analysis. At first the agencies thought the British jihadists were planning an attack inside Great Britain. But on August 3, British wiretaps picked up the plotters checking on airline schedules to the United States. Hulon placed Cummings in charge of the FBI's response.

Now the question was when to arrest the twenty-four plotters. If Scotland Yard and the British MI5 waited too long, some of the terrorists could proceed with their plans and kill thousands. If they moved on the terrorists too soon, the agencies risked not learning enough about who else might be involved and might be planning other attacks.

That quandary was at the heart of what Cummings did every day. It was a question that kept him awake at night, one that made other agents literally sick. One of Cummings's bosses told him flatly: "If there's another attack, it's your ass."

1

Cummings knew that was true in more ways than one. Al Qaeda was intent on acquiring devices that could kill millions of Americans and usher in another dark age.

"You make a mistake, there are dead people," Cummings would say.

An agent since 1987, Cummings had worked nearly every kind of FBI case—counterintelligence, violent crimes, drugs, child molestation— before focusing on terrorism. Cummings, forty-eight, was born in Washington, D.C., where his father was working with the Department of Agriculture. Later his father was assigned to Pakistan and Brazil, where Cummings lived as a kid. Once fluent in Portuguese, he now can't recall a single word. After graduating from Bowie High School in Maryland, Cummings joined the Navy SEALs, then attended the University of California. After college, he applied to the Drug Enforcement Agency and the FBI. Both offered him jobs, but the FBI offered more money.

The risk of being a federal agent would not bother him. In a way, he was used to taking risks. All through college and the Navy, Cummings had two motorcycles, a BMW 650 and a Honda 900. When he married his wife, Ellen, in 1982, she made him promise not to ride motorcycles, and he sold them. In the Navy and in the FBI, Cummings had made 160 parachute jumps from airplanes. When he decided to go skydiving for fun, she said, "I'm just going to require one thing: Why don't you sit down and write a good-bye letter to each of your kids, just in case?" That was the end of his skydiving.

Cummings was running a counterterrorism squad in the FBI's Richmond Field Office when 9/11 happened. That afternoon, Dale L. Watson, who was in charge of the FBI's national counterterrorism effort, called Cummings frantically. He considered Cummings a sharp operator who was not afraid to tell his bosses exactly what he thought. Watson needed him in Washington. He gave him until midnight to get there.

Cummings arrived at 11:30 P.M. Working fourteen-hour days, he wound up living in a Marriott Hotel at Ninth and F Streets NW for three months. After that, Cummings stayed in Washington, shuttling back and forth between headquarters, the Washington Field Office, and the NCTC in McLean, and going home to his wife in Richmond on the weekends. Cummings also did a stint at Guantánamo Bay where he interrogated prisoners.

Now, as a deputy assistant director of the Counterterrorism Division, Cummings was in charge of all international counterterrorism operations. When Joe Billy Jr., the chief of counterterrorism, was away, Cummings was the number one FBI official in charge of counterterrorism. So today, as the British plot reached a boiling point, Cummings had gotten the call to come to the NCTC and take charge of the FBI's response. That involved finding out if the plotters had accomplices who were planning a direct attack on the United States.

Cummings finally slowed his car down and turned off the flashing lights as he approached the winding drive to the NCTC. The restricted U.S. government installation, a six-story building, gleamed white in the summer sun. A nearby building with highly reflective glass looks more forbidding, but this one is the real thing and you can almost see into its windows. From overhead, the NCTC building looks like an ×, as in × marks the spot, they like to say.

A member of the "United States Police"—actually the CIA's security force—came out of the guard house to check Cummings's FBI credentials, as the officer's walkie-talkie crackled with ten-fours. Cummings parked his FBI car, leaving his .40 caliber Glock in the glove compartment.

Heading toward the NCTC entrance in the back of the building, he passed through a paved terrace that serves as informal meeting ground. Few people take the time to sit on the benches and enjoy the massed begonias in bloom and the dark blush of the crape myrtles. In the center of the terrace is a flagpole flying the Stars and Stripes. When he reached the lobby, he crossed two large welcome mats bearing the words *Liberty Crossing*.

Liberty Crossing is the name of the building that houses the

NCTC and large components of the FBI's and CIA's counterterrorism efforts. According to the media and politicians, the FBI and the CIA don't talk to each other. Cummings knew that was rubbish. Prior to 9/11, Cummings had to plead with his bosses to allow him to combine what he knew from intelligence sources and criminal sources, a result of the so-called wall that separated criminal and intelligence cases. But now those walls did not exist.

Established in 2005, the NCTC integrated the intelligence community. Here, dozens of analysts from the CIA, FBI, National Security Agency (NSA), and other intelligence agencies sit side by side, sharing intelligence and tracking threats twenty-four hours a day. In addition, major portions of the FBI's Counterterrorism Division and the CIA's Counterterrorism Center make their offices at the NCTC.

Cummings swiped his ID at a turnstile in the lobby. He wasn't required to pass through a metal detector, but he had still chosen to leave his Glock out in the car. The NCTC building is owned and operated by the CIA, which is hinky about weapons in the building. Besides, carrying a weapon feeds into the stereotype that many in the CIA have of FBI agents as dumb cops who want to arrest everyone, as opposed to intelligence operators who want to infiltrate plots and stop them.

As far as Cummings was concerned, that stereotype was a crock. Cummings considered intelligence a fancy name for information. The FBI had been using intelligence since it pursued tips to close in on John Dillinger on July 22, 1934, at the Biograph Theater in Chicago. But since 9/11, the FBI had expanded its ability to acquire and analyze intelligence. Moreover, under FBI Director Robert S. Mueller III, the FBI's primary goal had become preventing another attack. Those were the changes that the media missed. In fact, Cummings had been in many discussions where the FBI sat at the table with the intelligence community and argued for continued collection while the CIA argued for a takedown.

Cummings was at the forefront of the effort to change the FBI culture. When an agent says he wants to arrest a suspect on some alien violations, Cummings tells the agent: "So you're telling me you've done your job, you know everything there is to know about him, his organization, everything around him, all his travel, all his friends, and all family members? He's not a viable source, and he's not producing any productive intelligence whatsoever?"

Often, there's silence. Cummings is a master of eye contact, and his receding hairline emphasizes the intensity. His magnetic blue, power-point eyes direct energy toward his listener.

Cummings says to the agent, "This is a deliberate judgment you have to make. Your objective is not to make the arrest. Your objective is to make that suspect our collection platform. That guy now is going to tell us just how big and broad the threat might be. He now becomes a means to collection, instead of the target of collection. I want you to understand his entire universe." And, Cummings tells the agent, "If he's not a viable source, and his intelligence isn't productive, then knock yourself out and use your law enforcement powers to make that arrest."

Inside the NCTC, all sections of offices are secure, and most doors have a cipher lock, requiring the entry of lengthy codes on key pads to enter. The offices inside, with their desks of warm-colored wood and geometric-patterned carpeting in wheat and gray, appear to be all seriousness, except for the occasional personal touch to the name plate, such as multiple M&M stickers.

After British authorities let U.S. intelligence officials know about the latest developments, Cummings was briefed on the British airliner plot. From his office at the NCTC, he began issuing orders for wiretaps and physical surveillance of terrorist suspects in the United States. The objective was to pick up clues from how the suspects reacted when they heard the news of the arrests in Great Britain. "Our focus is: Is there anything bad that could kill us here?" Cummings said.

"Let's get this on. Let's go," Cummings told his agents. "Give me everything we've got on these guys. I need to know everybody who's ever touched any of these guys ever in their lives, from the time they were born. Every person these guys have ever spoken to, paid, run into. Who went to school with them, had any type of contact with them, any type of communication with family members, friends of family, all of them. I want financials, associates, travel. Start giving me numbers that I can start working with. Put on technical [wiretaps and bugs] surveillance 24/7, wake 'em up, put 'em to bed. Every single piece has to be reviewed and looked at, not just for threats, but for opportunity."

Cummings participated in daily secure video conferences with the British MI5. He considered the plotters to be "very operational, really serious guys, no games, with significant connections to al Qaeda." Indeed, it later developed that some of those involved in the operation in the United Kingdom had trained in Pakistan and had associations with al Qaeda figures there. The plot was, in fact, inspired by al Qaeda.

Cummings argued for continuing to monitor the plotters as long as possible. But the Pakistanis lost track of one of the suspects in Pakistan. When they finally found him, they arrested him. The dominoes started falling. News of his arrest would travel quickly to the other plotters, and they would be on the move.

"Either they're going to start killing people, or they're going to start running," Cummings figured. "That's it. They're not going to sit there and wait for the cops to come get them."

At 3:00 A.M. on August 10, 2006, FBI headquarters called Cummings at his apartment in Rosslyn, Virginia, to tell him the plot had been taken down. That meant the FBI would expand its investigation of the suspects and all of their contacts.

"Okay," he said. "I guess we gotta rock and roll."

1

"WE'RE AT WAR"

AT 8 A.M. ON Tuesday, September 11, 2001, President George W. Bush sat down for his daily intelligence briefing from the CIA's Michael Morell. They were in Bush's suite at the Colony Beach and Tennis Resort on Longboat Key, an eleven-mile-long barrier island between the Gulf of Mexico and Sarasota Bay off the coast of Florida. It was a gorgeous day, the sky crystal clear.

Morell is preppy and boyish with light brown hair tufted at the part. Soft spoken, he speaks the clear, precise language of the briefer, choosing his words well and effortlessly.

"As soon as the briefing was over, I went down and got into my place in the motorcade, which was the van carrying the senior staff, so it was Karl Rove and Dan Bartlett and Ari Fleischer," Morell recalls. "And it was on the drive from the Colony Resort to the school that Ari Fleischer's phone rang, and he answered his phone. He chatted with somebody for about five seconds, and he turned around and said, 'Michael, do you know anything about a plane hitting the World Trade Center?' And I said, 'No, I'll make some calls.'"

At that point, everyone thought a small airplane had lost its way. Morell called the CIA operations center and learned that the airplane was a commercial jet. A few minutes later, the second plane hit, clinching the fact that it was a terrorist attack.

As Bush read to children at Emma E. Booker Elementary School,

Andrew H. (Andy) Card, Jr., his chief of staff, whispered to him that a second plane had hit the south tower.

"America is under attack," Card said.

After letting the news sink in, Bush cut short his presentation, apologizing to the principal, Gwendolyn Tosé-Rigell. From a secure phone in the next room, he called Vice President Dick Cheney and FBI Director Mueller. Bush watched videos of the attacks on a television that had been wheeled in on a cart. Flame and smoke engulfed both towers, and people were jumping from windows.

"We're at war," Bush announced to his aides—Card, Fleischer, Rove, and Bartlett.

"The president wrote out what he was going to say to the nation when he went back into the classroom," Morell says. "He went back into the classroom, and the Secret Service said to us, as soon as he's done in there, we're going to *Air Force One*, so if you're not in the motorcade, you're going to be left behind. So everybody kind of rushed out into the motorcade and went back to *Air Force One*."

As they were flying from Barksdale Air Force Base in Louisiana to Omaha, Bush asked to see him.

"Who do you think did this?" Bush asked.

Morell's right hand is like another person in the room—tapping fingers, wiggling fingers, his index finger in the air to make a point. When he mentions George Bush, Morell makes a loose fist with the thumb sitting on top. When he refers to protecting the American people, his hand makes a kind of fence on the arm of his chair.

"There's a couple of countries who have the capability to do this—Iran and Iraq would have the capabilities to do this," Morell said. "But they've got nothing to gain, and everything to lose, in doing this. I don't think it's one of those countries. There's no evidence, there's no data, but I would pretty much bet everything I own that the trail will end with al Qaeda and bin Laden."

"When will we know?" Bush asked.

Morell reviewed previous al Qaeda attacks—the one of the USS

Cole and the detonation of two truck bombs that killed 224 people, including twelve Americans, at U.S. embassies in Kenya and Tanzania. He recounted how and when the United States determined that the terrorist group was behind them.

At that moment, the CIA had already linked three of the hijackers to al Qaeda.

"They had done name traces on the flight manifests," Morell says. "And when we got to Omaha, and we got to the briefing area, George Tenet [the director of Central Intelligence] briefed the president on the fact that we already knew three of these guys were al Qaeda."

At 8:30 that evening, Bush spoke to the nation. In a speech he gave in 1999 at The Citadel military academy, he had said that those who sponsored terrorism or attacks on the United States could expect a "devastating" response. Mike Gerson, Bush's chief speechwriter, enlarged on that text to say that the United States will "make no distinction between those who planned these acts and those who permitted or tolerated or encouraged them."

Bush felt that was "way too vague." Instead, he wanted to use the word "harbor." The final sentence read: "We will make no distinction between those who planned these acts and those who harbor them."

This not only expanded the definition of the enemy, but also shifted the burden of proof the United States would use in pursuing those who support terrorism. Instead of having to show that another country was aware of and permitted terrorists to operate within its borders, the United States would now use military force or apply diplomatic pressure on countries simply because terrorists lived there.

This declaration became known as the Bush Doctrine. It was a sea change in foreign policy, one that made all the difference in the war on terror; now Arab countries began turning over terrorists to the United States and providing intelligence leads.

"It was during those moments when I was with the president that

I saw this determination," Morell says. "And it was in the days after, in the Oval Office every morning, that I saw this determination for not only bringing to justice those folks who did 9/11, but doing everything in his power and authority to make sure that it didn't happen again."

2

DOUBLE WHAMMY

A T 8:45 ON the morning of September 11, Robert Mueller was planning a brown bag lunch with reporters when his secretary told him to turn on the TV. Wearing his usual dark blue Brooks Brothers suit, a white shirt, and a red tie, he had been sworn in as FBI director just seven days earlier.

A man with a craggy face, graying black hair, and ram-rod posture, Mueller rushed down the stark white corridors of FBI headquarters from the fifth floor to the Strategic Information Operations Center (SIOC). It was a twenty-million-dollar, twenty-room complex of phones, secure computers, and video screens.

A Princeton graduate, Mueller served in the Vietnam War and was awarded a Bronze Star and a Purple Heart. After the Marines, Mueller thought he would like to become an FBI agent. That in mind, he obtained a law degree in 1973 from the University of Virginia Law School. But instead of joining the FBI, Mueller became a prosecutor, first in the U.S. Attorney's office in San Francisco and then in Boston, where he was placed in charge of the Criminal Division. Along the way, Mueller married his high school sweetheart, Ann Standish.

In 1990, Mueller became assistant attorney general in charge of the Criminal Division of the Justice Department. In that position, he supervised prosecutions of John Gotti, the Libyan suspects indicted in the bombing of Pan Am 103, and Panamanian leader Manuel Noriega.

Mueller left Justice in 1993 to become a partner in the prestigious

11

Boston law firm of Hale and Dorr. But Mueller hated private practice. One day he called Eric H. Holder Jr., the U.S. Attorney in Washington. When Mueller headed the Criminal Division, Holder had reported to him. Now Mueller was calling him to apply for a job.

"He called up out of the blue and said he wanted to try murder cases," Holder says. "I was like, 'What?' Here's this guy who was the former assistant attorney general, the head of the Criminal Division. He came to the U.S. Attorney's office and tried cases as a line guy."

Having tossed aside his $400,000-a-year partnership for a government salary in May 1995, Mueller began prosecuting knifings, batterings, and shootings. He answered the phone, "Mueller, Homicide." Tough and businesslike in court, Mueller worked from color-coded files with plastic labels. A colleague called him a "well-organized pit bull."

In 1996, Mueller became chief of the Homicide Section. He poked his head into every corner of the criminal justice system, including the morgue.

Mueller went on to become U.S. attorney in San Francisco, at first on an interim basis. In August 1998, President Clinton nominated him for the position, and in October 1999 he was confirmed. After President Bush took office, Mueller became acting deputy attorney general.

Bush announced Mueller's nomination as FBI director in a Rose Garden press conference on July 5, 2001. Mueller, fifty-six, spoke for forty-eight seconds, thanking Bush several times.

Several weeks before taking over, Mueller met with Bob Dies, the FBI's new computer guru. Mueller listed standard software such as Microsoft Office that he wanted on his computer. Dies told him he could have it installed, but none of it would work with anything else in the bureau. Mueller was flabbergasted.

Mueller was a sharp contrast to Louis Freeh, the previous FBI director. Freeh, who was appointed by Bill Clinton in 1993, never used a computer or e-mail. Mueller was a proponent of new technology. In

1989, he bought a Gateway computer for his home so he could tally items for taxes more easily with a Quicken program. When he was U.S. Attorney in San Francisco, he tasked a talented computer programmer to create new software for tracking cases. The program—called Alcatraz—was adopted by U.S. Attorney offices throughout the country.

The state of the FBI's computers went back to Freeh and his aversion to technology. Freeh's concept of investigations was limited to what he had done as an agent ten years earlier—knocking on doors and interviewing people. He did not understand how essential technology had become to law enforcement.

Weldon L. Kennedy, who was appointed by Freeh to be associate deputy director for administration, remembers that Freeh kept a computer on the credenza behind his desk.

"I never saw him use it, nor did I ever see it turned on," Kennedy says.

Because of the lack of computers, the FBI could not handle all the intelligence that poured in. While the agents were smart and dedicated, they had few analysts who could sift through the data and connect the dots to try to zero in on potential investigative targets.

Robert M. Blitzer, who was in charge of counterterrorism in headquarters, recalled being inundated by threats and leads coming in from the CIA, State Department, NSA, and Defense Intelligence Agency (DIA).

"The FBI, because of lack of resources, was not able to analyze and exploit all of the intelligence on bin Laden," Blitzer says. "I would have reams of stuff on my desk. It was frantic. I came in on weekends. There was an ocean of work. We got thousands of threats every year. I would ask myself, 'What should we do with this? Is it real or not? Where should I send it?' We were trying to make sense of it. I don't think we ever came to grips with it."

The FBI should have been recruiting Arab-American agents to develop informants, Blitzer says. "We had no infrastructure. We had no analysts. Agents had to share computers. . . . If an agent could find a computer, he typed up his reports himself. We couldn't afford to pay stenographers. We were paying agents $80,000 to $90,000 a year to type up reports."

While the terrorists communicated by code on the Internet, agents had computers that lacked CD-ROM drives. Because of the lack of analysts and computers, "We didn't know what we had," says Robert M. "Bear" Bryant, a former deputy director. "We didn't know what we knew."

When Mueller took over, the FBI's personal computers were so primitive that no one would take them even as a donation to a church. They were pre-Pentium machines, incapable of using the current software or even working with a mouse. "I am good on computers and couldn't figure out the FBI's computers, which were 386s," Blitzer says. The FBI's internal e-mail was so slow that agents used their personal e-mail addresses instead. The FBI system did not allow e-mail outside the agency. Often because of funds from the Justice Department, local police were far more technologically advanced than the bureau. Because few of the FBI's computers could handle graphics, agents would ask local police departments to e-mail photos of suspects to their home computers.

Just before 9/11, Mueller began ordering thousands of new Dell computers. But the bureau's mainframe computer system was so flawed that memos sent to agents never arrived, and there was no way for the sender to know if a memo had been received. To store a single document on the FBI's Automated Case Support system required twelve separate computer commands. On these green-screen terminals, the FBI could search for the word "flight" or the word "schools"—retrieving millions of documents each time—but not for "flight schools." The CIA, in contrast, had been able to perform searches for "flight schools" on its computers since 1958.

Mueller, having just moved into his office on September 4, was hit with the double-whammy of dealing with the attacks and trying to uncover plans for new attacks while learning what his job entailed.

When the second plane hit the World Trade Center, Dale Watson, chief of counterterrorism, was already in the command center conducting a briefing. Mueller placed Tom Pickard, deputy FBI director, in charge of the investigation with Dale Watson under him.

Assuming that FBI headquarters would be the next target, nonessential employees were being evacuated from the J. Edgar Hoover Building, a monstrosity on Pennsylvania Avenue between Ninth and Tenth Streets NW, and a monument to the former FBI director's authoritarian rule.

The building, which was occupied by the FBI in 1974, is a skewed tetrahedron, not quite a square. To conform with local restrictions, the building is seven stories along Pennsylvania Avenue and rises to eleven stories in the rear. From the side, the grotesque overhang at the rear gives the impression that the building is about to topple over on pedestrians below.

On 9/11, the backup to leave the FBI's underground garage was half an hour. Police blocked off Ninth and Tenth Streets alongside headquarters. Bomb-sniffing dogs and the FBI Police armed with submachine guns patrolled the perimeter. The FBI tour was canceled indefinitely.

Because flight attendants on the doomed planes had called in the seat numbers of some of the hijackers, FBI agents began matching seat assignments with the hijackers' names on flight manifests. Agents ran out leads from credit card and telephone records. Anyone who shared a residence or a hotel room with a hijacker was placed on a growing watch list.

Attorney General John Ashcroft asked the FBI for a list of terrorist suspects who might be under surveillance. He was told the FBI had no such list. The files were spread over the country, and they were all paper records. When Ashcroft asked why the FBI did not have such information in computers, he was told the bureau had at least forty computer systems, but most of them could not talk to each other.

To work around the primitive Automated Case Support System,

FBI agents had designed Rapid Start. This makeshift system kept track of investigative reports at the scene of a crime but it could not manage a big case. Still, because of Freeh's contempt for technology, that was all the bureau had. As reports and leads poured in about the attacks, Rapid Start became so overloaded that documents could not be retrieved. This led to more delays.

Even worse, because Rapid Start had no links to field offices, reports had to be downloaded and individually transmitted to the Automated Case Support System in each field office. The process was unreliable, and agents at the SIOC would often call and fax leads to the field. Dozens of fax machines lined the walls, flooding the Strategic Information Operations Center (SIOC) with paper.

"Sometimes, three teams of agents were dispatched to one house when only one team should have been sent, because we had three duplicative leads being sent out," Bob Dies says. "Meanwhile, we needed those extra agents to work other leads."

In some cases, leads were not covered for days because the downloaded material never showed up, so no follow-up calls were made or faxes sent.

There was "a degree of pandemonium," according to one of the FBI officials in the SIOC.

Within a day, the FBI noticed that no family members were calling airlines to learn about the fate of certain passengers.

"All of a sudden, it was clear to us from the manifest, working with the airlines, there were nineteen guys whose relatives didn't call," Art Cummings says. "That immediately pointed to the hijackers."

The next question was, who was supporting them and were more attacks coming?

"I didn't believe for one minute there were nineteen guys in the U.S. who didn't have an infrastructure within the U.S.," Cummings says. "We were going a thousand miles an hour looking for somebody that was going to come back and hit us. We were on our knees, and we thought if we were hit again, we really were going to be crushed."

Since all four planes had five hijackers (except Flight 93, which crashed in Pennsylvania), it appeared there was a twentieth hijacker somewhere.

"We were frantic to find him," Cummings says. "The guy right now who's probably the best guess is al-Qahtani."

The Saudi, identified only as al-Qahtani, was turned away by a U.S. immigration agent at Orlando International Airport in late August 2001. The agent became suspicious when al-Qahtani provided only vague answers to questions about what he was doing in the United States. He could not provide names of people meeting him at the airport or describe where he was staying.

"He came into Orlando previously, was denied entry, and was fingerprinted," Cummings says. "While he was in the airport the second time, Mohammed Atta received a phone call from that airport. We never knew who made the call. And then this guy showed up in Gitmo. They picked him up on the battlefield, and they ran his print. That print was the same print of a guy that showed up at the airport before 9/11. Then a smart analyst went, 'Wait a minute, whoa, what airport?' The answer was Orlando. So he goes, 'Wait a minute. There was a call to Mohammed Atta on exactly that same day, from that airport, and it was exactly in the one-hour window that the guy was there.' So we knew it was this guy. Then we did a little searching, and it looked like he was coming in to be the twentieth hijacker and was denied entry."

U.S. agents put al-Qahtani on a plane back to Saudi Arabia. He later wound up in Afghanistan, where U.S. forces captured him. Eventually, he was transferred to the detention center at Guantánamo Bay in Cuba.

In Cummings's opinion, Zacarias Moussaoui, who claimed to be the twentieth hijacker, saw himself as someone of the stature of Mohammed Atta, the leader of the 9/11 attack team. A thirty-three-year-old French national of Moroccan descent, Moussaoui was taking lessons at the Pan Am Flight Academy in Eagan, Minnesota, before

9/11. On August 15, 2001, a school official called the FBI and reported that Moussaoui wanted to concentrate on navigation and midair turns, not landings or takeoffs. He lacked flight skills and was belligerent and evasive about his background. He paid $6,800 of the $8,300 fee in cash. The biggest plane he had ever flown was a single-engine Cessna, and then only with an instructor. Yet he wanted to learn to fly "one of these Big Bird," as he put it in an e-mail to the flight school—a Boeing 747-400 or an Airbus A-300.

After 9/11, when more evidence linked him to the hijackers, the FBI finally was able to look at his hard drive. It had information about airplanes, crop dusting, and wind currents.

"There's no doubt that he was slated to conduct an operation on behalf of and at the direction of al Qaeda," Cummings says of Moussaoui, who was sentenced to life in prison after pleading guilty. "And there is intelligence that shows he had significant contacts with individuals responsible for 9/11."

3

"THE WALL"

IN PURSUING COUNTERTERRORISM cases before 9/11, Art Cummings had been constantly frustrated by the so-called "wall." It was hard to believe that a 1995 interpretation of law by Richard Scruggs, a Justice Department official, had essentially paralyzed the nation's effort to hunt down terrorists before they killed people.

As chief counsel of Justice's Office of Intelligence Policy and Review, Scruggs decided that in applications made for electronic surveillance in foreign counterintelligence or counterterrorism cases, the information gathered in the criminal investigation would be kept separate from information gathered from intelligence sources. The Foreign Intelligence Surveillance Act of 1978 (FISA) had established a court to hear requests for electronic intercepts in such cases.

Until Scruggs came along, there had been no problem. John L. Martin, head of the Justice Department's espionage section, successfully prosecuted more than seventy-six spies by properly distinguishing between information developed for purposes of intelligence gathering and that developed for purposes of a criminal investigation.

When advising FBI agents, Martin made the point that while watching KGB officers who have diplomatic immunity as part of a routine counterintelligence investigation, they might very well develop information that implicates a government employee in passing secrets to the Russians. FISA specifically recognized that this routinely happens and that therefore a counterintelligence investigation and an espionage investigation were often indivisible. Under court rulings, as long as the "primary purpose" of the initial investigation was to gather intelligence, the evidence collected could also be used to support a prosecution. To preserve that option, Martin needed to consult with agents as soon as they suspected they might have an espionage case. But Scruggs said that to demonstrate that the primary purpose of an investigation was originally counterintelligence and not a prosecution, those who worked on the case initially should have absolutely no contact with prosecutors.

Suddenly, the cooperation between the FBI and Justice that had allowed Martin to prosecute spies without any allegation of improper conduct or illegality evaporated. Scruggs's interpretation had the same effect on terrorism investigations.

In his memo on the subject, Scruggs stated, "The simple legal response to parallel investigations is a 'Chinese Wall,' which divides the attorneys as well as the investigators." After Deputy Attorney General Jamie Gorelick and Attorney General Janet Reno approved Scruggs's memo, Scruggs's staff at the Justice Department enforced his dictum by warning that FBI agents could be fired if they overstepped the boundaries.

Overreacting to the warning, the FBI and CIA soon began separating information from criminal and intelligence sources even if no application was being made for a FISA warrant. As a result, the wall became so rigid that FBI agents on the same counterterrorism squad were prohibited from discussing the same case with each other. Within the FBI, files on the same case were kept separate. The criminal side of the case was assigned a 265 classification number, while the intelligence side was assigned a 199 number.

"They anticipated there were going to be huge problems with the FISA court if we mixed and matched," Cummings says. "This was somebody's opinion. Never asked the court! So all of a sudden, there was this rock-solid policy."

"There was no basis for Scruggs's interpretation of the law," according to John Martin. "Janet Reno knew little about the subject and fell for Scruggs's construction hook, line, and sinker."

Scruggs, when asked why he made an issue of contact between the FBI and Justice Department prosecutors in view of the record of success in prosecutions, said a court had held that Justice acted "improperly" in the prosecution of Ronald Humphrey, an employee of the U.S. Information Agency, and David Truong, who turned over top-secret State Department documents from Humphrey to the North Vietnamese. But that case, brought in early 1978, was before the enactment of FISA. It was therefore irrelevant. Moreover, an appeals court found no impropriety and upheld the convictions. Asked about that, Scruggs said he "thought" the case occurred after FISA was passed.

Cummings remembers saying to Marion "Spike" Bowman, the FBI lawyer who headed the National Security Law Unit and was in charge of the issue, "Spike, this is stupid! I can't live with this."

"Oh, you don't have a choice," Bowman replied.

Cummings devised a way around the wall—a subterfuge, really. He told Bowman, "I'm going to open a 199 case. I'm going to work this as an intel case. But I'm going to have a criminal subfile."

"Well, you're supposed to open a 265," Bowman replied.

Cummings said he wasn't going to do that. He didn't have the luxury of adding a second agent to a case so that one could pursue it as a criminal matter and another as an intelligence matter.

With only 11,500 agents, the FBI was a quarter of the size of the New York City Police Department. Fewer than 10 percent of its agents were then assigned to domestic and foreign counterterrorism. The rest pursued white collar crime, kidnappings, espionage, organized crime, and drug cases. Assigning two agents to pursue parallel investigations of the same terrorism case because Richard Scruggs had suddenly decided that the rules should be changed was almost criminally negligent.

The misinterpretations and overinterpretations of the Scruggs memo soon spread. Not only was the wall used to prevent FBI agents from sharing information with each other about the same case, it prevented the CIA and NSA from sharing vital intelligence with the FBI.

"Agents in the field began to believe—incorrectly—that no FISA information could be shared with agents working criminal investigations," the 9/11 commission later concluded. "This perception evolved into the still more exaggerated belief that the FBI could not share any intelligence with criminal investigators, even if no FISA procedures had been used."

Thus, the commission said, relevant information from the CIA never made its way to criminal investigators. In effect, the U.S. government had tied itself in knots, preventing vital information from flowing to the people who needed to know it, and putting Americans at risk. Al Qaeda itself could not have devised a more effective way to thwart terrorism investigations.

Looking back, Cummings and others thought that if that obstacle had been removed, it might have prevented the 9/11 attacks. The CIA did not tell the FBI in January 2001 that two of the eventual hijackers, Khalid al-Mihdhar and Nawaf al-Hazmi, were in the United States and had flown to Los Angeles. When the CIA finally informed the FBI that they were in the country in late August, it was too late. If the information had been passed to the FBI early on, the FBI might have had some chance to uncover aspects of the plot.

When he learned from the CIA on August 29, 2001, that al-Hazmi and al-Mihdhar were in the country, Ali Soufan, a twenty-nine-year-old Lebanese-American FBI agent based in New York, wrote in an e-mail to headquarters, "Someday someone will die—and wall or not, the public will not understand why we were not more effective and throwing every resource we had at certain 'problems.'"

Even after the FBI learned that the two terrorists were in the country, supervisors cited the wall to block Soufan's urgent request that the bureau open a criminal case to find the two men.

"We basically honored this wall, and we only engaged the intelligence side of the New York office in the search for these two guys—instead of using everybody," Cummings says. "If we had found them, whether or not we would have known that they were in the actual execution phase of an operation, I don't know. Whether we would have prevented them from getting on an aircraft or would have followed them onboard that aircraft is also unknown."

"Had we been made aware of al-Hamzi's and al-Midhar's presence in the U.S. back in January 2001 when the CIA became aware, we would have been all over it," says Kenneth Maxwell, the FBI agent who was in charge of counterterrorism in New York. "It would have been unprecedented—a genuine al Qaeda member in the U.S."

After 9/11, when Soufan realized that the CIA had known for most of the year that the two hijackers were in the country yet did not notify the FBI, he ran into a men's room and threw up.

"We did everything by the book," Soufan's supervisor told him.

4

CROSS-EXAMINING
AGENTS

O N THE MORNING of Friday, September 14, 2001, Andy
Card arrived at his office at 5:45 A.M. As usual, Bush's chief
of staff skimmed the newspapers, read over intelligence reports, and reviewed the president's schedule. From the Secret Service
locator box, he could see that POTUS was on the south grounds of
the White House. At 6:45 A.M., Bush walked into the Oval Office.

Card started to go over the day's schedule, but Bush stopped him.
The previous evening, the president had developed plans for reshaping
the government's response to terrorism. Instead of passively waiting
for the next attack, the United States would become the aggressor,
taking on terrorists wherever they were. Instead of focusing on catching and prosecuting terrorists after they had done their damage, the
government would switch its priorities to preventing attacks. Instead
of relying on laws that created impediments to tracking down terrorists, the government would enact new laws so the FBI and other government agencies would not be handcuffed.

Bush told Card to rearrange the day's schedule so he could implement those plans. After the daily CIA briefing at 8:00 A.M., FBI Director Mueller and Attorney General John Ashcroft began to brief Bush.

"They talked about how the terrorists got plane tickets, got on
planes, moved from one airport to another, and then attacked our citizens," Card says. "And the president, while he was very interested in
that report, said, 'Mr. Director, that's building a case for prosecution.

I want to know what you have to say about the terrorist threats that haven't materialized yet and how we can prevent them.' "

Mueller got the message and took it back to headquarters.

"The director said, 'We've got this new mission. It's a prevention mission,' " Cummings remembers.

Many agents scratched their heads.

"There was a communication problem," says Cummings. "All of us sat there saying, 'I've been working terrorism almost my entire career. What does the boss think we've been doing except preventing attacks?' "

The difference is that when the FBI arrested Ramzi Yousef, the mastermind of the first World Trade Center bombing, rather than pursuing leads to uncover more cells and plots, the FBI thought that was the end of the matter. In the six years before 9/11, the bureau stopped forty terrorist plots before they happened. The FBI foiled an attempt by al Qaeda to blow up the Holland and Lincoln tunnels, the United Nations, and the FBI's New York Field Office. The bureau also determined that al Qaeda had connections through Al Kifah Refugee Center in Brooklyn to some of those convicted in the 1993 attack on the World Trade Center. But under Louis Freeh's leadership, the FBI tended to treat each incident as a separate case instead of recognizing the larger threat and mounting an effort against the entire al Qaeda organization, as the bureau did with the Ku Klux Klan and the Mafia.

"Pre-9/11, the first consideration was, I got an indictment in my pocket," Cummings says. "The CIA would have run the other way, rightfully so. They didn't want anything to do with testifying in a court of law. And we ran on the assumption that if you had an indictment, you used the indictment. Slap it down on the table, pick the guy up, you throw him on an airplane. You bring him home, you put him in jail, and you go, 'Okay, I've done a great job today.' "

If that were to happen today, Cummings says, "I would have told my agents they basically just put Americans more in jeopardy rather than less in jeopardy. It's a completely different approach and bears little resemblance to the previous one."

Like a giant ocean liner, the FBI does not change course quickly. In turning the FBI into an agency that emphasizes prevention, Mueller had to deal with a bureaucracy that often resisted change and did not always give him straight answers. Early on, Mueller removed Sheila Horan as acting director of the Counterintelligence Division. Besides finding that she was generally not on top of the subject, he felt that she did not appropriately brief him on a Chinese counterintelligence case in Los Angeles, failing to warn him of problems with it.

Perhaps more than anything else, that defined the difference between Mueller and Freeh. Freeh had the habit of punishing anyone who disagreed with him or brought him bad news. In contrast, Mueller banished those who did not give him the facts.

"Freeh said he wants everything straight. The first person who told it to him straight, he cut his head off," says Weldon Kennedy, whom Freeh promoted to deputy director.

Under Freeh, the FBI lurched from one botched case to another. As detailed in the author's *The Bureau: The Secret History of the FBI*, Freeh contributed in one way or another to the problems at the FBI laboratory, the flawed indictment of Los Alamos nuclear scientist Wen Ho Lee, the fiasco involving innocent bystander Richard Jewell in the Olympics bombing in Atlanta, the security breaches that allowed Robert Hanssen to spy for the Russians, the failure to turn over documents relating to Oklahoma City bomber Timothy McVeigh, and the FBI's counterterrorism failure before the 9/11 attacks.

"I think we all breathed a sigh of relief that Freeh was not here on September 11," says a longtime bureau supervisor.

As Cummings rose in the FBI, he briefed Mueller every morning and in the late afternoon on weekdays. He briefed him on Saturdays as well.

Mueller was not a diplomat. When he headed the Justice Department's Criminal Division, Mueller would throw office parties at his home. He would signal that the festivities were over by flicking the lights on and off. As a former Marine, Mueller expected his orders to be carried out without any need for hand-holding. When officials did not meet Mueller's standards or ignored his directives, he quietly forced them out.

Within the bureau, Mueller's forcefulness and restructuring of operations evoked the kind of low-grade grumbling that usually accompanies change in an organization. Rather than looking at the big picture and focusing on what the FBI needed to do to protect the country better, many agents focused on their own discomfort at changing their routine.

That same shortsightedness manifested itself during Louis Freeh's tenure—in the opposite direction. Under Freeh, a new botched case came to light nearly every six months. Yet about half the FBI's agents thought he was the best thing since sliced bread. As a former agent, they felt he was one of them.

In visiting field offices, Freeh spent most of his time talking with field agents, often without the special agent in charge present. In Miami, he went for a run on the beach at 6:00 A.M., then talked with agents on each squad for the rest of the day. In Chicago, Freeh spent just a half an hour with top officials, then devoted the day to talking with agents.

While Mueller supported agents, he was not trying to win a popularity contest. As with Bush, he woke up every morning with the pressure of knowing that stopping the next attack depended on him.

"I want people to tell me they are unhappy and that this change is wrong for these reasons," Mueller would say. "I don't want people to come in and say we should do it this way because we have always done it this way. That argument doesn't go very far."

In the months after 9/11, Mueller occasionally raised his voice when he found agents had done a sloppy job or raised objections to the new direction. But usually he showed his impatience by cross-examining agents who seemed to be giving him a song and dance.

With Mueller, "you can't go in there not engaged," Cummings says. "If you ask me a question about the case, more times than not I'm going to have the answer. I better at least understand the strategy, what it is we are doing against the guy, and how and why and where we're going with it. If I set a pattern that I'm not engaged, I'm out of here. I'm gone."

"He will ask rapid-fire questions, where there's no chance to answer," says a counterterrorism agent. "When that happens, you know you're done. We used to sit back, we used to push away from the conference table, so he could have a direct line at the guy he was questioning. You didn't even want to get in the way of it. And then he would ask, 'Did you do this? Did you do this? How about this? Did you think of this?' There's no chance to answer. None."

Prior to 9/11, the FBI designated a so-called "office of origin" to direct each terrorism investigation. Before the first World Trade Center bombing, New York was considered the office of origin for al Qaeda. Thus, the New York Field Office was in charge of anything related to Osama bin Laden.

Given the global nature of terrorism, Mueller decided that headquarters should direct all terrorism investigations. That would centralize information and leads and better coordinate the bureau's response. In the parlance adopted after 9/11, it was a way to connect the dots. But that change encountered resistance as well.

5

RISK AVERSION

SINCE PASQUALE "PAT" D'Amuro had been running counter-terrorism in New York, Mueller moved him to headquarters, appointing him inspector in charge of the 9/11 investigation. Later, Mueller named him assistant director of the counterterrorism branch. Eventually, D'Amuro became assistant director over counterterrorism and counterintelligence.

Like Art Cummings, D'Amuro had railed against the "wall" before he came to Washington. He thought it was crazy.

"The agency [CIA] and NSA took it upon themselves to expand the wall, saying we're not going to determine if it was or was not FISA-derived," D'Amuro says. "We're going to label everything 'Can't be shared with those individuals.' And I remember arguing with headquarters, saying, 'You guys gotta push back on this, this is wrong. We've got to share in that intelligence.'"

D'Amuro also remembers that the CIA failed to inform the FBI about al-Mihdhar, the hijacker who entered the United States in January 2001 and then re-entered on July 4.

"If we had known al-Mihdhar was here, the bureau would have acted as it did during the Millennium investigation of December 2000," D'Amuro says. That was a time when the bureau aggressively sought FISAs and followed individuals who were involved with Ahmed Ressam. After a U.S. Customs officer became suspicious of him, Ressam was arrested in the plot to bomb Los Angeles International Airport on New Year's Eve 1999.

"We would have pulled out all the stops to find out what the hell this guy al-Mihdhar was doing here," D'Amuro says. "And maybe—maybe, because we'll never know—we would've picked something up that could've stopped 9/11."

Contrary to the impressions created by the media and politicians, nothing else has turned up that would have led to uncovering the 9/11 plot, D'Amuro says. Senator Arlen Specter, for example, claimed that evidence the FBI had before 9/11 would have provided a "veritable blueprint" for the attacks. That was bs, D'Amuro thought.

The media focused on a memo that Kenneth Williams, a Phoenix agent, wrote to headquarters on July 10, 2001, suggesting that the FBI look into Middle Eastern men who were enrolled in flight training schools. Headquarters ignored the suggestion. When he wrote the Phoenix memo, Williams was investigating an individual who was a member of the al-Muhajiroun, an Islamic extremist group whose spiritual leader was a supporter of bin Laden. The man was taking aviation-related security courses at Embry Riddle Aeronautical University. Why was he interested in aviation security? Perhaps so he could hijack a plane, Williams thought. Others taking flight training could have the same nefarious purpose.

Headquarters passed the memo off to low-level analysts, who wondered whether interviewing Middle Eastern men taking flight lessons or aviation security courses would raise issues of racial profiling. New York agents who received a copy of the memo considered it speculative. They figured bin Laden needed pilots to transport goods in Afghanistan.

At the time, FBI counterterrorism agents were focused on investigating the bombing of the USS *Cole* in Yemen in 2000 and the earlier attacks on two American embassies in East Africa, all ordered by bin Laden. There are a thousand flight schools in the United States. Even if the FBI had had the manpower, in the political climate at the time, an effort to investigate Middle Eastern men because they were taking aviation courses likely would have resulted in a congressional investigation. In fact, by the time Williams wrote the memo, none of the 9/11 hijackers was still taking flight lessons.

Williams said that when he drafted the memo, he envisioned the possibility of a standard hijacking, not the kind when planes were flown into buildings. He marked the memo for "routine" attention. Yet these distinctions were lost in the media reports, and the public was left with the impression that the FBI could have averted disaster by responding to Williams's memo. The victims' survivors said as much in Congressional hearings, blaming the FBI and CIA for their loss.

Mueller considered the Phoenix memo a very good intelligence product and cited it as an example of what FBI analysts should be turning out today.

On the other hand, "the fact that an agent in Phoenix writes a very good intelligence report saying we have a lot of Middle Easterners taking flight lessons here and asking why did they take flight lessons here would not have led to the plot," D'Amuro says. "A lot of people do that, taking flight lessons here because it's cheaper in the U.S. than in other places. Even in today's world, if we had that intelligence, we couldn't stop these people from taking lessons if they were here legally." Interestingly, when the author wrote the first national story on the FBI's profiling program in the February 20, 1984, *Washington Post*, the term *profiling* had no law enforcement connotation. It has since taken on a sinister meaning, referring to singling out suspects solely because of their race or ethnicity. That is neither good profiling nor good law enforcement.

What was far more damning than the Phoenix memo was Coleen M. Rowley's June 2002 testimony before the Senate Judiciary Committee. The Minneapolis Field Office's legal counsel, Rowley arrived to testify with a blue fanny pack strapped beneath her suit jacket. She wore large glasses and no makeup. As television networks carried her testimony live, millions of Americans got to see perhaps for the first time what an FBI field agent was like. Tough, honest, and unintimidated, Rowley lashed out at FBI bureaucracy and interrupted senators in midsentence.

In her testimony, Rowley described what had led her to write a thirteen-page, single-spaced letter to Mueller the previous month. In the letter, she poured out her frustration at the lack of head-quarters support for an application to search the computer of Zacarias Moussaoui, who would later be charged in the September 11 attacks. Rowley outlined how a supervisor at headquarters rejected the Minneapolis Field Office's efforts to obtain permission to search Moussaoui's computer under the provisions of the FISA. The FBI had learned from French intelligence that Moussaoui had links to terrorists, but the supervisor mistakenly thought that to obtain ap-proval for the search, the FBI would have to tie Moussaoui to a "recognized foreign power" rather than to a terrorist group that is not necessarily associated with a foreign country.

The supervisor nonetheless submitted the request to the FBI's National Security Law Unit, where attorneys failed to clarify the issue. In fact, one lawyer confirmed that the agents would have to tie Moussaoui to a "recognized foreign power," a term that does not even exist in FISA. Nor did the FBI consult with the Justice Depart-ment, which ultimately rules on such applications. If the FBI had done so, Justice lawyers would have corrected the misinterpretation and advised the agents on how to cite enough evidence to show Moussaoui's possible ties to a terrorist organization.

Like so many problems at the FBI before 9/11, the failure to properly handle the Minneapolis request was a legacy of Louis Freeh. As a former agent, Freeh had always hated headquarters. As FBI di-rector, he decided that it should be downsized.

Freeh began slashing headquarters personnel and sending them to the field. Freeh's policy of transferring headquarters agents to the street gave preference to agents with seniority, so the most experi-enced agents elected to return to the field in areas where they wished to someday retire. Yet they were the personnel the bureau most needed to supervise sensitive investigations.

Freeh also compelled experienced attorneys at headquarters who knew the intricacies of FISA and FBI procedures to retire or transfer to field offices where they chased drug dealers. In addition, the "climate of fear"—a phrase Rowley used in her testimony—that Freeh created made it far easier for those who remained at headquarters to do nothing rather than take a chance on supporting a controversial surveillance application.

"There was a hell of a lot of risk aversion coming from headquarters," says Barry Mawn, who was assistant FBI director in charge of the New York Field Office and oversaw the bin Laden investigations.

Yet, as in the case of the Phoenix memo, a search of Moussaoui's computer before September 11 would not have yielded anything directly tying him to the plot. When the FBI finally searched the computer, agents found information about such matters as using airplanes for crop dusting. It did contain telephone numbers that, if pursued, might have tied Moussaoui to one of the plotters in Hamburg. But even an aggressive investigation of that link would most likely not have uncovered the plot before September 11.

In her letter to Mueller, Rowley conceded that point, but she said that it was "at least possible we could have gotten lucky and uncovered one or two more of the terrorists in flight training prior to September 11, just as Moussaoui was discovered, after making contact with his flight instructors." In retrospect, Rowley says, the agents should have sought a criminal search warrant from a local magistrate.

Aside from these errors, the FBI operated in a politically correct atmosphere that Congress, the Clinton administration, and the media fostered. Focusing on Arab men was a no-no.

"Remember, under the administration of the day before 9/11, the Justice Department was investigating the Pittsburgh police department for profiling," Cummings says. "Profiling was a really, really bad thing back then. Imagine in those pre-9/11 days going to flight schools and saying, 'We want you to give us a list of all your Middle Eastern students.' They would've said, 'Excuse me? Is there a problem with Middle Eastern students we aren't aware of? Why don't you go to the ACLU and American Arab Anti-discrimination Council and talk to them about it?' We'd have had more knocks on our door. In the case of Arab men taking flight training, we would not have been able to justify an investigation."

The critics had the notion that the FBI and CIA could uncover plots by moving a cursor around on a computer screen. But in no way would that have uncovered the kind of carefully compartmentalized scheme devised by bin Laden and a few of the top people in his organization. The problem before 9/11 was that the information that would uncover the plots simply was not there: There were no dots to connect.

Still, bringing all the existing information together coherently and analyzing it properly would most likely have led to more aggressive investigations, possibly uncovering more leads. Whether those investigations would have stopped the plots is anybody's guess. Whether such investigations are necessary to uncover future plots is a certainty.

6

POCKET LITTER

WHEN BOB MUELLER first asked Pat D'Amuro to move to Washington to run the 9/11 investigation, D'Amuro said he had to ask his family how they felt. D'Amuro was devoted to his wife, Laura, and his son from his first marriage. Because his son was still in school, he wanted his family to remain in New York. Laura urged him to accept the position at headquarters, but three weeks after Mueller named him assistant director of counterterrorism, she was diagnosed with uterine cancer.

"Listen, I don't know how this is going to work," D'Amuro told Mueller. "I gotta go home and see what I have to do. You could put somebody else in this job, and you won't hear one complaint from me, because this is too important right now."

"You were the guy I wanted," Mueller said. "You're still the guy I want. We'll somehow make this work. You go up to New York and work two days a week in New York if you want."

D'Amuro couldn't see it.

"I need to be here. Or back with my wife," he told Mueller. "I don't see how both of them work."

When D'Amuro told Laura he was thinking of giving up the position, she started crying.

"This is everything you've worked for," she said. "You know what? A lot of times it's bs when the director tells you you're the guy that's needed on this job. But this is what you do. And you are needed

35

down there. I'll feel worse if you come home. I want you to stay there. I want you to do the job."

After President Bush announced strikes against al Qaeda training camps and the Taliban in Afghanistan, D'Amuro urged Mueller to begin sending agents to exploit items confiscated from al Qaeda leaders—cell phones, computers, even pocket litter. The FBI later used the same approach in Iraq.

Bush signed an intelligence finding, or order, directing the CIA to destroy bin Laden and al Qaeda. George Tenet, as director of Central Intelligence, promised Bush that he would present him with a plan for covert action. The CIA had been working with the Northern Alliance in Afghanistan for years, doling out millions in exchange for intelligence. The plan would make use of these assets and tribal leaders in southern Afghanistan. Being inseparable from al Qaeda, the Taliban had to go. Tenet warned Bush that the plan would be expensive. To get up to speed, the agency might need as much as an additional $1 billion—about half the cost of a B-2 stealth bomber.

By September 17, Bush had decided to grant all of Tenet's requests, including an extra $1 billion. Bush wanted the CIA to be first on the ground, preparing the way for the military with both intelligence officers and paramilitary officers.

In fact, according to an intelligence source, "Bin Laden believed that 9/11 would lead the U.S. to invade Afghanistan, with exactly the same consequences as the Soviet invasion of Afghanistan—that the U.S. would have to leave in humiliation."

Instead, "we fought the war very differently than the Soviets fought the war," says an intelligence official. "But that's what al Qaeda is after, that kind of history-changing attack."

By December 7, it was almost over. The Taliban had abandoned Kandahar, their last stronghold, where the CIA had helped create a force of 3,000 fighters. The CIA had spent $70 million on getting the Northern Alliance and tribal leaders to work for the agency. Much of the money went for equipment, light weapons, four-wheel drive vehicles, and communication devices like satellite phones. Working in the shadows, the CIA had broken the enemy's spine.

In mid-December, U.S. and Afghan troops surrounded a giant cave complex in the eastern Afghan region of Tora Bora, where a radio transmission was believed to have come from bin Laden. The CIA had acquired maps of the caves from Russia, which compiled them during the ten-year Soviet occupation of Afghanistan.

The United States sent warplanes to blanket the area with bombs but relied largely on local Afghan ground forces. Hundreds of al Qaeda suspects escaped across the border into Pakistan. Bin Laden was believed to be among them.

Besides military action, the chief way to fight al Qaeda was to obtain intelligence so that plots could be rolled up and operatives captured, killed, or arrested. Obtaining intelligence meant developing informants, seizing records, and conducting electronic surveillance. To make sure the FBI got such intelligence, Bush asked his counsel, Alberto Gonzales, to begin working with the Justice Department to craft what would become known as the USA Patriot Act. Congress passed the new law in record time, and Bush signed it in the East Room forty-five days after the attacks.

The Patriot Act removed the wall—real and imagined—between criminal and intelligence work so that leads could be shared between agencies and within them. However, it was not until summer 2004 that the bureau finally combined terrorism classification numbers, making it clear that criminal and intelligence cases are one and the same.

The Patriot Act also allowed the FBI to wiretap a terrorist regardless of what phone he used. Incredibly, the FBI could employ what are known as roving wiretaps in organized crime or drug trafficking cases, but not in terrorism cases, which could threaten the country's survival.

Before passage of the law, if a terrorist switched from a home phone to a disposable cell phone or a pay phone, the FBI would have to apply all over again for a FISA order, a process that took weeks. In the meantime, the terrorist had gone on to use a different phone.

With the new legal procedures, the FBI had powerful new tools to fight al Qaeda, but it was still creeping along on technology from the early 1980s.

"Mueller comes in as director, and within a week, he's got 9/11 placed on his plate," D'Amuro says. "He doesn't know the bureau, he doesn't know the people, he doesn't know the capabilities. Everybody talked about the bureau being broken. I explained to him that the piece of the FBI that was broken was the information technology. It wasn't so much the people; it was our ability to manage the massive amounts of information that the bureau was collecting and being able to utilize that information."

When D'Amuro was still in New York, an agent told him that an optical disk drive for information storage was being taken out of service.

"The Smithsonian wanted it, because it was the last known optical drive of its type being used to store data, and here the FBI was using it," D'Amuro says. "That's how sad it was."

Back then, D'Amuro thought about picking up the phone and trying to reach Microsoft founder Bill Gates to plead for his help.

"The computer technology is a mess! It's a disaster!" D'Amuro told Mueller. "We should be going to some of the top people in the private sector like Microsoft and all these other companies that are out there."

Early on, D'Amuro had an argument with Mueller over the director's insistence on centralization. Mueller had said, "Anything you need to do down here, get it down here."

But headquarters had never been an operational entity. That was especially true under Freeh. Because of his disdain for headquarters, experienced supervisors in Chinese counterintelligence had been sent to the field or encouraged to retire. As a result, no one was in a position to properly direct an espionage investigation of Wen Ho Lee.

This led to critical errors in pursuing the case against the Taiwanese-born scientist at Los Alamos. More than any other screwup, FBI officials thought the case damaged the bureau's credibility. On September 13, 2000, Judge James A. Parker freed the sixty-one-year-old Lee, saying his jailing "embarrassed our entire nation and each of us who is a citizen of it."

When D'Amuro discovered that headquarters was not analyzing phone numbers from the cell phones of the 9/11 hijackers properly, he decided that he could get the job done faster and better in New York. He asked the New York Field Office to take over the task.

When Mueller found out, he confronted D'Amuro: "I told you I wanted this done down here."

"Listen, you brought me down here, and I told you I was going to do the best job I could," D'Amuro said. "I can get this done in New York faster and better than it can be done down here."

Three times that day, they went at it. Finally, that weekend, Mueller ran into one of the agents who was running down the numbers. He asked him questions, and the agent gave him wrong information, saying a link from one phone number had been established when it had not been.

"We discussed it, and I proved to the director that the information he was given on that weekend, when he was walking around asking questions, was wrong," D'Amuro says. "And he looked at me and said, 'You're not going to kill the agent, are ya?'"

"No," D'Amuro replied. "But you stop walking around asking questions before this stuff gets vetted out and we present it to you in a briefing. Because you're going to have stuff that isn't correct. And you've got to be careful, whatever you bring to the White House has got to be dead accurate."

"I'm just upset that you're telling me you can get something done in New York that I can't get done down here at FBI headquarters," Mueller said.

"You gotta remember what headquarters was created for,"

D'Amuro replied. "It was not an operational entity. You're changing the entire game here. The fear that I have about headquarters being the all-encompassing operational agency with respect to terrorism is that the field is waiting for headquarters to tell them what to do now. That's a real danger. Because as much as you want to hold the assistant director of counterterrorism responsible for all the investigations, you have to hold the SACs [special agents in charge of each field office] accountable for those investigations also."

After that, Mueller eased off on having all the telecommunications data run through headquarters.

Tough as Mueller was, it was nothing compared to working for the legendary John O'Neill, D'Amuro thought. O'Neill headed international counterterrorism when D'Amuro was in New York, and later headed the National Security Division at FBI headquarters. O'Neill retired a week before 9/11 to head security at the World Trade Center. He died helping others escape as the Twin Towers were collapsing.

O'Neill taught D'Amuro everything he knew about counterterrorism. D'Amuro thought they bonded because they both favored Chivas and water. But O'Neill could be overly demanding. D'Amuro remembered when an agent in New York overstepped his bounds in dealing with a source, telling the source he could take a crucial step in a case without having first obtained the proper authorization.

"O'Neill reduced this guy to just ashes in his office, in front of other agents, in front of supervisors, in front of me," D'Amuro says.

D'Amuro remembered taking O'Neill aside, telling him he would take care of the agent and asking to meet with him in his office.

"You know something?" D'Amuro said to O'Neill. "The agent's wrong. He doesn't have the authority to do that without us knowing about it. But we stopped it. You can't reduce people to ashes and then try to rebuild them. This guy's going to hate you till the day he dies or you die. You're never going to resurrect your relationship with this agent. You can't do that to people."

"Mueller was a cupcake compared to John O'Neill," D'Amuro

says. And while Mueller was not warm and fuzzy, he did occasionally praise agents. One day, Mueller asked D'Amuro to brief President Bush in his place. The next day, D'Amuro was meeting with a new special agent in charge when Mueller came in to his office.

"Can you excuse us?" Mueller said.

D'Amuro thought he had screwed up. But Mueller said, "You know, I got three compliments on you today. One of them was from the president of the United States. One was from George Tenet. And the other one was from Don Evans, the Commerce secretary."

Evans, a close friend of Bush, was not in the briefing, so D'Amuro wasn't sure how that compliment even arose.

"You're kidding me," D'Amuro said.

"No," Mueller said. "The president commented that you did an excellent job in the briefing, that you weren't in awe of being in the Oval Office—because a lot of people go in there and lose it."

7

SECOND WAVE

ALL THE INTELLIGENCE pouring in pointed to a second
wave of attacks, perhaps within months of 9/11. The Library Tower in Los Angeles was to be one target. The pressure to stop those attacks was enormous.

"Listen, guys, we got another one hit, and we're all gone," Pat
D'Amuro told Art Cummings and other section chiefs at a meeting.

At first, Cummings had been on temporary assignment at headquarters. But after D'Amuro saw him give a PowerPoint presentation, he decided to bring Cummings to headquarters permanently.
D'Amuro made Cummings chief of the document exploitation section, then the communications exploitation section. After that, he
placed him in charge of the first national Joint Terrorism Task Force,
which brought together dozens of intelligence and law enforcement
agencies to go after terrorism. Eventually, the FBI had 101 local
Joint Terrorism Task forces, compared with 35 before 9/11. By
March 2003, Mueller had placed Cummings in charge of International Terrorism Operations Section 1 (ITOS 1), which directs operations having to do with al Qaeda.

"The real anxiety was, 'Okay, if they're here, how do we make
sure they don't do another one?'" Cummings says. "We don't have
the luxury of time. If they're here, they're already planning. They may
have been disrupted with this first wave, but if there's going to be a
second wave, we need to get out in front of it."

The FBI came up with a disruption strategy.

"We went to all our field offices and said we want them to do surveillance on all of their subjects," Cummings says. "We wanted arrests of everyone who was arrestable, anyone whom we can show has violated a criminal law. If they're here illegally, arrest them, get them out of here."

On November 12, 2001, American Airlines flight 587 crashed on takeoff from Kennedy International Airport. The plane was heading for Santo Domingo in the Dominican Republic. The crash killed 260 people on the plane and another five on the ground in the Rockaway section of Queens.

The question was whether this was the start of a second wave of attacks.

"It was brutal," Cummings says. "We ran to another room where we had Federal Aviation Administration systems online. We were listening to the FAA traffic. There was real concern that that was the start of a second wave. Everyone was just holding their breath going, 'Okay, okay, what we got?'"

Tracing the manifest, Cummings found that a passenger killed on the plane had survived the World Trade Center attack.

"Everybody started thinking, whoa whoa, hold on," Cummings says. "But it was pure coincidence."

Despite the pressure, Mueller always seemed calm.

"The director's very focused, very calculating," Cummings says. "I've never seen him lose his composure at all."

Mueller put out the word that no lead would be overlooked. Prior to 9/11, if an e-mail came in saying that somebody was going to bomb the Sears Tower, "We would've looked at it and said, 'This is just not realistic,'" Cummings says. "Now we began knocking on every door. A lead may seem to be 99.9 percent absolute garbage. But we have no tolerance for the one-tenth of one percent. That could get somebody killed."

Hundreds of leads came in about Arab men acting suspiciously—talking in a bar about a terrorist operation, for example.

"Now, is it realistic that Arab men, speaking English, drinking beer, would talk about an operation in public where people can over-hear them?" Cummings asks. "That's six different factors, none of which makes any sense. I'd love to be able to say, 'No, sorry, nothing's going on in there.' But maybe, just maybe, someone had a foolish moment, talked about something they were actually planning. No way would most of our counterparts go out on that. It may or may not make us better. Makes us busier. Because none of those kinds of leads has panned out."

What did pay off was captures of al Qaeda operatives. Finding them overseas was primarily the job of the CIA, along with the military. In seeking to penetrate al Qaeda, the CIA made extensive use of bugging devices provided by the CIA's Directorate of Science and Technology. The CIA targeted mosques, where al Qaeda operatives would pray but also hatch terrorist plots. Besides recruiting agents and intercepting communications, the CIA made extensive use of information gathered by foreign security services. When the CIA had difficulty with a foreign service, President Bush would occasionally place a call to the leader of its country.

Yet it was a lowly intelligence analyst, going through a bunch of e-mails, who was able to narrow the search for Abu Zubaydah, bin Laden's field commander or chief of operations.

Zubaydah is believed to have been born to Palestinian parents in Saudi Arabia. He had strong connections with Jordanian and Palestinian groups and was sentenced to death in absentia by a Jordanian court for his role in a thwarted plot to bomb hotels there during millennium celebrations. Officials believe he was also connected to a plan to blow up the U.S. embassy in Sarajevo and a plot to attack the American embassy in Paris.

Zubaydah had run a terrorist camp in Afghanistan where some of the 9/11 hijackers trained. He was, says an FBI official, like a U.S. Army recruiting station for al Qaeda. He was based in Pakistan near the border, and people who were looking to join the jihad would come through Zubaydah and he would assess them: Are they reliable?

Do they come from trustworthy people? Does somebody vouch for them? Are they infiltrators?

Once he was done with his vetting process, he would decide where they should go—to a camp for making bombs, to a camp for combat training.

"We talk about him in terms of being a high-ranking al Qaeda operative," says an FBI official. "It's not so much that he was high-ranking as that he had access to all of the most high-ranking people, because he was a funnel through which people came."

The analyst zeroed in on Zubaydah's locations because she noticed similarities in e-mails from different points using different screen names and concluded they were all written by him. Combined with other intelligence from intercepts, the CIA came up with more than a dozen possible targets for raids in Pakistan in March 2002.

"It was a combined, all-source effort," says Robert L. Grenier, who was the CIA's station chief in Islamabad and later headed the agency's Counterterrorism Center. "There was so much information, and so much of it was very fractured data, you had to take a lot of little bits and put it all together to make the mosaic."

With the Pakistanis and the FBI, the CIA developed a plan to raid all the possible locations at the same time.

"We were concerned that if you just raid one or two a night, for instance, then obviously they'd all flee, they'd realize what was happening," Grenier says. "The point was to raid as many of these places as possible simultaneously, which we did."

Even then, Grenier rated the chance of getting the terrorist at fifty-fifty.

"You just never know—perhaps he's not home, and it's hard to perfectly sequence these things," Grenier says. "Maybe they'd get some advance warning, maybe he'd flee. There were a couple of places at least that we thought he might flee to. And so we were prepared to hit those very rapidly in a second wave once the dust had settled from those initial raids."

Abu Zubaydah turned out to be in a two-story house in Faisal-abad, an industrial city in Punjab Province in western Pakistan. The Pakistanis took the lead and ran up to scale the fence, which turned out to be electrified. They were shocked off the fence. Then they cut through the gate, but now they had lost the element of surprise, so they hit the door with a ramrod. It turned out to be a steel-reinforced door with multiple locks.

Finally, they broke through the door. A terrorist inside wrapped a piano wire across the neck of the first Pakistani soldier to enter and pulled on it. A second soldier shot the terrorist. Then they heard footsteps everywhere, running up through the stairs and down the hallways.

They went upstairs and captured a half dozen people. One terrorist ran away over a rooftop. A soldier confronted him with an AK-47.

"The first thing the guy does is, he grabs the barrel of it and tries to wrestle the gun away," says an FBI official. "This turns out to be Abu Zubaydah. So he is at the other end of the gun. The Pakistani soldier, judging the path of least resistance, pulls the trigger. So Abu Zubaydah's pulling the gun, which shoots him in the stomach and groin and puts numerous rounds through him, and he goes down."

Bullet fragments ripped through his abdomen and groin. Nobody knew he was Abu Zubaydah. They carried him and other wounded terrorists to a truck. A CIA officer said, "I think this is our guy."

At the hospital, FBI agents identified him as the wanted al Qaeda operative. As George Tenet writes in his book *At the Center of the Storm*, Buzzy Krongard, the CIA's executive director, was on the board of Johns Hopkins Medical Center. He used his contacts to persuade a world-class medical expert to hop on a chartered CIA plane and fly to Pakistan to save the killer's life.

A treasure trove of computer discs, notebooks, and phone numbers discovered in the safe house was flown to CIA headquarters in Washington.

Meanwhile, the FBI agents and CIA officers had urgent business:

They both knew that Jose Padilla had gone through Abu Zubaydah's operation on his way to al Qaeda, and they believed that Padilla had been tasked to detonate a radiological "dirty" bomb in the United States.

"They were showing Abu Zubaydah different photos, trying to get him to identify Jose Padilla," says an FBI official. "And it was within the course of trying to get him to identify Padilla that he hesitated on Khalid Sheikh Mohammed."

Known as KSM, Khalid Sheikh Mohammed was the mastermind of the 9/11 plot.

Bluffing, an FBI agent said, "No, no, no. I know all about him. I ask the questions, you give the answers. I want to know about this other guy."

They went on to the photo of Padilla. But recognizing that the first photo had alerted Abu Zubaydah to something, the agent began thinking about how he would get back to it. As a ruse, he said, "We know Khalid Sheikh Mohammed was the mastermind behind the 9/11 attacks."

"How did you know he was the mastermind?" Abu Zubaydah said.

In fact, the agent did not know. "He tricked him," an FBI official says. Later, Abu Zubaydah said, "I want to know how you knew that that guy was the mastermind?"

The agent replied, "Oh, we just did."

Abu Zubaydah mentioned that KSM used the moniker "Mukhtar," which allowed analysts to comb through previously collected intelligence and develop leads that eventually led to his capture.

Soon after that, Abu Zubaydah stopped cooperating. Propelled by fear that another attack was in the works, the CIA began developing coercive interrogation techniques—water-boarding high value terrorists or subjecting them to ear-splitting music or to icy temperatures and forcing them to stand for hours.

"We weren't getting very much from him at all," Grenier says. "And that's when we began the process of putting together a properly focused interrogation process. It was refined a good deal subsequently, but he was the test."

Before the interrogation procedures were employed, the Justice Department reviewed them and determined that they were legally permissible. After a few months, the CIA began using some of the techniques on Abu Zubaydah. As the interrogation of Abu Zubaydah and other detained terrorists progressed, the agency briefed the chairs, ranking members, and majority and minority staff directors of the House and Senate intelligence committees on the details of the procedures used.

Before confronting a terrorist, each interrogator was given 250 hours of specialized training. In addition to the interrogators, detainees were questioned by experts with years of experience in studying and tracking al Qaeda. That expertise allowed them to fire rapid questions at detainees, to follow up on their answers, and to quickly verify their truthfulness.

The FBI has always found that, even though it may take longer, a soft approach works better and leads to more accurate information. Moreover, as a law enforcement organization, the FBI could not become involved in questionable tactics that might come to light in a criminal proceeding in a courtroom.

Even though the CIA never engaged in torture, D'Amuro was adamantly opposed to using coercive techniques.

"Mueller listened to me," D'Amuro says. "Later, he said, 'You kept us out of that, and you were right.'"

Cummings found it was difficult for others to understand how FBI agents could turn murderers into cooperative sources without aggressive tactics. But, he says, "We've had case after case following 9/11 of genuine, real, true-to-life bad guys who have sat down in hotel rooms with us, for weeks on end, just pouring it out."

While the FBI likes to think it takes the moral high ground, "That's not really the driving reason," Cummings says. "The driving reason's, frankly, because we think we are much more effective as an organization working that way. And it doesn't take that much time. It's something you learn as you go. You work with somebody, you see what resonates with him. Is it family that drives him? Is it children that drives him? Is it career that drives him? Is it freedom that drives him? What is it that motivates him and keeps him motivated?"

The approach is the same as in working a criminal case.

"You have a drunk driver, you work everything from rationalization to all kinds of different themes," Cummings says. "You say, 'I know you didn't mean it. Of course you didn't. You left the scene, it was kind of stupid, we've all done that.' When really it's not the case. When you see a little sparkle, then you work that theme."

On the other hand, the CIA could point to a string of successes and dozens of plots that were rolled up because of coercive interrogation techniques. CIA officials say that regardless of what techniques are used, they try to corroborate any information gleaned from a terrorist. Even intercepts of conversations are not infallible, they say. A conversation could be a setup, so the CIA has to try to verify any information it obtains.

Some media reports later suggested that Abu Zubaydah, who is now at Guantánamo Bay, was crazy.

"One agent looked at one of his notebooks and decided it didn't make any sense at all," D'Amuro says. But, he says, Abu Zubaydah was no more crazy than any other terrorist.

"He turned out to be incredibly valuable," D'Amuro observes. "Abu Zubaydah provided information that helped stop a terrorist attack being planned against the Library Tower and other buildings on the West Coast, the so-called second wave. He provided physical descriptions of the operatives and information on their general location. Based on the information he provided, the operatives were detained, one while traveling to the United States."

Al Qaeda had set aside some $20,000 to fund the second wave.

Abu Zubaydah also identified Ramzi bin al Shibh, who was captured in Karachi in September 2002. He was a top al Qaeda recruiter and a member of bin Laden's inner circle. Zubaydah identified him as one of KSM's accomplices in the 9/11 attacks.

Together, these two terrorists provided information that would help in the planning and execution of the operation that captured Khalid Sheikh Mohammed. If it had not been for coercive interrogation techniques used on Abu Zubaydah, CIA officials suggest, the second wave of attacks might have occurred and KSM could be free and planning more attacks.

8

KSM

O N MAY 8, 2002, the FBI arrested Jose Padilla at Chicago
O'Hare International Airport on a material witness warrant. By then, Abu Zubaydah had identified Padilla, an
American citizen who was tasked by KSM to detonate a dirty bomb,
from a passport photograph. He told interrogators that Padilla and
Binyam Muhammad had been working on a plot to detonate the
bomb somewhere in the United States.

Muhammad, who was later captured, told investigators that he
and Padilla researched the bomb plot and were trained in explosives
wiring. But he said that al Qaeda leaders ultimately directed Padilla to
return to the United States to conduct reconnaissance on behalf of al
Qaeda within the United States.

"Abu Zubaydah's basic feeling was, having spent time with
him, that Jose Padilla was not sophisticated enough to pull together a radiological device by himself," says an FBI official.
"Abu Zubaydah was trying to convince KSM, if we're going to
give the kid a job, let's make it something deadly but something
simple enough that he can pull off. Let's try something realistic like
renting apartments in apartment buildings and filling the whole
building full of gas and large amounts of explosives. Blow the
buildings up from the inside instead of from the outside with a
truck bomb."

So, even though KSM's original draft of the plot was to set off a radiological bomb, Padilla was tasked by Abu Zubaydah to scout for

those kinds of projects in America and by KSM to try to set off a dirty bomb as well.

When arrested, Padilla was carrying $10,526, a cell phone, and e-mail addresses of al Qaeda operatives. The FBI said it believed it had disrupted a plot to blow up apartment buildings and to detonate a dirty bomb.

"Padilla was true to life, a guy who was recruited, offered his services, wanted to come to the U.S. to do something and was going to do something," Art Cummings says. "We just got enough intelligence on him in advance to show that he was going to do something. That was the early days. We wouldn't treat it that way today. When he came here to the States, he was arrested. I'd have collected against him, for a long time, and I would've worked him after that."

To conduct around-the-clock surveillance, Cummings would have assigned two teams of seven agents each.

"If you're going to run twenty-four hours a day, you need to give people time off, so that'd probably be four or five teams, plus aviation support," Cummings says. When the FBI was "no longer comfortable that we could control him or that surveillance was productive, then I would have taken him to a five-star hotel and worked to get his cooperation."

On September 10, 2002, the U.S. government raised the threat level to orange—high risk of terrorist attacks—in response to information about a possible anniversary attack on September 11. Meanwhile, the FBI began arresting terrorists who were not necessarily part of al Qaeda but had been inspired by it. These so-called homegrown terrorists often sought support from al Qaeda but were not controlled by the organization, which was in disarray because of rollups by the CIA and the military with help from foreign countries.

By the end of 2002, FBI Director Mueller could point to about a hundred terrorist attacks that had been thwarted by the U.S. government since 9/11, including some intended to take place on U.S. soil. Other plots involved planned attacks on the U.S. embassies in Paris,

Yemen, and Albania; an American building in Turkey; and a NATO building in Brussels.

The United States got its biggest break on March 1, 2003, when Khalid Sheikh Mohammed, the architect of the 9/11 attacks, was captured in a predawn raid in Pakistan. He was involved in planning the bombings that killed more than 180 people in Bali.

The CIA and FBI first became interested in Mohammed because of his role in a Philippines-based plan hatched by him and his nephew, Ramzi Yousef, to blow up as many as a dozen airplanes crossing the Pacific. Mohammed would meet associates in karaoke bars and go-go clubs. He would hold meetings at four-star hotels to plan the plot, code-named Bojinka.

The men also discussed assassinating Benazir Bhutto, then prime minister of Pakistan, and blowing up the American consulate in Karachi, U.S. nuclear power plants, and a range of U.S. government buildings in the United States and elsewhere.

The Bojinka plot was foiled when Yousef, who was the explosives expert, accidentally set fire to his one-room apartment. A police detective became suspicious when Yousef claimed that firecrackers had started the fire. Police were already on edge because the apartment was a block from where Pope John Paul II was to stay during his upcoming visit. They returned to the apartment with a search warrant. On a computer, the police uncovered details of the airliner plot.

In an interview with al-Jazeera television on the first anniversary of the 9/11 attacks, Mohammed, a Kuwaiti national of Pakistani ancestry, said planning for the 9/11 plot had begun in 1999.

"The attacks were designed to produce as many deaths as possible and havoc, and to be a big slap for America on American soil," he said.

Back in early 1996, the CIA traced Mohammed to Qatar, where he was working for the Qatar Water department. A CIA agent took a job with the department so he could obtain Mohammed's fingerprints and make a positive identification. Aware that the Qatar government might compromise a plan to seize him, the Clinton National

Security Council tried to arrange to fly Mohammed out secretly. But the CIA said it lacked sufficient resources.

"The CIA's paramilitary force had been dismantled," says Michael Battles, a former Army Ranger who joined the CIA in the Special Activities Division. "What we were doing was considered unseemly."

Since the CIA would not help, the NSC asked the Pentagon to devise a plan to seize Mohammed. The plan entailed flying helicopters into Qatar, but the NSC feared that the country would think it was being attacked by Bahrain, triggering a war. So the CIA wound up asking the Qatar government if it would help the FBI arrest Mohammed. The result was that Mohammed was tipped off and got away.

Mohammed came close to being arrested five more times. Each time, he escaped or did not show up as expected. Finally, intercepts and information developed months earlier allowed the CIA to trace Mohammed to the posh Westridge neighborhood of Rawalpindi in Pakistan.

In capturing key al Qaeda operatives in countries like Pakistan, the CIA, usually working with the Department of Defense, sometimes with help from the FBI, pinpoints the locations of the terrorists and informs the local security service. As an example, the Inter-Services Intelligence Directorate of the Pakistan Military (ISI) might make the arrests. However, being aware that the Taliban has penetrated the ISI in the past, the CIA and FBI often stake out the neighborhood where arrests are to take place. Agency and bureau operatives may wear disguises. Sometimes, the local arresting officers include CIA assets, as happened with the capture of Abu Zubaydah.

"You can't take the risk that they will get away like in the movies," a former CIA official says.

In pinpointing targets, the CIA uses an array of high-tech techniques. The agency regularly bugs offices, embassies, or mosques by training laser beams on simple objects like dishes or ceramic or glass lampshades. The beams pick up vibrations from the objects and beam conversations back to CIA officers.

The CIA developed a method to introduce laser beams into fiber-optic strands as fine as human hair. The laser beams turn the end of the strand into a microphone, creating an almost invisible bugging device. To further conceal them, the ends of the strands could appear inside a hole in the wall smaller than a pin hole. The bugs are essentially invisible and undetectable electronically.

To communicate with agents, the CIA issues devices ranging from satellite phones concealed in rifles to laptop computers that send and receive encrypted documents. The programs are secreted on hard drives in innocuous games or graphics. At pre-arranged times when satellites pass overhead, the agents aim the computers out a window, and the secret messages are sent or received.

To help hunt terrorists, the CIA operates the Gnat, a 24-foot unmanned plane equipped with radar called Lynx. Made by General Atomics, the plane can detect objects as small as four inches—about what a satellite can see—at a distance of up to sixteen miles, day or night, rain or shine. It relays still photos or videos via satellite to remote locations. The Gnat flies quietly at four or five miles above the earth. It can stay aloft for forty-eight hours without refueling.

When Khalid Sheikh Mohammed took a plane to Islamabad on February 28, 2003, ISI officers followed him. At 3:00 A.M. on March 1, ISI and the CIA closed in on Mohammed, who was sleeping in a white t-shirt in a spacious two-story villa. Besides snatching him, the CIA also picked up Mustafa Ahmed al-Hawsawi, who allegedly oversaw the hijacking plot's finances through bank accounts in the United Arab Emirates.

The arrest was a turning point in the war on terror. It showed that Bush meant what he said at Barksdale Air Force Base on September 11, 2001: "Make no mistake: The United States will hunt down and punish those responsible for these cowardly acts."

Within a few months, the transcripts of KSM's interrogations were four feet high. The CIA shipped his computers, telephone records, and other seized evidence under armed guard to Langley. The material disclosed plans, operatives, and sources of financing.

Mohammed, thirty-seven, told the CIA about a range of planned attacks—on U.S. convoys in Afghanistan, nightclubs in Dubai, targets in Turkey, and an Israeli embassy in the Middle East. He revealed that another al Qaeda operative he knew was in CIA custody, a terrorist named Majid Khan. KSM revealed that Khan had been told to deliver $50,000 to individuals working for a suspected terrorist leader named Hambali, the leader of al Qaeda's Southeast Asian affiliate known as J-I.

When CIA officers confronted Khan with this information, he confirmed that the money had been delivered to an operative named Zubair, and he provided both a physical description and a contact number for this operative.

Based on that information, Zubair was captured in June of 2003. He soon provided information that helped lead to the capture of Hambali. After Hambali's arrest, KSM was questioned again. He identified Hambali's brother as the leader of a J-I cell and Hambali's conduit for communications with al Qaeda.

Hambali's brother was captured in Pakistan. That capture in turn led to a cell of seventeen southeast Asian J-I operatives. When confronted with the news that his terror cell had been broken up, Hambali admitted that the operatives were being groomed at KSM's request for a second wave of attacks inside the United States, probably using airplanes.

As with Abu Zubaydah, the CIA used aggressive tactics in persuading KSM to talk, and the FBI refused to participate. A March 4, 2003, story in the *New York Times* said his captors "are likely to use tactics like sleep deprivation and psychological manipulation in trying to pry information from him, officials said today."

Because that story appeared on page A13, it had no impact, and there was no outcry from civil libertarians. A previous story that appeared in the *Washington Post* on December 26, 2002, said that when captured al Qaeda operatives refused to cooperate, they were sometimes kept standing for hours in black hoods or spray-painted goggles. At other times, they were deprived of sleep and bombarded with lights. Again, there was no outcry.

Illustrating how reactions are influenced by the play the major media give to certain stories, those same disclosures led to denunciations, investigations, and a Pulitzer Prize for a *Washington Post* reporter when given bigger play in 2005 and 2006.

As questioning of KSM proceeded, he provided details of other plots to kill innocent Americans. For example, he described planned attacks on buildings like the Library Tower in Los Angeles. He outlined how operatives were directed to carry them out. He said the operatives had been instructed to ensure that the explosives went off at a point high enough to prevent the people trapped above from escaping out the windows.

Subsequently, at a military hearing at Guantánamo Bay in March 2007, KSM confessed to planning both attacks on the World Trade Center. He described himself as bin Laden's operational director for the 9/11 attacks and as al Qaeda's military operational commander for "all foreign operations around the world."

KSM said he had also planned the failed missile attack on an Israeli passenger jet after it took off from Mombasa, Kenya. He said he was responsible for the 2002 bombing of a nightclub in Bali, Indonesia, an attack that killed 202 people.

Other plots he said he was responsible for included planned attacks against the Sears Tower in Chicago, the Empire State Building and New York Stock Exchange, the Panama Canal, and Big Ben and Heathrow Airport in London—none of which happened. He said he was involved in planning assassination attempts against former presidents Carter and Clinton, attacks on U.S. nuclear power plants and suspension bridges in New York, the destruction of American and Israeli embassies in Asia and Australia, attacks on American naval vessels and oil tankers around the world, and an attempt to "destroy" an oil company he said was owned by former secretary of state Henry Kissinger on Sumatra in Indonesia.

KSM also claimed he shared responsibility for assassination attempts against Pope John Paul II and Pakistan president Pervez Musharraf. Finally, KSM said he personally killed *Wall Street Journal* reporter Danny Pearl, who was kidnapped and murdered in Pakistan in 2002. KSM said he "decapitated with my blessed right hand the head of the American Jew Daniel Pearl," but that the incident was not part of an al Qaeda operation.

In all, Mr. Mohammed said he was responsible for planning twenty-eight attacks and assisting in three others. The comments were included in a twenty-six-page transcript released by the Pentagon.

KSM contended that he and al Qaeda are not terrorists but are engaged in a long struggle against U.S. oppression in the Middle East. He said he wants to make a "great awakening" to force the United States to stop foreign policy "in our land."

He apologized for killing children in the September 11 attacks. "Because war, for sure, there will be victims," he said. "When I said I'm not happy that three thousand been killed in America. I feel sorry even. I don't like to kill children and the kids."

He likened al Qaeda's quest to Colonial America's struggles in America's Revolutionary War. "So when we made any war against America, we are jackals fighting in the nights," he said, adding later that had George Washington been arrested by the British, he, too, would have been considered an enemy combatant.

In the initial CIA questioning, KSM provided vital information on al Qaeda's efforts to secure biological weapons. He admitted having met three individuals involved in the organization's efforts to produce anthrax, a deadly biological agent. One of the individuals he identified as a terrorist named Yazid Sufat.

Khalid al-Mihdhar and Nawaf al-Hazmi, the two hijackers who slipped into the United States in July 2001, were known by the intelligence community to have attended an al Qaeda summit in January 2000 at Sufat's apartment in Kuala Lumpur.

KSM apparently believed that the United States already knew about Sufat, because Sufat had been captured and taken into foreign custody before KSM's arrest. In fact, U.S. intelligence did not know about Sufat's role in al Qaeda's anthrax program.

Information from Sufat then helped lead to the capture of his two principal assistants in the anthrax program, preventing al Qaeda from developing anthrax for attacks against the United States.

Finally, KSM's information led indirectly to the arrest in Ohio of Iyman Faris, whom Mohammed had tasked to take down the Brooklyn Bridge. The Pakistanis were about to arrest a relative of KSM. Art Cummings asked the CIA to get them to hold off until surveillance could be put in place on others who could be expected to react to the man's arrest.

The Pakistanis "gave us four hours, total," Cummings says. "We basically identified that guy's associates in the U.S. in four hours— we knew about some of them—and basically put collection in place, leading to Faris."

After a FISA application was approved, the FBI began wiretapping Faris. In most cases, the FBI does not physically attach a wire to a line in order to wiretap. It simply asks the appropriate telephone provider to electronically shunt the line to be tapped to the appropriate FBI field office for monitoring.

To make sure the FBI can intercept terrorists' e-mails, the FBI goes so far as to ply them with offers of free computers or phone equipment to make sure the bureau does not have a problem intercepting their communications.

"We gave somebody technical equipment because his equipment was so old and hardly working that we couldn't get the technical collection we needed," Cummings says. "In this case, we arranged for him to stumble into a great promotional deal—as in free—to upgrade his technology. When I worked terrorism back in the 1990s, if we had an opportunity to send equipment to a terrorist organization, and it enhanced that terrorist organization's capability, almost under no circumstances would that have been approved."

In the case of Iyman Faris, the FBI's surveillance led the bureau to discover the Brooklyn Bridge plot.

"Faris was someone who had gone overseas and reached out for al Qaeda," Cummings says. "He had some connections in Pakistan. He met KSM, who tasked him to come back into the U.S. and study how to drop the Brooklyn Bridge."

Faris "actually was looking at some cutting devices for cutting the cable," Cummings says. "You can imagine some idiot sitting up there straddling an eighteen-inch cable, with a cutting torch trying to cut the cable. He would have been tackled and probably beaten to death by New Yorkers before he got very far. But he was looking at a number of other things at the same time. The problem was, he was a research conduit for al Qaeda central, directly. So eventually he probably would have gotten to a point where they would have given him something useful. He also knew a lot of people."

Before 9/11, Cummings says, "We would have indicted him, taken him to jail, and worked with his lawyers to see if he wants to cooperate. Absolutely. After 9/11? No way. We approach him, using smart agents with lots of experience to convince him that it's in his best interest to work with us."

Faris quickly agreed to cooperate.

"We worked him for over a month—worked him and worked him and then worked him some more," Cummings says. "We had the agency and military and everybody on board with us."

Faris eventually pleaded guilty. On October 28, 2003, he was sentenced to twenty years in prison.

9

STIRRING UP LIBRARIANS

ON MARCH 31, 2003, the 9/11 Commission held its first public hearing, To focus attention on the 9/11 attack and its victims, the hearing was held at the Alexander Hamilton Customs House in New York City. The ensuing hearings in Washington and the commission's scathing reports brought to a crescendo the criticism that began within an hour of the attacks about the "intelligence failure."

The truth was the government had never taken the al Qaeda threat seriously enough and dealt with it in a coherent, aggressive fashion. Moreover, even with the most focused effort, no country can stop every plot, any more than every bank robbery can be stopped.

In a videotape recovered in Afghanistan, bin Laden was seen chatting with followers. According to an early translation, bin Laden told them that few within his own organization knew of the plot, and most of the hijackers recruited for the "martyrdom operation" were not aware until the last minute that they were going to their deaths. According to a later, more precise translation, bin Laden said they knew they were going on a martyrdom operation but did not know until the last minute what the targets were.

The 9/11 commission made much of the fact that, in the months before 9/11, the CIA received and distributed reports on hundreds of terrorist threats. When read with the benefit of hindsight, they all sounded ominous. Yet none of them pinpointed the plot that finally unfolded. Most were third-hand accounts that were not credible. For example, a 1998 report about a plot to crash a bomb-laden plane into the World Trade Center originated with a police chief in the Caribbean. The chief said he had heard from Islamic militants in his country that Libyan officials were planning the attack on behalf of Iraq. The CIA considered such an attack highly unlikely but distributed the report anyway. Nevertheless, the headline over one story said: U.S. FAILED TO ACT ON WARNINGS IN '98 OF A PLANE ATTACK.

An August 1998 report said a group of unidentified Arabs planned to fly an explosives-laden plane from a foreign county into the World Trade Center. In November 1998, a report said an Islamic extremist group in Turkey was considering crashing an airplane into the tomb of a Turkish leader.

"We had threats to malls, threats to power plants, threats of assassinations, across the board we had threats coming in every day," says Dale Watson, who was in charge of counterterrorism at the FBI.

The implication of the 9/11 Commission hearings was that because these tips were not pursued, the government had goofed again. Yet without specifics, there was no way to follow up on any of those tips. In fact, none of the threatened attacks occurred.

More egregious, the final report of the commission almost totally disregarded the changes that had occurred in the intelligence community in the intervening three years.

"The criticism by the 9/11 Commission in terms of people not working together was a snapshot of the tenth of September, 2001," says a CIA official who worked closely with the commission. "By the time the 9/11 Commission wrote its report, that wasn't reality anymore."

President Bush recognized that the failure to catch the hijackers was systemic. Instead of assigning blame, Bush began taking steps to correct the problems, making it clear that lack of cooperation between the FBI and CIA would not be tolerated and asking Congress for billions in additional funds for the CIA.

Bush took the approach that to protect America, the help of FBI agents and CIA officers was critical. They risked their lives simply going to work. Along with the Capitol and the White House, the headquarters of the CIA and FBI were the most likely terrorist targets. Yet after 9/11, the FBI and CIA came under constant criticism. Nothing they did was portrayed by the press in a positive light.

Rather than castigate the two agencies, Bush visited the FBI and the CIA to tell employees how crucial they were to winning the war on terror.

"One week after 9/11, Bush came to the CIA," George Tenet recalls. "He said, 'I trust you, and I need you.' It doesn't often happen that way in Washington, D.C. The president could have easily cut us off at the knees. Instead, he came to us and said, 'I have enormous confidence in the men and women of this organization. I know what your work has been like.' If you don't think that made a difference in everything that has happened since," Tenet said, "you don't understand the relationship between the CIA and the president. It gave us peace of mind so we could do our jobs. Our boss was at our back. There isn't enough money in the world to tell you what that meant."

Yet by spring 2003, the tools Bush had put in place to gather intelligence to stop another attack were under assault. In particular, the Patriot Act became a symbol of an alleged assault on civil liberties.

"This law is based on the faulty assumption that safety must come at the expense of civil liberties," said Laura Murphy of the American Civil Liberties Union. "The USA Patriot Act gives law enforcement agencies nationwide extraordinary new powers unchecked by meaningful judicial review."

"We have begun to tamper with some of the basic laws—laws that strike at the heart of what this democracy is about," Anthony Romero, executive director of the ACLU, said.

Gregory Nojeim, associate director of the ACLU's national office, said that giving the FBI more powers was "rewarding failure at the FBI."

In fact, the legislation was an effort to update existing law to keep up with technology and give the FBI the same powers in terrorism cases that it already had in cases targeting drug traffickers, spies, and Mafia figures. Since under the new law each roving wiretap had to be approved by a judge, there was no question about infringing on civil liberties, any more than when a judge approved a search of the house of a suspected child molester. It was a question of making it at least as easy for the FBI to do its job as it was for a terrorist to do his.

The critics seemed to think that FBI agents relished wiretapping and that allowing them to do it somehow rewarded them. In fact, because of the paperwork involved, it was the least appealing part of an agent's job. As it was, the FBI literally did not have the personnel to transcribe and translate all the wiretapped material it received.

Since the days when J. Edgar Hoover ordered illegal wiretaps and improper surveillance, the FBI as an organization had not engaged in illegal conduct. If the FBI could not be trusted to wiretap within the framework of the law, then why trust agents to make arrests or carry weapons? What was the point of having an FBI if civil libertarians hobbled it so it could not perform its mission? Whose rights were being violated more, those whose phones were tapped by court order or those who died in the 9/11 attacks?

If the FBI ever did abuse its authority, the appropriate response would be to prosecute those responsible and institute more oversight—not to make it more difficult to wiretap so that terrorists could avoid detection and kill again.

In its effort to repeal the Patriot Act, the ACLU claimed that the FBI now could use "sneak and peek" tactics in libraries to probe the reading habits of sinless grandmothers without informing the targets until after a search. But the FBI always had authority, with a judge's approval, to conduct a search without telling the suspect until a later point in the investigation. If the FBI were trying to stop a terrorist bombing and needed to search the computer of a suspect in order to round up the plotters without tipping them off, would anyone want the FBI to inform the suspect that his computer was about to be searched?

Neither did the FBI have any interest in anyone's reading habits. Its interest was in finding the bad guys before they killed again. Since some of the 9/11 hijackers used Internet connections at libraries to communicate, the FBI might ask a judge for authority to search a particular library's computers to find such communications.

The ACLU whipped librarians into hysteria, and they began destroying charge-out records of library patrons so the bureau would not get them. In Seattle, the public library printed 3,000 bookmarks to warn patrons that the FBI could obtain permission to look at their reading or computer records.

"The FBI . . . is all over the library threat, seizing library records at will under the Patriot Act," Naomi Klein wrote in the *Nation*.

Five years after the enactment of the Patriot Act, the number of searches of charge-out or computer records conducted at libraries under the business records provision of the new act was one. The provision allowing for roving wiretaps had been used forty-nine times.

Undaunted, some members of Congress—including Republican Representative C. L. "Butch" Otter of Idaho—insisted that perhaps agents were clandestinely conducting searches of library records on their own. Otter added that "some of these provisions place more power in the hands of law enforcement than our Founding Fathers could have dreamt and severely compromises [sic] the civil liberties of law-abiding Americans."

Since only one library had been searched, critics said the provision in the act should be repealed.

"If they haven't used it, they shouldn't have any problems with our efforts to get it repealed," Representative Dennis J. Kucinich, a Democratic presidential candidate, said.

That was like saying that because a policeman had never used his gun, it should be taken away. If the provision were needed to stop a dirty radiological bomb attack that might kill hundreds of thousands of people, would Kucinich oppose the law? Bush wanted the provision in place before it was needed, not when it was too late.

The ACLU had a field day with the one search the FBI conducted in the summer of 2005 at the Library Connection, a consortium of twenty-six libraries in the Bridgeport, Connecticut area.

"This is further evidence that the FBI is indeed using provisions of the USA Patriot Act to obtain library patron reading records, an activity the American Library Association (ALA) has fought since the passage of the legislation in 2001," the ACLU said in announcing that it was suing the FBI on behalf of the library. "Such open-ended fishing expeditions expose all library users to the search and seizure of their records and to the invasion of their privacy."

In fact, the FBI had used what is called a national security letter to try to find out who had sent a detailed, threatening e-mail to a government agency from one of the Library Connection's computers. The FBI was not interested in anyone's reading habits or general Internet usage, as the ACLU claimed. Rather, it wanted to nab the person who had sent the anonymous e-mail before he killed hundreds of people. Moreover, because it knew which computer had originated the e-mail, the FBI only wanted transmission data for that one computer during a forty-five-minute period on the day the e-mail had been sent.

This was the modern-day equivalent of trying to find out who had set off a false alarm from a fire box. The police would dust the fire box for fingerprints and check out any nearby surveillance cameras. In this case, because the FBI wanted to catch the suspect before he got away, secrecy was critically important.

The ACLU complained that under the Patriot Act, it was barred from disclosing the identity of the institution or other details of the FBI's demand. Newspapers, magazines, and TV shows ran hundreds of stories on the ACLU's complaint and its suggestion that the FBI was engaged in a sinister subversion of civil liberties.

In fact, in this case, the secrecy imposed by the Patriot Act worked to the ACLU's advantage. Library officials knew that the FBI was not looking for patrons' charge-out records, but for data from a particular computer from which an e-mailed threat had been sent. But because neither the ACLU, the library, nor the FBI could disclose that fact, the ACLU was able to make up chilling charges that the FBI was trying to obtain patrons' reading records, hiding from the public the real reason for the FBI's interest.

In the end, the FBI decided that the threat was a hoax. But if it had been real and the FBI had failed to track down the perpetrator in time, the media would have pounced on the bureau for having failed to do its job.

In attacking the USA Patriot Act, the ACLU argued that Bush was exploiting the 9/11 tragedy to gain wider powers. That was like saying that President Franklin Roosevelt exploited the Japanese attack on Pearl Harbor to get the United States into World War II. The ACLU warned ominously that the number of wiretaps was increasing. That was like complaining that arrests were increasing. The reason the number of wiretaps was increasing was that the FBI was doing a better job of tracking down terrorists and other criminals. When Democratic Senator Dianne Feinstein of California asked the ACLU if it knew of any actual abuses by the FBI under the Patriot Act, the organization admitted that it knew of none.

In fact, before 9/11, relentless media criticism and a lack of clear authority under Justice Department guidelines had caused the FBI to become so gun shy and politically correct that even though terrorists were known to hatch their plots in mosques, the FBI was averse to following suspects there, a restriction that since has been rescinded. Because he was a cleric, FBI and Justice Department lawyers debated for months whether to open an investigation of Sheik Omar Abdel Rahman, who was later convicted in the first World Trade Center bombing.

Under the guidelines in place before 9/11, FBI agents could not even look at online chat rooms to develop leads on people who might be recruiting terrorists or distributing information on making explosives. The FBI had to first determine that there was a sound investigative basis before it could sign on to chat rooms any twelve-year-old could enter.

In other words, "A crime practically had to be committed before you could investigate," Weldon Kennedy, the former FBI deputy director, says. "If you didn't have that, you couldn't open an investigation."

"We were told before 9/11 that we were not allowed to conduct investigative activity on the Internet, even though it's public," Cummings says. "Same thing with a mosque. It's a gathering open to the public, but we were absolutely precluded from going into a mosque as an FBI agent. And precluded from having a source in a mosque report on anything in the mosque, or look at anything in the mosque, unless we had a specific target within the mosque."

"I remember discussions when we said that unfortunately, it will take a tragedy before the issue of the tools we need is recognized for what it us," says Larry Collins, a former FBI special agent in charge in Chicago. "Maybe a congressman's daughter has to be kidnapped, and we can't track her. Congress tied our hands."

Meanwhile, having initially criticized the government for doing too little to stop the next attack, the media now switched to criticizing the government for doing too much. Even though no abuse was involved, any classified FBI or CIA program became fair game.

If the FBI collected the same personal credit information anyone can obtain for $25 by going on the Web, the media said the bureau was "spying." Often, the media mischaracterized the administration position or reserved facts that undercut the lead of a story until the last few paragraphs of the story.

When the 9/11 Commission reported that it found no "collaborative relationship" between Iraq and al Qaeda, the *Washington Post* said in its lead that the conclusion challenged "one of the Bush administration's main justifications for the war in Iraq." Yet Bush had never said that Saddam and al Qaeda were working together as partners. He said there had been many contacts between them, a fact that the 9/11 Commission confirmed. But the *Washington Post* story mentioned that point in the fourth paragraph under the headline AL QAEDA-HUSSEIN LINK IS DISMISSED.

Taking a similar approach, the *New York Times* buried the 9/11 Commission's confirmation of contacts between al Qaeda and Saddam in the eighth paragraph of its story.

In other cases, the media simply ignored evidence that undercut its theme. On April 23, 2006, Tyler Drumheller, a former chief of the CIA's Europe Division, said on *60 Minutes* that he was shocked that the Bush administration and the CIA were claiming that Iraq had weapons of mass destruction and that Saddam was trying to obtain uranium from Niger. He said Bush knew then that a CIA source—later identified as Naji Sabri, the former Iraqi foreign minister—was secretly telling the CIA that Saddam had no WMD.

"He [the source] told us that they had no active weapons of mass destruction program," Drumheller told Ed Bradley in a segment called "A Spy Speaks Out."

"So in the fall of 2002, before going to war, we had it on good authority from a source within Saddam's inner circle that he didn't have an active program for weapons of mass destruction?" Bradley asked.

"Yes," Drumheller said.

Drumheller maintained that the White House brushed aside the CIA report because the policy was "set." Drumheller claimed, "The war in Iraq was coming, and they were looking for intelligence to fit into the policy, to justify the policy."

But according to an addendum to a report by the Senate Select Committee on Intelligence on postwar findings about Iraq's WMD program, Drumheller's entire story was untrue. In fact, CIA documents showed that Sabri—referred to in the report only as a source—warned the Bush administration that Saddam did indeed have WMD.

"Both the operations cable and the intelligence report prepared for high-level policymakers [based on interrogation of the source] said that while Saddam Hussein did not have a nuclear weapon, 'he was aggressively and covertly developing such a weapon,' " the Senate report said.

Both CIA documents said "Iraq was producing and stockpiling chemical weapons." They both said Iraq's weapon of last resort was mobile launched chemical weapons, which would be fired at enemy forces and Israel, the report said.

Moreover, there is "not a single document relating to this case which indicates that the source said Iraq had no WMD programs," stated the addendum. "On the contrary, all of the information about this case so far indicates that the information from this source was that Iraq did have WMD programs."

Pointedly, the report added: "The committee is still exploring why the former Chief/EUR's public remarks differ so markedly from the documentation."

Prior to issuance of the Senate report, the media had run at least 134 stories referring to Drumheller's claims and his criticism of the CIA and Bush administration in general. One of the stories ran as the second lead of the June 25, 2006 *Washington Post*.

WARNINGS ON WMD 'FABRICATOR' WERE IGNORED, EX-CIA AIDE SAYS, read the headline. According to the story, Drumheller was dumbfounded when he saw a classified version of the speech Colin Powell was about to give to the United Nations citing Iraq's biological weapons factories on wheels. Drumheller claimed he had warned both George Tenet, the director of Central Intelligence, and John McLaughlin, the deputy director, that the source for that claim was a fabricator.

Buried in the eighth paragraph of the *Washington Post* story was a single line saying that Tenet "now" says he did not learn of the problems with the defector, known as Curveball, until much later. By using the word "now," the paper implied that Tenet had changed his story and was therefore being misleading.

Not until almost the end of the story did the reader learn that both Tenet and McLaughlin said they had no recollection of warnings

Drumheller allegedly gave them in person or on the phone. Nor did the reporter ask Drumheller why, if he was so incensed, he did not send a written communication to document his concerns.

According to Ed Bradley's introduction to the *60 Minutes* piece, Drumheller saw how the Bush administration "time and time again welcomed intelligence that fit the president's determination to go to war and turned a blind eye to intelligence that did not."

In fact, it was the media that was in the business of suppressing the truth. In the weeks after its release, no media outlet ran the Senate committee's findings demolishing Drumheller's claims and the report by *60 Minutes*. Still, most of the major TV and cable networks continued to invite Drumheller back to repeat his discredited claims.

10

"SPYING ON AMERICANS"

AS IMPROVEMENTS IN intelligence collection and coordination progressed, the media adopted a new term to describe any secret method for catching terrorists: spying on ordinary Americans. By playing stories about intelligence gathering as if they revealed scandals, the media succeeded in making it appear that the government's efforts to protect Americans were abuses.

Thus, on November 6, 2005, the *Washington Post* ran a story stripped across the top of page one. It was headlined THE FBI'S SECRET SCRUTINY. The subhead claimed that in the hunt for terrorists, the FBI EXAMINES RECORDS OF ORDINARY AMERICANS.

The story by Barton Gellman claimed the FBI issues 30,000 national security letters a year, allowing the bureau to "sweep up records of many people" and "extending the bureau's reach as never before into the telephone calls, correspondence, and financial lives of ordinary Americans."

Despite the chilling language of the article, national security letters are similar to grand jury subpoenas, which are normally issued at the direction of a prosecutor and allow the FBI to obtain records of calls, e-mails, and searches on the Web in criminal investigations. National security letters are issued in international terrorism and espionage investigations. They do not allow the FBI to wiretap or to see the contents of e-mails. In contrast to grand-jury subpoenas, compliance is not required.

The FBI has similar authority, through what are called administrative subpoenas, to obtain records in drug, health care fraud, and child abuse criminal investigations. Since grand jury subpoenas are normally approved by the clerk of the court after a prosecutor requests them, they do not undergo judicial review any more than the FBI's national security letters do.

As it turned out, the actual number of national security letters issued by the FBI each year averages around 50,000. While that number may sound like a lot, an investigation of one suspected terrorist may entail issuance of hundreds of national security letters to track down data from each bank account, credit card, cell phone, telephone, e-mail, and Internet account he may have used over time.

The 9/11 hijackers used computers in libraries to evade detection. If the FBI had received a tip that those men had seemed suspicious, the bureau could have immediately used national security letters to obtain a listing of the recipients of their e-mails to see if, in fact, those suspicions had any basis. Waiting for additional approvals from a prosecutor or judge before obtaining the list of e-mail recipients might have meant that the FBI would have been too late to stop the plot.

In any case, the *Washington Post* story reported no abuse of national security letters. Instead of forthrightly conceding that, the story buried in the fortieth paragraph this line: "Those who favor the new rules maintain—as Senator Pat Roberts (R-Kan.), chairman of the Senate Select Committee on Intelligence, put it in a prepared statement—that 'there has not been one substantiated allegation of abuse of these lawful intelligence tools.' "

By using the word "maintain" instead of "said" and attributing the fact that there had been no abuses to "those who favor the new rules," the *Washington Post* sought to undercut the simple fact that its story in fact revealed no abuses. Instead, in issuing national security letters, the FBI was doing its job, trying to stop the next attack. Yet through clever language and positioning of the story at the top of page one, the *Washington Post* presented a legitimate, lawful operation as a scandal.

In a later audit, Justice Department Inspector General Glenn A. Fine found minor deficiencies associated with 22 of the 293 national security letters he examined from 2003 to 2005. In some cases, the letters were issued after the authorized investigation period, or an agent had accidentally transposed the digits in a telephone number of a person under investigation.

In about half the cases, the problems were not the fault of the FBI: According to Fine's report, recipients of the letters sometimes turned over more information than requested or provided information about the wrong phone number. These problems never should have been lumped in with FBI violations.

Mueller brought that up with Fine, who insisted he was right to do so.

Mueller says the reason the FBI did not keep proper track of requests for national security letters is that no separate system had been set up to keep track of them.

"What we did not have is a compliance program or a mechanism to test the procedures we put in place," Mueller says. "The biggest fix in my mind cuts across not just NSLs but across the organization," he said. "We need a compliance entity that looks at the weak points in terms of our procedures, does red-cell–testing of those procedures to see where the weaknesses are, and makes certain that the procedures are being followed."

By the time the report came out, Mueller had already taken twelve steps to correct the problems, including installing a Web-based data system to keep better track of national security letters and instituting new review processes and additional training. In fact, during the period examined, the FBI itself had found twenty-six errors and appropriately corrected and reported them.

Fine specifically found that the FBI had not intentionally violated any rules. He determined that, with the exception of situations where the recipient made an error, the FBI in most cases had obtained information to which it was, in fact, entitled. He noted the tremendous workload of FBI agents trying to stop the next attack. And he concluded that NSLs have contributed significantly to the FBI's counterterrorism effort.

The news accounts either ignored or downplayed these findings. Instead, they played up the story as a massive intrusion into people's personal lives, suggesting NSLs had something to do with monitoring calls rather than simply obtaining subscriber information associated with telephone numbers and e-mail addresses or obtaining financial records.

The news accounts routinely referred to the findings as "abuses." An abuse was when J. Edgar Hoover wiretapped individuals to obtain political secrets or blackmailed members of Congress to obtain a higher budget, as detailed in the author's *The Bureau: The Secret History of the FBI*. Transposing digits in telephone numbers, while inexcusable, amounts to sloppiness. Ironically, a table accompanying the *Washington Post's* page one story about Fine's report itself contained a typo, listing as 273 instead of 293 the number of cases examined by Fine.

On November 2, 2005, the *Washington Post* again stripped across the top of page one a story by Dana Priest. CIA HOLDS TERROR SUSPECTS IN SECRET PRISONS, the headline said. The story said some of the CIA's most important captives had been held at a "Soviet-era compound in Eastern Europe." Subsequent stories in the media suggested the CIA held thousands in prisons.

In fact, the CIA held most al Qaeda operatives in detention rooms on military bases in Afghanistan, not in a Soviet-era compound in Europe. During the course of the program, fewer than a hundred were detained. More important, the CIA was doing what it was supposed to be doing. If the agency held captives at federal prisons in the United States, they would be killed by fellow prisoners. Nor could the CIA interrogate them easily in a federal prison. Yet the *Washington Post* story caused an international uproar. For political reasons, a number of European countries informed the CIA that they could no longer cooperate with the agency on other matters like passing along leads on terrorists.

In the same vein, an Associated Press story was headlined, "Navy Secretly Contracted Jets Used by the CIA." The planes were used to return terror suspects to countries that practice torture, the story reported breathlessly. Of course, if the suspects came from countries that practice torture, the relevant question should have been, "Why should the U.S. give them a safe haven from the laws and practices of their own countries?" And the fact that the CIA uses Navy planes should be useful news to no one but terrorists.

Almost three years earlier, the *Los Angeles Times* disclosed on its front page of January 15, 2002, that the CIA was recruiting Iranian-Americans in southern California, home to the largest concentration of Iranian émigrés in the United States. According to the paper, the agency was "offering cash for useful information" to Iranian-Americans who "have business connections [in Iran] or relatives in [a] position to provide valuable information from inside the largely impenetrable republic."

As with stories about secret CIA prisons and use of Navy planes to transport terror suspects, the agency was doing exactly what it should be doing—in this case, trying to develop intelligence about the Iranian nuclear program. When George Tenet learned about the story, he called Dean Baquet, the paper's editor, to plead with him not to run it because of the harm it would do, but Baquet ran the story anyway, claiming everyone in the Iranian community already knew about the CIA's efforts. Even if that obvious exaggeration were true, running the story in the paper guaranteed that the Iranian government would be alerted to a program that entailed no abuse and therefore was not news.

In a 2006 interview with *Frontline*, Baquet was asked if it was his job to run stories that reveal secrets that the government says will help the enemy.

"Yes, because it's not my job to believe everything the government tells me," Baquet, now Washington bureau chief of the *New York Times*, said. "If the government had offered compelling proof that a life would be threatened, or if the government offered compelling proof that an ongoing operation would have been threatened, I would have felt differently."

There is no way to prove that the publicity scared off a potential recruit who might have provided the CIA with information that ultimately would have opened a window on Iran's nuclear program or even plans for a possible attack. But in 2007, the Iranian government began detaining Americans who were not connected with the CIA on charges they were spies. Those detained, like Haleh Esfandiari of the Woodrow Wilson International Center for Scholars, and Kian Tajbakhsh, an urban-planning consultant, were the sort of people the *Los Angeles Times* revealed the CIA was trying to recruit. CIA officials believe the story fueled those Iranian suspicions.

Robert Grenier, who headed the CIA's Counterterrorism Center when the *Washington Post* began writing about secret prisons and other aspects of cooperation with the CIA by foreign intelligence services, says the stories had a devastating effect, even though they were mostly wrong.

"For the most part, they were the usual pastiche of rumor, half-truth, and innuendo, generally attributed to unidentified sources whose grasp of what was happening in most cases was—to us—transparently half-baked," Grenier says. "By citing the alleged cooperation of specific countries in highly sensitive areas, however, these leaks were having a chilling effect. They made it appear to many of our partners that we couldn't keep a secret—that we couldn't protect them under circumstances when they were cooperating with us in good faith for the benefit of their countries but in ways which would have been highly unpopular with their own populations."

Cooperation with America in the war on terror is seen in much of the world as a war against Muslims.

"Though most of what was published was untrue, our partners couldn't know that," Grenier says. "Our protestations to that effect seemed self-serving to them."

Perhaps half a dozen countries—most critically important in the war on terror—said they would have to ratchet down cooperation with the CIA on sensitive projects. All did, in fact, scale back such cooperation.

By December 2005, the effect of the leaks was becoming intolerable.

"Looking at my senior lieutenants around our conference table one morning, I was at the point of distraction," Grenier says. "We can't go on like this," he told them.

While it was clear that most of the leakers were no longer working for CIA, some of the leaked information seemed to be coming from inside the building.

"In a series of verbal messages to the workforce, I invited anyone who had misgivings about what the agency was doing to speak directly with me about it, and I told them clearly that anyone betraying the trust placed in them, to leak information anonymously, was not a hero, but a coward," Grenier says. "Press accounts claimed that there was open dissent about aspects of our CT program within the organization. Nothing could be further from the truth. There was no such debate, though I would have been happy to foster open discussion."

In prosecuting the war on terror, "the CIA has depended utterly upon the good will and cooperation of foreign partners, and it was just those relations which a few journalists were sacrificing for the benefit of their own egos," Grenier says. "The reward for Dana Priest became clear in April 2006: She won the Pulitzer Prize."

Meanwhile, "when it became the expectation in the intelligence community that vital information was going to be leaked, it had a big impact on morale," says Grenier. "The press's pattern of irresponsibility had a vitiating, corroding effect on all of us."

With the media reporting nothing but criticism of the government's counterterrorism efforts, a finding that the FBI and CIA were successfully prosecuting the war on terror should have been news. But when the House Intelligence Committee's Subcommittee on Oversight issued a report with that conclusion, the *Washington Post* buried it at the end of an eleven-paragraph story on July 28, 2006.

The subcommittee found that while some areas still need work, overall "we do have a relatively successful counterterrorism capability," which it attributed to "exceptional individuals overcoming organization and planning pitfalls."

While the *Washington Post* tacked the conclusion onto the end of its story, the *New York Times* didn't mention it at all. The paper ran only the subcommittee's criticism that some reforms were not proceeding fast enough.

Ironically, before 9/11, the *New York Times* was even more clueless about bin Laden than the government was. Three days before the 9/11 attacks, the paper shelved a story by John F. Burns about a two-hour videotape that was appearing on Islamic Web sites throughout the world. The tape featured bin Laden saluting the bombing of the USS *Cole* in Yemen and promising more attacks.

"Mr. bin Laden uses the tape to spell out a continuing nightmare for his principal enemies, the United States and Israel," Burns wrote. "He promises an intensified holy war that includes aid to Palestinians fighting Israel—an important shift in emphasis, according to intelligence analysts. In recent years, through a series of violent attacks, Mr. bin Laden's main focus has been on driving American forces from the Arabian Peninsula."

The story noted, "With his mockery of American power, Mr. bin Laden seems to be taunting the United States. Although FBI investigators believe he was behind the World Trade Center bombing in 1993, two bombings in Saudi Arabia, and the bombings of two American embassies in East Africa, the United States has found no way, so far, of containing him."

The story ran on September 8, 2001, on the paper's Web site, but the paper's editors decided the story was not important enough to run in the *New York Times* itself. They pulled it for "space reasons," according to Burns. When the story did not run in the paper, the Web site expunged the story from its database. By September 11, the story had disappeared.

Asked about the matter by the *Washington Post*, Bernard Gwertzman, editor of Nytimes.com, admitted "a bad screw-up." The *New York Times* ran thousands of stories about the government's alleged failures, but the paper never ran a story on its own journalistic failure. Dismissive as they were about bin Laden before 9/11, the editors of the *New York Times* quickly became experts on how flawed the government's response was to the al Qaeda threat.

Meanwhile, politicians found that they were guaranteed air time if they criticized the FBI or CIA. Senator Bob Graham, the Florida Democrat who headed the Senate Select Committee on Intelligence, claimed the FBI "still doesn't know where the terrorists are, how many are here, what their intentions are, what kind of support network they have." He added, "They have so little to show for their work, and we have so little time to take action now. No evidence I've seen shows they have a sense of urgency or a thoughtful plan or very much information to predicate a plan on."

Mueller met with Graham and showed him a seventy-four-page report listing hundreds of changes the bureau had made since 9/11 to combat terrorism. The number of agents working counterterrorism had been doubled to 2,398. The number of intelligence analysts had doubled to 2,161. The number of emergency FISA applications had increased to 170 a year, more than three times the number in the twenty-three years after enactment of the law.

Before 9/11, the FBI produced few intelligence reports. After 9/11, it was producing 2,450 a year. Before 9/11, the FBI was not capable of giving a comprehensive intelligence briefing. After 9/11, it regularly conducted such briefings with the president, the attorney general, and other government officials.

"Graham's comments were a joke," D'Amuro says. "I'd go in to see Graham with the director, and I'd push back and say, 'Your analysis is wrong, and here's why.' Then Graham would leave and go out and hold a press conference and say how the bureau's all screwed up."

Pat D'Amuro thought Mueller should go on the offensive to combat the unfair congressional and media criticism. But Mueller didn't want to go on the attack.

"He wanted to be seen as making changes," D'Amuro says, "but agents want you to protect them, want you to be challenging the misinformation that's out there."

If the CIA and FBI had no sense of urgency, that was news to D'Amuro, Cummings, and other agents who were working fourteen-hour days to prevent another attack. Their families rarely saw them but had to watch constant reports about how incompetent they were.

In case he was called to testify in one of the many investigations into the FBI and the intelligence community, Cummings kept a journal with notes on important conversations.

"Every time you turn around, somebody is looking for another way to say the FBI dropped the ball," he says. "We don't take it personally, but we do shake our heads in disgust."

11

EAVESDROPPING
ON BIN LADEN

EFORE 9/11, THE CIA was far more alert to the al Qaeda threat than the FBI. In a December 4, 1998, memo to his deputies, George Tenet declared, "We must now enter a new phase in our effort against bin Laden." He said, "We are at war. . . . I want no resources spared in this effort, either inside the CIA or the community."

Robert Grenier, who was station chief in Islamabad and became chief of the Counterterrorism Center, remembered Tenet's reaction when Grenier proposed trying to foment hostility between the Taliban and al Qaeda in 2001.

"Very much to my surprise, when I came back on R&R in July 2001, I got a phone call saying the director wants to see you in his office at seven o'clock tomorrow morning," Grenier says. "Senior counselors and senior folks in the CIA were there around the table, and George pulled out these cables that I had written over previous months. And clearly he had studied them very, very closely. They'd been highlighted, they were annotated in his hand, and he started asking me very detailed questions about what it was that we were proposing, how we would go about it, and how we would sequence it."

Two months later, the World Trade Center was attacked, and the U.S. uprooted the Taliban militarily. But Grenier says, "Very clearly, in George Tenet's mind, the threat from al Qaeda was the greatest priority that he had to deal with. He essentially was the headquarters' action officer on these issues."

Nonetheless, the media and Congress ignored the fact that the CIA was far more focused on al Qaeda before 9/11 than they were. Instead, they lambasted the agency over its failings. Senator Bob Graham, who chaired Congress' Joint Inquiry into the 9/11 attacks, described the agency's lapses as "inexcusable" and "outrageous." But when Tenet finally had a chance to testify publicly in October 2002, Graham tried to limit his prepared statement to ten minutes. As Tenet endeavored to plow ahead, Graham kept cutting him off.

"Mr. Tenet, twenty-one minutes, now," Graham said at one point.

"Well, sir, I just have to say, I have been waiting a year," Tenet responded.

After other members sided with Tenet, Graham allowed him to continue. Tenet pointed out that in the previous decade, Congress had cut the CIA's budget 18 percent after inflation was taken into account. The number of employees had declined by 16 percent. Covert officers had been cut by 25 percent.

Another committee member, Senator Richard C. Shelby, a Republican from Alabama, repeatedly called for Tenet's resignation. Obtusely, Shelby lamented that he could find no one in the intelligence community who knew about the plots of 9/11 and had failed to issue a warning. In other words, he wished the failure had been worse than it was.

"It would be nice to find a smoking gun," Shelby said wistfully. "But absent that, we're looking for problems that need to be solved."

Ironically, federal investigators later concluded that Shelby leaked the top secret contents of two messages intercepted by NSA just before 9/11. Fox News chief political correspondent Carl Cameron confirmed to FBI agents that Shelby verbally divulged the information to him during a June 19, 2002, interview, minutes after Shelby's Senate Select Committee on Intelligence received the information in a classified briefing.

Cameron did not air the material, but Shelby then met with CNN reporter Dana Bash. Half an hour after that, CNN broadcast the material.

The disclosure involved two messages that NSA intercepted on the eve of the September 11 attacks but which were not translated until September 12. The messages said in Arabic, "The match is about to begin" and "Tomorrow is zero hour." The *Washington Post*, citing senior U.S. intelligence officials, reported on the same messages in its June 20, 2002, editions.

Shelby issued a statement saying he never "knowingly compromised classified information." The Senate Ethics Committee declined to take any action.

Like the rest of the information the intelligence community received before 9/11, the messages intercepted by NSA could not have begun to lead investigators to the al Qaeda plot. Their reference to something that was about to happen could have related to almost anything. However, from its first briefing with President-elect Bush in Crawford in December 2000, the CIA had been warning him about Osama bin Laden and al Qaeda. In April and May, CIA briefer Michael Morell began conveying reports of chatter indicating that terrorists could be planning a major attack. During the summer, Bush asked several times whether the CIA had any information indicating an attack might occur within the United States. The answer was that while bin Laden wished to launch a direct attack and had made such plans in the past—including the thwarted plot to bomb Los Angeles International Airport—no intercepted communications suggested it was about to happen.

On August 6, the CIA gave Bush a background paper on bin Laden's interest in attacking the United States. Full of vague, uncorroborated information, it was mainly an historical document and showed just how little the CIA and FBI knew about al Qaeda's presence in the country.

While the CIA had agents in al Qaeda at low levels, it had not penetrated bin Laden's inner sanctum. Back in 1998, NSA had succeeded in intercepting bin Laden's satellite phone calls. But on August 17, 1998, the *Washington Post* ran a story citing a claim by Vincent Cannistraro, a former CIA counterterrorism official in the late 1980s, that the United States was intercepting bin Laden's calls. The story ran ten days after al Qaeda bombed American embassies in Kenya and Tanzania.

The article paraphrased Cannistraro's claim that he was "aware of intercepted electronic communications among bin Laden associates in the aftermath of the embassy bombings in which they take credit for the attacks and exchange warm congratulations."

In a subsequent letter to the editor, Cannistraro, without denying that he had made the claim, backpedaled from his own quote. "I do not have current access to intelligence collection techniques, nor am I aware of the specific nature of any intelligence information the U.S. intelligence community has on bin Laden's alleged responsibility," Cannistraro wrote.

Within a few days of the publication of Cannistraro's claim, bin Laden and his people stopped using the phone. Based in part on the location of the phone, Clinton ordered a Cruise missile attack on August 20 on an al Qaeda paramilitary training camp in Khost, Afghanistan, and on the El Shifa pharmaceutical plant in Khartoum, Sudan's capital. The attack killed twenty-one al Qaeda trainees from Pakistan but missed bin Laden.

"Today we have struck back," Clinton said after the missile attacks.

Even if bin Laden had been killed, such an attack could never inflict real damage on al Qaeda. If the statement was laughable, it diverted public attention from Clinton's televised admission three days earlier that he had misled the American people about his relationship with White House intern Monica Lewinsky.

Regardless of the strike, intelligence officials believe bin Laden would have continued to use the phone if the intercepts had not been compromised.

Two days before the *Washington Post* ran Cannistraro's claim, a Knight-Ridder story that appeared in nine local papers quoted Cannistraro on the bombings. The story included unattributed quotes saying that "U.S. intelligence officials" reported that "an exhaustive review of electronic intercepts of traffic on bin Laden's communications network has uncovered some evidence that bin Laden helped plan the attacks, along with some congratulatory messages after the August 7 bombings in Nairobi and Dar es Salaam."

That statement was vaguer than the one in the *Washington Post* and appeared in papers such as the *New Orleans Times-Picayune* and the *Dayton Daily News*. As a result, the CIA did not consider it as significant a compromise. An on-the-record comment in the *Washington Post* by a former CIA counterterrorism official was an entirely different matter. The story was also available on the paper's Web site.

Once the comments appeared, subsequent press stories speculated about whether NSA was intercepting bin Laden's communications. Because those stories were not as specific or credible and appeared days after bin Laden stopped using the phone, they were not considered as significant as the original *Washington Post* story.

In congressional testimony, then NSA Director Michael V. Hayden described the press compromise as a "setback of inestimable consequences."

Cannistraro's public statements years earlier calling the CIA a "dinosaur" and more recently a bureaucratic "mush factory" had not endeared him to his former colleagues. But the intelligence community never fingered him for compromising the bin Laden intercepts because any SIGINT (signals intelligence) information is highly classified and because intelligence officials as a rule do not want to call even more attention to the fact that NSA intercepts communications of terrorists. In addition, no one is eager to single out for criticism a powerful media outlet like the *Washington Post*.

Asked about his comments, Cannistraro said he had no comment on the matter beyond his letter to the editor. But had the *Washington Post* not run the story, bin Laden's location could have been pinpointed through his satellite phone. As a result, he might have been captured before 9/11. Moreover, NSA could have still been listening to his calls in the months before 9/11.

Thus, long before 9/11, the media was undercutting the government's efforts to catch terrorists in the most damaging way possible. Nor was President Clinton helpful. Clinton had no use for intelligence. While he read the President's Daily Brief, Clinton stopped the CIA's morning briefings six months after he became president.

R. James Woolsey, Clinton's first director of Central Intelligence, loved to tell the joke he heard about the plane that crashed into the White House. "They said it was just Woolsey trying to get an appointment with Clinton," Woolsey deadpans.

"I didn't have bad relations with Clinton," Woolsey says. "I just didn't have any relations with him. Clinton was interested in balancing the budget, health care, NAFTA. He did not want to accomplish much in the foreign policy arena."

Bush thought the Clinton's administration's response to bin Laden only confirmed that the United States would do little to go after him. In effect, tossing Cruise missiles into tents was like waving a red handkerchief in front of a bull and goading it to attack again. Condoleezza Rice called the policy "feckless."

Meanwhile, John M. Deutch, Clinton's second appointee as director of Central Intelligence, imposed a damaging rule that CIA officers obtain high-level clearance before recruiting an agent with so-called human rights violations. Yet agents who had murdered or tortured people were the ones who would know what the bad guys were up to. It was as if the FBI had said it was no longer interested in getting help from Mafia members like Sammy Gravanno—whose testimony was critical in convicting Mafia boss John Gotti—because Gravanno had murdered nineteen people.

Deutch's rule sent a message to CIA officers throughout the agency that it was better to sit in their offices and collect paychecks than to take risks.

A former MIT chemistry professor who was appointed by Clinton to be deputy secretary of Defense, Deutch further shattered morale at the agency by saying publicly that CIA officers were not as competent as military people. He would tell guests at Washington dinner parties that the military was far superior to the CIA.

Deutch made no secret of the fact that he had never wanted the CIA job anyway. In a characteristic parting shot after he resigned, Deutch peevishly told the *Washington Post*, "Everybody says it's a job I've been pushed out of, but I would recall it's a job I was pushed into."

"The human rights violation rule had a chilling effect on recruitment [of spies]," says William Lofgren, who was chief of the CIA's Eurasian Division, which includes Russia. "If faced with two possible recruitments, are you going to go after the one with a human rights violation or the other one with no human rights violation?" The result was that "people retired in place or left," Lofgren says. "Our spirit was broken. At the CIA, you have to be able to inspire people to take outrageous risks. Deutch didn't care about us at all."

As a chemist, Deutch felt comfortable with the certainty of science: Two chemicals mixed together react predictably. A chemical formula is neat, clean, unassailable. Gathering human intelligence is quite the opposite. It is fraught with uncertainty, entailing far greater risk than collecting technical intelligence. Ultimately, the job of the CIA's clandestine side is messy. Because CIA officers commit espionage in other countries, they can create big diplomatic and political trouble—flaps, the CIA calls it with typical understatement.

Deutch made it clear that he thought human collection was secondary to technical collection. In retrospect, as the need to penetrate terrorist organizations became clearer, it was an attitude that was chilling.

"I'm a technical guy," Deutch told an interviewer. "I'm a satellite guy. I'm a SIGINT [signals intelligence] guy."

To succeed Deutch, Clinton appointed Tenet, a former staff director of the Senate Select Committee on Intelligence who had been the CIA's deputy director and then acting director. When Bush became president, he took a liking to Tenet and asked him to stay on as director.

Both men were focused, prized action over words, and were highly patriotic. Accepting the Ellis Island Medal of Honor on November 6, 1997, Tenet described how his Greek mother had fled from southern Albania on a British submarine to escape Communism. She never saw her family again.

Like Bush, Tenet could be blunt. Neither man was given to pretense or "hand-wringing," the phrase Bush applied contemptuously to those who endlessly worried about taking decisive action. With Tenet, there was no meandering academic analysis, just straight talk.

When Michael Morell, now CIA associate deputy director, first briefed the newly inaugurated President Bush the day before the president was to go to Mexico, a White House steward entered the Oval Office with coffee. Bush motioned to his guest to stop talking while the steward was in the room. Mike was impressed. Bush cared about security.

At the end of the briefing, Bush brought up a planned trip to see President Vicente Fox of Mexico.

"Are you coming with me?" the president asked.

From that point on, Morell or alternate CIA briefers traveled with Bush on every trip. They saw him six and often seven days a week, whether at Bush's ranch in Crawford, his parents' home in Kennebunkport, at Camp David, or in the White House. Since the founding of the agency in 1947, no other president had wanted to be briefed by the CIA when he was out of town.

Every morning when Bush met with Mueller and Tenet, Bush reviewed the latest threats, following up on previous ones and demanding to know what the CIA and FBI were doing to make the country safer. As Mueller would say, nothing concentrates the mind so much as having to report every morning to the president of the United States. Bush was nothing if not focused.

"His concern is not the number of indictments and arrests," Mueller says. "It's what we have we done to assure that there will not be another September 11. That covers disrupting terrorist cells but also anticipating the attacks, looking at the threats, and making sure we track down every piece of information related to threat, whether it's here or overseas. He gets a report on that integrated investigation daily."

Having ramped up its efforts after 9/11, the CIA began seeing results. By the middle of 2002, the CIA had rolled up 3,000 terrorists in a hundred countries. Usually, a foreign service made the arrest based on CIA information. It became so common that Jim Pavitt, who headed the clandestine service, stopped telling Tenet about each success. In other cases, the suspect was sent to another country and held or prosecuted. The process was called rendering.

If an arrest took place within the United States, a cover story was developed so that it appeared that the FBI or Customs Service had arrested the suspects without receiving any inside information from the CIA. The idea was to hide sources and methods as much as possible.

Planned attacks on U.S. embassies in Italy, France, Yemen, and Albania and on other U.S. facilities in Turkey and Saudi Arabia were thwarted.

Symbolizing the agency's new approach to terrorism, in November 2002, a CIA-operated Predator armed with Hellfire missiles killed Abu Ali al-Harethi, an al Qaeda operative in Yemen. He was one of the top dozen al Qaeda figures in the world. The strike killed five associates as well as they traveled with him by car in northwestern Yemen.

Yemeni officials had given the CIA permission to operate the aircraft in their air space, but they did not want the fact publicized. When news of the strike leaked, they were furious. Back when FBI agents went to Yemen to investigate the bombing of the USS *Cole*, they had been frustrated by the lack of cooperation. Yemen's help now illustrated how profoundly relations with Arab countries had changed since 9/11. The fact that al Qaeda often ended up killing more Muslims than Americans in countries like Saudi Arabia only galvanized Arab countries to help the Americas in the war on terror.

The CIA interrogated captured terrorists at Guantánamo Bay and at secret locations throughout the world such as Bagram Air Force Base, an American installation in Afghanistan. While the CIA used coercive methods like depriving suspects of sleep and forcing them to kneel for hours, the CIA believed that actual torture involving infliction of pain produced bad information. Simply offering terrorists tea and sympathy was often enough to get al Qaeda members to talk. Often, the Stockholm Syndrome took over. Most al Qaeda members cooperated after a day or two. If not, they might be turned over to intelligence services in Egypt, Morocco, or Jordan where rough techniques could be used.

"You start by getting him talking to you," David Manners, the former station chief in Jordan, says. "You start with items you already know about. That shows him you know a lot. His defenses diminish. Then you ask about items you don't know about. Beating a guy up doesn't work. He will tell you anything to stop the pain. We never used such tactics."

Both responsible for the country's security and subject to urgent calls in the middle of the night, Tenet and Mueller became soul mates.

Like Tenet, Mueller had an aversion to talking to the press. He associated it with calling attention to himself and being boastful. In his three years as U.S. Attorney in San Francisco, he gave two press conferences. He told aides that when he had something to say, he would say it. His interest was in looking forward, not backward. Reputations are based on actions, not words.

After Mueller became FBI director in September 2001, he had to overcome his distaste and met regularly with the reporters who covered the FBI.

With far more experience in Washington than Mueller, Tenet became his mentor, guiding him in how to respond to press attacks, fair or unfair. For Mueller, the nadir was when the *Wall Street Journal* called for his resignation over the failures of 9/11 in an editorial, even though Mueller had become FBI director one week before the attacks took place. Democratic Senator Patrick J. Leahy of Vermont said it was "a parody of Washington scapegoating."

With the press continuing to maintain that the CIA and FBI don't talk to each other, Mueller and Tenet would socialize over dinner every three weeks with their wives, Stephanie and Ann, at DeCarlo's. An unremarkable neighborhood restaurant in Washington's Spring Valley section, DeCarlo's serves skimpy portions of linguine but is located about halfway between their homes. The two couples were left to themselves in the restaurant as FBI agents and CIA security officers hovered discreetly nearby.

12

THE TERRORIST
MIND-SET

I N APRIL 2004, the FBI, working with the Joint Terrorism Task
Force in New York, arrested Mohammed Junaid Babar on Long
Island.

Babar was an American citizen based in London who traveled pe-
riodically to the United States and Pakistan. The FBI became suspicious of him when NSA found he was e-mailing al Qaeda operatives
from a New York City library. Attorney General John Ashcroft later
cited that fact to show how important it was for the FBI to be able to
monitor computers in libraries. Meanwhile, the Brits picked up intelligence in London on a plot to blow up locations in London. Clues
from that cell led to Babar.

"We were working with them, and they gave us intel about the cell
that they had in the U.K. and the ties to Babar," Cummings says. "We
took all of that, and we began to run it through all of our systems—
CIA, FBI, NSA. We then tracked him. He was flying into the U.S.
There was an initial impulse on the part of the community, at large, to
react directly to him coming to the U.S. They said, 'Okay, what are we
going to do about this guy right now? We can't let him come in.'"

Cummings argued that the FBI should use him as a collection
platform.

"Everybody stay back, stay away from this guy," Cummings
would say. "We got his picture, we know when he's coming in, what
flight he's coming on, we've got all of that. It does the U.S. government

and the counterterrorism mission no good to take him off the street. It does nothing for us. I don't know why he's coming here, I don't know what his connections are. But I need the opportunity to spend as long as I need to spend collecting against him."

Working with the other agencies, the FBI did just that.

"New York had the case, and headquarters micromanaged the day-lights out of it," Cummings says. "We worked everything we could possibly work against Babar. We surrounded him with everything—a full net of collection. Technical, physical, airplanes, surveillance teams, everybody."

Conducting twenty-four-hour physical surveillance of a suspect requires dozens of agents. They may dress as homeless people, nuns, mail carriers, or ice-cream vendors. In following suspects on a street, agents are in constant communication. They may wear stereo head-sets to give the impression they are listening to rock music when in-stead they are receiving instructions on where to go next. Meanwhile, FBI agents in cars or trucks may pass the suspect or move with him along parallel streets. The agents may switch vehicles to further con-fuse the suspect. The vehicles may be Corvettes, old rattletraps, bull-dozers, buses, or ice cream trucks.

"A lot of it seems like overkill, but it's not," Cummings says. "Babar was an operator. He had sent some guys through training, and they were now going to murder some people. And we clearly needed to give the attorney general and the director confidence that we had this under control and could work him on the street and leave him on the street while we collected against him. It was that balance that's weighed every single day on an operation like this. The daily discus-sion was: 'What's the current intel on Babar? What's the current threat? And can we tell the attorney general and director that we have a hundred percent confidence that he's not going to get away and kill somebody?' We could only assure a confidence level of 99.9 percent. There's always a chance that something is going to happen."

Once the FBI knew everything about him, agents moved in to

have a chat with him. Facing the possibility of life in jail, he quickly flipped and agreed to cooperate.

Cummings set up the FBI's interrogation operations at Guantánamo and learned first hand how to get terrorists to cooperate without using coercive methods.

When Cummings first showed up at Guantánamo, the general in charge said, "I don't know why you are here. You're not going to arrest any of these guys."

"General, you have a fundamental lack of understanding of what the FBI does for a living," Cummings said. "We're not going to come here with handcuffs. My job is intel collection. I need to get what's in their head out of their head."

At the time, the military was using coercive interrogation methods. In addition, Cummings and other agents reported back to headquarters more egregious conduct. In October 2002, a Marine captain squatted over a copy of the Koran during intensive questioning of a Muslim prisoner. That same month, interrogators wrapped a bearded prisoner's head in duct tape "because he would not stop quoting the Koran." One interrogator bragged to an FBI agent that he had forced a prisoner to listen to "Satanic black metal music for hours," then dressed as a Catholic priest before "baptizing" him. Such conduct was not condoned by military policies.

Cummings argued coercive and degrading techniques wouldn't work.

"Okay, let me understand this," he would say. "You are going to somehow coerce a young jihadist who has just traveled a thousand miles through desert and unfamiliar territory to go put his ass on the line to die in really austere, dirty, nasty, rocky conditions, wholly untrained. And you think you're going to somehow make this guy uncomfortable? You found this guy in a cave starving and drinking only water, and what are you going to do to this guy that will compel him to do anything except hate you more?"

Coercive techniques were nothing new to Cummings. During

training as a Navy SEAL, Cummings had been subjected to coercive techniques that might be used if he were captured.

"If you're going against Johnny White Boy down the street, who was brought up in middle class America, yeah, it would probably work," Cummings says. "When talking about a jihadist, maybe it would work, maybe it wouldn't. I know what does work."

In seeking cooperation from a terrorist, Cummings tries out different themes.

"You try to understand the kid, whoever it is," he says. "Most of them are very young. You try to find out what's driving him, what's important to him based on his culture. It could be about marriage and children."

Cummings would say: "You're never going to see your mother again."

"Kids will be tough, but one of the values that should never be lost is compassion," Cummings says. "You're never unkind for the sole purpose of being unkind. Not because we're just a bunch of great people, but because compassion actually works. We will sit down in front of a bank robber and tell him his life is completely off track, and if he ever wants to live the life of a normal human again, he needs to get it back on track. It's a compelling argument."

Cummings found that what drives terrorists most is a look at their future.

"You understand, you're going to die in this steel box," Cummings would say. "And when you're dead, your life is nothing. You will die, and you will be nothing to anyone. When you die, you will be in an unmarked grave, and no one will know how you died, when you died, or where you're buried."

Cummings would look for body language that would tip him off to whether his approach was working. If not, he might take another tack.

"I saw one kid who was sitting there, not moving," Cummings says. "The tears were coming down by the gallons when I started talking to him about never having a child," he recalled. "He wasn't blubbering, but I knew I had him. Maybe it takes a couple days. But I'm not going to slap him on the side of the head. All that does is steel him—steel his courage. It reinforces why he hates me so much."

Instead, Cummings would offer hope: "If you ever want me to make the argument for you, I'm the conduit that gets you out of here," he would say. "I'm it. Look at me directly in the eyes. I'm it! No one else in the world. That's it. You'll have to help me out, and I'll help you out."

Most are susceptible to creature comforts as well.

"That's the one thing plenty of time will always give you," Cummings says. "Eventually, these guys just get tired of living in austere conditions, and the government offers them different accommodations based on different levels of cooperation. I got this guy who was in Guantánamo Bay and had tried to go on a jihad. He saw a little snuff on my lip—I don't dip anymore. He asked for some, so I said, 'Sure.' I gave him some."

The doctors at the base "went nuts because I was giving him snuff," Cummings says.

"I said, 'Okay, enlighten me here. What's the problem?'

" 'Well, it's not healthy.' "

"The only reason he's talking to me is because I'm supplying him with snuff," Cummings told the doctors. "So I'm going to be bringing a tin of Copenhagen every time I interrogate this guy," Cummings said. "And I guarantee you that, every time before he starts talking, he's going to put a big ol' mighty healthy dip in his lip."

The terrorist wound up talking to Cummings.

When Cummings returned from Cuba, Mueller asked what he had learned.

"What we got was a general understanding of this whole mind-set."

"Are we getting any tactical answers?" Mueller asked.

"Well, tactical stuff is only good for a week or two weeks after they're captured," Cummings said. "These guys have been in for months. But they can teach us everything about how the organization moves its money, moves its people, where did they get their education, when did they get radicalized, when did that happen, at what age?

"Our understanding of the enemy early on was wrong, heavily weighted toward the religious fanatic," Cummings says. "It became apparent to us in a very short period of time down in Guantánamo Bay that that wasn't the biggest factor driving them. Islamic extremism was a factor. But a lot of these guys were young and adventure-seeking. A lot of them were pressured by their families to go check that box: They wanted the jihadi badge of honor. But believing that when they died they would have seventy-two virgins waiting for them and that this was just a wonderful thing to die in the service of Allah was not the driver."

Cummings interrogated a Saudi who had gone to Afghanistan to fight.

"You know in my world, you're called a mercenary," Cummings told the jihadist.

The man started laughing.

"You don't get it," he said. "You think I draw the line at the Saudi border? You Americans are so selfish. All you think about is America. Well, I think about humanity, the *ummah*—the Islamic community that follows Mohammed. I'm coming here for you, to fight the broader cause, for Islam."

Cummings interrogated another prisoner who cried because he was only in Afghanistan one day.

"All he wanted to do was go touch Afghanistan," Cummings says. "Because once you've done that, you've got your badge. Done, been there. He said, 'I was there only one day, and they sweep in and grab me. I never did anything.' "

Of course, "They all claimed to be bakers or Koran salesmen," Cummings says. "That was the joke in Gitmo. I found that amazing. I remember saying to one guy, 'Oh, another Koran salesman.' And he said, 'Oh, selling Koran was good.' I said, 'Yeah, but it's an Islamic country, why do you need to sell Korans? They're all over the place.' He said, 'Oh, you've got to sell lots of Koran.' "

Armed with an understanding of the terrorist mind-set, the FBI worked Babar for weeks after he was arrested in Long Island.

"The key was convincing him, when it may not be in his best interest to speak to us," Cummings says. "We put him up in a four-star hotel, treated him like a star. We have done this half a dozen times. Sometimes we want to bring them back out, we want to put them back out on the street. Other times, they have no intel value after they're finished, and so we wouldn't put them back on the street if they weren't some exceptional source."

Babar revealed an ongoing plot to blow up London pubs and train stations. He also confessed to supplying al Qaeda members with ammonium nitrate fertilizer to make bombs and to set up a terrorist training camp in rural Oregon.

Meanwhile, the Brits took down Babar's fellow plotters in London. They rolled up eight terrorist suspects and seized one thousand pounds of ammonium nitrate fertilizer from a storage locker near central London.

In June 2004, Babar pleaded guilty to conspiring to provide material support to al Qaeda. He was sentenced to twenty years in prison.

13

AN AMERICAN MI5

On May 6, 2004, the FBI arrested Brandon Mayfield, an American lawyer, in his home city, Portland, Oregon, in connection with the March 11 terror bombings of commuter trains in Spain. The bombings had killed 191 people.

Mayfield had been identified through a partial fingerprint found on a blue plastic bag filled with detonators. The bag was in a van parked near the Alcala de Heneres train station in Madrid. All of the trains involved on the fatal day had originated from that station.

"When this came to us, we went, 'Holy cow!'" Cummings says. "We got a guy in Portland whose fingerprint is matching directly to the fingerprint on this bag. So my brief to the director was that we have an operative here. He's either witting or unwitting. He either gave somebody something in that bag and then they reused it, or he knows something about this. So we have some work to do against this guy."

The FBI found Mayfield was a former military man who had converted to Islam. As a lawyer, he had represented a high-profile terror suspect in a child custody case.

"This was a case where there was just coincidence after coincidence," Cummings says. "This guy is a Muslim convert. Okay, that gives me something, I've gotta look at him. It doesn't mean anything, but it means more than if his name is Jimmy O'Reilly and he's not a Muslim convert. He's not a terrorist, but he knows the wife of a terrorist."

The FBI found out that Mayfield had planned to travel to Barcelona.

"Okay," Cummings said. "We got a problem. Then we find out he's given money to the Holy Land Foundation, the funnel organization for Hamas."

Cummings told FBI fingerprint examiners to fly to Spain.

"What happened was prior to that, the Spanish had recovered the bag and the Spanish had submitted it to Interpol for comparison," Cummings says. "That's how we got a hit on him. Then before our raid, the Spanish National Police said they don't think the prints match."

When the examiners came back, they said the Spanish police had erred.

"They come back and go, 'No, that's not it, they're wrong,'" Cummings says. "In the middle of all this, we advised the court that the Spanish are doubting the fingerprint. So the judge said, fine, hold him on a material witness warrant. Mayfield got his own court-appointed fingerprint expert who affirmed the FBI's opinion that it was an identical match."

Then Spanish authorities raided an apartment where the terrorists were hiding out.

"They blew themselves up inside this apartment, and a finger comes out, and the finger matches the fingerprint found on the bag," Cummings says. "It was an exact match to the print."

Cummings asked the FBI examiners to return to Spain.

"You guys better figure this one out now," Cummings told them.

The examiners called Cummings from Madrid.

"We made a mistake," one of them said. "There was an anomaly that no one ever told me about."

"Oh, my God," Cummings says. "I was mad."

When prints are taken, the impressions are not always perfect.

"In this case, the fingerprints were from when he was in the military," Cummings says. "There was one area that looked kind of obscure, but we thought we didn't have to worry about that. But it was very different, once they saw the finger in person."

The problem was compounded by the fact that there were a re-markable number of points of similarity between Mayfield's prints and the prints submitted to the FBI from the bombing.

Cummings knew the press would slaughter the FBI, and Mayfield would be a multimillionaire. Every morning at 6:45 and again at 5:00 P.M., Cummings briefed Mueller on the latest twists and turns in the case. When Cummings told him about the debacle involving the fingerprints, the FBI director cocked his head to one side.

"How'd that happen?" he asked.

"Sir, we did everything by the numbers," Cummings said. "We'll be fine, but it's going to cost us."

"Yes, it is," Mueller said.

Cummings informed the FISA court, shutting down all technical collection relating to Mayfield. He informed the judge, who threw out charges against Mayfield on May 24, 2004. The FBI issued a formal apology. In November 2006, the government settled with Mayfield, agreeing to pay him $2 million.

Mueller asked an international panel of fingerprint specialists to devise ways to try to prevent such a misidentification in the future, and he implemented their recommendations.

Having stubbed its toe on the Mayfield case, the FBI faced a new threat: an ill-conceived proposal to do away with the FBI's counterterrorism effort and replace it with a new terror-fighting agency similar to the British MI5. Such an agency would have investigative powers but no law enforcement powers, as the FBI has.

The idea was first floated by former NSA director William E. Odom, a retired general and former head of NSA. In a *Washington Post* op-ed headlined WHY THE FBI CAN'T BE REFORMED, Odom wrote that the FBI's shortcomings in fighting the terrorist threat are systemic.

"No one can turn a law enforcement agency into an effective intelligence agency," he said. "Police work and intelligence work don't mix. The skills and organizational incentives for each are antithetical. One might just as well expect baseball's Washington Nationals to win football's Super Bowl as believe the FBI can become competent at intelligence work."

Richard A. Posner, a U.S. appeals court judge who wrote a book on intelligence, chimed in, advocating creation of an American MI5. In a *Washington Post* op-ed, he claimed that the FBI is oriented toward "arrest and prosecution rather than toward the patient gathering of intelligence with a view to understanding and penetrating a terrorist network."

These and other similar proposals came from people who had never investigated terrorism cases and seemed to have no clue about how the FBI investigates terrorism. That did not stop members of Congress from endorsing the idea, giving them another chance to go on TV.

In fact, the MI5 idea made little sense. It meant creating a new wall that would bifurcate the counterterrorism effort. In Great Britain, when an arrest must be made, the MI5 presents the case to a police agency such as the Metropolitan Police based at New Scotland Yard. MI5 then has the task of trying to persuade that agency to pursue it. Thus, rather than tearing down walls that impede cooperation and sharing of information, an American agency patterned after MI5 would create a new wall.

Even more important, without law enforcement powers, MI5 cannot use the threat of prosecution to try to elicit cooperation and recruit informants. Because terrorists often finance their activities by smuggling cigarettes, selling stolen designer clothing, or dealing in drugs, the FBI's structure makes it easy for the bureau to pass along leads from agents pursuing these cases to agents focused on counterterrorism.

During creation of a new agency, the country would be vulnerable to attack as investigators are recruited and trained. The well-publicized chaos at the Department of Homeland Security, which combined twenty-two agencies and departments, is an illustration of what can happen initially when a new agency is created.

The beauty of the FBI is that its focus on violations of criminal laws keeps FBI agents from violating civil liberties. Without that framework, agents might begin to stray into investigating political beliefs or dissent or even gathering personal information for the purpose of blackmailing political leaders, as they did when J. Edgar Hoover was FBI director. In doing so, they would lose their compass, forgetting what their target is and botching investigations because of a lack of proper focus.

A bureau legend is illustrative. According to that story, a New York FBI agent went to lunch at a deli around the corner from the field office's old location on Sixty-ninth Street at Third Avenue. The agent thought the deli was an establishment that offered a discount or more food to FBI agents and police officers. He ordered a roast beef sandwich and watched the counterman make it. The deli man slid the plate toward the agent. To the agent's chagrin, the sandwich looked no bigger than any other roast beef sandwich. Showing the deli man his credentials, the agent said, "FBI! More roast beef."

The counterman didn't know about any special deals and looked at the agent dumbfounded. The story soon spread to the FBI's fifty-six field offices. Probably no story is more widely known within the bureau, and it always brings a laugh. When they are dissatisfied with anything, FBI agents say, "More roast beef!" When they tell their bosses they showed their credentials, they say, "I roast-beefed him."

The roast beef story is so appealing to agents because it underscores what it means—and doesn't mean—to be an FBI agent. FBI agents have awesome power. They are authorized to carry weapons and can shoot to kill. They can deprive a suspect of his freedom and send him to jail for life. They can eavesdrop on private phone conversations, videotape what goes on in bedrooms, subpoena witnesses to testify before a grand jury, open mail boxes and read mail, and obtain telephone toll records and other confidential documents, including income tax returns. By consulting their files, they can learn the most damaging personal information. By showing their credentials, they can bypass airport security, take their weapons on airplanes, get into movie theaters free, and park illegally without getting a ticket. But unless an agent is on bureau business, has proper authorization, and, in many cases, has a court order, he has no more power than any other citizen. Showing "creds," as they are called, to obtain more food at the local deli violates the most basic credo of the FBI.

Cummings considered nutty the idea of handing over such awesome powers to a new agency that is not trained in law enforcement. Moreover, Cummings and other agents who worked with MI5 in Great Britain knew that their work was constantly impeded by their lack of law enforcement powers.

"I find it astounding that anyone would take the position that what you want to do is essentially to strip away the law enforcement powers and say, 'Now go fight terrorism,'" Cummings says. "To think that you're going to develop a domestic intelligence service from the ground up and do it in anything short of a decade before they can even walk, let alone crawl, is crazy. And then to think that they could do that and still have the organization grounded in the Constitution and the civil liberties that go with that, I think is crazy as well."

Posner's claim that the FBI focuses only on arrest and prosecution showed how misinformed he was about changes since 9/11.

"The day we arrest someone is the day I can't collect against him anymore," Cummings observes. "I don't know anything about him, I'm operating in the blind. And the day I take somebody off the street, leaving someone on the street who's going to kill me tomorrow, that is the day I haven't done my job."

Having the option of using the FBI's law enforcement powers as leverage is critically important. "Perhaps we found out that a suspect was committing some type of criminal violation," Cummings says. "That could potentially give us leverage to approach him. Most individuals who have been at a training camp have nefarious associates. They're going to be talking to like-minded individuals most of the time in the U.S. So then you look into whether he is being influenced or directed by an outside source. That's what intelligence is about, to figure it out."

"The FBI model of combining intelligence and law enforcement responsibility is the envy of allied services, including the British," says John L. Martin, who, as chief of the U.S. Justice Department's counterespionage section for twenty-five years, prosecuted seventy-six spies, and had extensive dealings with MI5.

"Indeed," he says, "MI5 is constantly impeded by its inability to quickly translate intelligence operations into arrests and prosecutions. Setting up an MI5 in the United States would create a significant and unnecessary barrier to fighting terrorism at a time when this country needs to enhance its communications among agencies and to quickly react to terrorist threats."

14

DUMB COPS

A S CRITICS CALLED the FBI broken, the bureau began rolling up terrorists every few months. Besides the arrests of Iyman Faris in Ohio and Jose Padilla in Chicago, the FBI in August 2002 arrested Karim Koubriti, Ahmed Hannan, and Farouk Ali-Haimoud in Detroit for conspiring to support al Qaeda. A search of their apartment revealed a cache of false documents, a day planner detailing planned attacks in Turkey and Jordan, and a videotape prepared for casing landmarks like Disneyland in California and the MGM Grand Hotel and Casino in Las Vegas.

In Seattle, Earnest James Ujaama was accused of providing support and resources to al Qaeda. Specifically, the indictment accused him of being a leader in discussions of firebombing vehicles and poisoning people. He pleaded guilty. Then on September 13, 2002, the FBI arrested five men in Lackawanna, New York, for providing material support to al Qaeda. A sixth man was rendered—or turned over—by Bahrain.

The men were U.S. citizens of Yemeni descent who lived in a tight-knit rural community. In summer 2001 the group flew to Afghanistan to train at Osama bin Laden's al-Farouq jihad camp. There, they studied how to make explosives, rocket-propelled grenade launchers, land mines, and other military equipment.

Nobody suspected them of terrorist activities. Indeed, Yasein Taher had been voted the friendliest person in his class in 1996. A former captain of the high school soccer team, he married his high school sweetheart, a former cheerleader. Sahim Alwan was a counselor at the Iroquois Job Center in Medina, New York.

George Tenet's book says the case began when the CIA picked up information about some of the suspects from computers and phone records in Afghanistan. But according to Cummings, "The initial reporting started with an anonymous letter to the FBI followed by the development of a source within the group by the FBI."

While the information from the CIA was valuable, "It wasn't until eight or nine months later that the agency provided additional valuable information on the group's overseas connections," Cummings says.

Initially, FBI agents found that the group professed to support bin Laden.

"There was a lot of rhetoric, but you know rhetoric's rhetoric," Cummings says. "Jihadi bravado we call it. But in terms of law enforcement, Jihadi bravado doesn't get you anywhere other than show someone thinks that way. But that does give us enough predication to take a look at them."

As the FBI began investigating further, however, the bureau found that "these guys are serious, really serious," Cummings says. "They really wanted to do something. They went to training camps overseas, they came back, they lived in very, very austere conditions, lived in trailers. But they were second generation Americans. At that time," Cummings says, "we kinda go, what's with these guys? These aren't immigrants. They were born and raised on American soil. How do you become an extremist that way?"

In March 2003, the suspects all agreed to plead guilty and cooperate with the FBI. They were sentenced to prison terms ranging from eight to ten years.

Meanwhile, on October 3, 2002, six individuals were indicted in Portland, Oregon, for providing material support and resources to a terrorist organization. They were Ahmed Bilal, his brother Mohammad Bilal, Habes Al-Saoub, Patrice Ford, Jeffrey Battle, and October Lewis.

Both the Lackawanna and Portland groups were home-grown. The Portland group tried to get to Afghanistan by going through China. "They tried to get the training and were not successful," Cummings says. "But they did enough to get them prosecuted."

In contrast, the Lackawanna Six, as they were called, did train at terrorist camps.

"They reached out, and they did get to a pretty connected guy with al Qaeda, but we got to them before they could actually get down to execution," Cummings says.

This new variety of operative is a combination wannabe and serious terrorist. Looking for any way to criticize the bureau, the media seized on the fact that the FBI usually arrested them before they had had a chance to advance their plots. News reports questioned whether those arrested could have ever executed their plans.

"The problem with a wannabe is that they can buy fertilizer and buy fuel and make something," says Philip Mudd, a CIA officer whom Mueller brought in as associate executive assistant director of the National Security Branch. In that role, Mudd is in charge of the FBI's analytical operations.

Having worked at the CIA and the FBI, Mudd has a unique perspective. He found that the stereotype of FBI agents as dumb cops who just want to make arrests is dead wrong. That stereotype is particularly prevalent among CIA officers who don't work with the FBI.

"Those who think all we want to do is arrest people are misinformed," says an FBI counterterrorism agent. "I don't want to just arrest people. I want to make cases and make them stick. I don't need to arrest people. I need to neutralize the cells."

The stereotype appears in the press routinely. On October 10, 2006, a *New York Times* story said, "Five years after the Sept. 11 attacks spurred a new mission, FBI culture still respects door-kicking investigators more than deskbound analysts sifting through tidbits of data."

In turn, politicians like Senator Charles E. Grassley, an Iowa Republican, got airtime with such comments as, "The FBI deserves a chance to get its act together. But their time to move from investigating Bonnie-and-Clyde–type crimes to preventing terrorist activities is getting shorter."

By Bonnie-and-Clyde–type crimes, Grassley was referring to non-terrorist crimes the FBI pursues, such as kidnappings, organized crime extortions, serial killings and rapes, fraud schemes, and looting of major publicly traded corporations like WorldCom and Enron. Grassley's suggestion that solving such crimes is not very important would come as news to their victims.

To be sure, despite the new emphasis on collecting intelligence, a small minority of agents resisted change, complaining that the FBI's traditional role of putting people in jail was being given short shrift. Mueller had no patience with laggards, accounting in part for a high turnover rate. Mueller either suggested that they find jobs elsewhere, or they became embittered and decided on their own to move on. The fact that industry offered salaries to FBI agents that were up to four times what they were making also meant that key counterterrorism jobs became revolving doors, a fact the press highlighted.

In the criminal arena, Mueller tried to prioritize, emphasizing organized crime and corruption cases and de-emphasizing drug cases.

FBI investigations led to the convictions of more than a thousand federal, state, and local employees on corruption charges over a period of two years. The highest profile cases were in Congress, including a probe into the web of corruption surrounding former lobbyist Jack Abramoff. That investigation led to guilty pleas from former Congressman Robert W. Ney, an Ohio Republican, and some congressional aides. A separate FBI investigation led to a guilty plea from former congressman Randy "Duke" Cunningham, a California Republican.

"I hate when the press talks about changing the culture of the FBI," an agent says. "We will do what we're told to do, and the culture has always been to stop evil. It hasn't always been to arrest people. When the reporters put the FBI down by referring to traditional

G-men, they forget, since the bureau was created, half of the bureau was devoted to intelligence, finding Soviet spies and espionage, like the CIA. These people seem to have no clue what we do for a living."

Mudd notes that an occasional agent will long for the days when criminal cases were the FBI's top priority. But throughout its history, the FBI has used intelligence. Through intelligence gathering, the FBI took down the Mafia and pulled off one of the biggest coups in the history of intelligence and counterintelligence by penetrating the Soviet leadership during the Cold War.

In 1954, the FBI began running a top-secret operation code-named SOLO, which entailed operating as an informant Morris Childs, the principal deputy to Gus Hall, the head of the American Communist Party. In effect, Childs—referred to by the FBI as Agent 58—was the second-ranking official of the party.

Carl N. Freyman, an FBI agent in Chicago, recruited Childs, a Ukrainian-born Jew and a former editor of the party newspaper the *Daily Worker*, after visiting him in his Chicago apartment. Since Childs was in ill health, the agent arranged for him to be treated at the Mayo Clinic in Rochester, Minnesota. Freyman managed to convince Childs that Soviet leader Josef Stalin had betrayed Marxist ideals.

Childs reported for twenty-seven years on party activities and strategy. In addition, he made fifty-two clandestine trips to the Soviet Union, China, Eastern Europe, and Cuba. The Soviets so trusted him that on his seventy-fifth birthday, Leonid Brezhnev, the Soviet leader, gave Childs a birthday party at the Kremlin. Meanwhile, on behalf of the Soviets, Morris Childs and his brother Jack Childs distributed $28 million in cash for Communist activities in the United States.

The FBI held the secret of SOLO so tightly that officials of the CIA, NSA, Defense Department, State Department, and National Security Council could only read reports of the operation while agents waited to return them to bureau headquarters. Not until 1975 did the FBI inform the president and secretary of state of the true source of the information.

Morris Childs reported on such items as the Sino-Soviet split, Nikita Khrushchev's speech documenting Josef Stalin's mass murders, and the Soviet invasion of Czechoslovakia.

In the FBI's effort against the Mafia, "We drew a picture of the families, figured out who the leadership was, took chump-change targets off the table, and said we're going to take the families down," Mudd says. "That was an intelligence-driven operation."

The press and others "would lead you to believe that there's a generation of the bureau that's out there saying, 'Let's not do this,' or 'What are we doing to the FBI?' " Mudd says. "I have not seen that here. What I see is people saying, 'Give us good training, give us the tools, give us the guidance to do what you want us to do.' "

As home-grown terrorists have sprung up, the antiterrorism effort has severely damaged al Qaeda, Mudd says.

"All of us thought on September twelfth it's going to happen again and again," Mudd says. "It has not."

Mudd was on the team at the CIA putting together a new Afghan government in the fall 2001.

"If you had said much of al Qaeda would be removed from Afghanistan, there will be a political process in Afghanistan, you will have a committed network of intelligence partners around the world, most of al Qaeda leadership will be gone, there won't be a major attack in the United States, no one would have believed it," he says.

According to Mudd, al Qaeda no longer can count on safe haven in Afghanistan. That has an impact on training, fund-raising, production of ideological materials, and operational plans. In fact, 80 percent of the original al Qaeda leaders have been rolled up.

Al Qaeda is "a very committed organization but they don't have anywhere near the same capability they had in 1998 or with the USS *Cole* bombing or the 9/11 attacks here." Those who are replacing operatives like Khalid Sheik Mohammed "do not have the same experience and capabilities. They're not as respected in the organization.

But nonetheless there are people moving up the ranks, so it's not like those spots on the bench go vacant."

On the other hand, Mudd says, "I would say that they look at attacks in places like Bali or Madrid or London, or attempted attacks in places like Canada. They would say they intended to inspire a new generation of people whom they may never train or never pay. I see an increasing number of plots, people, and occasionally attacks that fit that profile."

Besides the counterterrorism effort, increased security measures have made a difference, one that terrorists discuss among themselves.

"The billions that have been sunk into things like cockpit hardening have had an impact," Mudd says. "It's not as measurable as taking down Khalid Sheik Mohammed. But the adversary talks about the post 9/11 complications, they talk about airline security, they talk about screening rules. So when I see the adversary talk about how hard it is to operate here, I know it's had an impact."

The difference between this and a conventional war is that the adversary will keep coming.

"You negotiate a truce after World War II, and once that's negotiated, people go home," Mudd says. "In this war, this adversary will not go home. First of all, he can't. The local services will pick him up. And second of all, this is a very committed adversary. So you can take out rows and rows of sharks' teeth, but regardless of that risk to them, they're still going to talk about coming after us—recruiting, planning operations, raising funds."

What Mudd sees as having changed the most in the intelligence community is that now there is a presumption that every piece of information must be shared.

"It's been drilled into every single one of us," he says. "I need a compelling reason why we can't put a bit of information out. Whereas before, someone would say, 'Well, that's sensitive information, we can't release it.' That paradigm has been flipped. People simply will not sit on threat reporting. The cultural shift in the intelligence community is: get it out to people who can act on it. And if it's sensitive, figure out a way to mask it so people can't figure out where it came from. We're taking risks all the time to put stuff out the door that potentially reveals sources and methods, because you can't sit on threat reporting."

Yet the possibility remains that an attack could occur tomorrow.

"If you combine the seriousness of the problem we face and the commitment of the adversary, the intensity of the terrorism business kind of surrounds you," says Mudd. "Turn on the radio, it's on. You think about it over the weekend. Think about, what are they going to do next? It never leaves you. It's like going into a cigar bar, and you go home, and that's going to be in your jacket all the time, until you get it dry-cleaned. It's always there, it permeates you. I think we're doing a good job, but the tension is just that the stakes are so high, and there's so many adversaries out there, and it only takes one."

Terrorists are constantly plotting, waiting for an opening.

"There's someone out there trying to find a weapon, trying to build a bomb, and it never changes," he says. "You can't forget the faces that stared out from those *New York Times* pages, the victims of the 9/11 attacks. I drive home every night remembering those, the faces of the fallen. I remember watching the towers come down. You know, there's a lot of kids out there who will never see a parent again because an adversary had no respect for the sanctity of human life."

15

"YOU OKAY, DAD?"

SINCE 9/11, THE FBI and CIA had been grappling with how to warn Americans of terrorist threats. The media portrayed threats as if they were warning lights at railroad crossings, triggered when a train is coming. But terrorism takes place in a realm of uncertainty. Perhaps someone passes along a conversation overheard in a restaurant. It may sound like a lead to a plot, but the source could be making up the story or could have misheard what was said. No one can be absolutely sure if information about a possible plot is or is not valid. But no one in the FBI or CIA wanted to relive being second-guessed about whether information they picked up could have led to uncovering the next plot and was not disclosed to the public.

No matter what course they chose, counterterrorism officials realized that they would be criticized. If they raised the threat level and nothing happened, then the media would say they were trying to scare people for political purposes. If they issued no threat warning and an attack occurred, then the media would criticize the agencies for not knowing about the plot.

Decisions on raising or lowering threat levels were made in consultation with the Department of Homeland Security. Bush made the final decisions. Like department store detectives, the Homeland Security Department works with potential targets like power generating plants to improve their security. The agency warns them and the rest of the country of threats. In contrast, the FBI and CIA try to uncover and stop terrorist plots before they happen.

As officials gained experience, they were able to refine the procedures so that the threat level could be raised only for particular economic sectors, like airlines or financial institutions. Early on, some questionable decisions were made.

On December 27, 2003, the threat level was raised to orange because of a fear of multiple al Qaeda attacks. Just before that, Air France, British Air, and some United Airlines flights were delayed for hours to check out passengers who might be terrorists with bombs. It went back to a warning from an NSA contractor who claimed that, through mathematical formulas, he could detect coded messages sent by al Qaeda indicating that a particular flight would be targeted.

In this case, most FBI and CIA personnel were highly skeptical, but no one wanted to take the chance of ignoring the warning even though, when asked to disclose his methodology, the contractor refused.

"It was all hocus-pocus," an FBI agent says. "We were stopping planes all over the world. We had to scrub 'em, searching for the terrorists on board. It was all because some guy had developed some system—and this was very close to voodoo—that some other people believed in. He came up with this great theory. It was serious mumbo jumbo. There was a lot of disagreement in the community about this, and finally someone said, 'This is nonsense.'"

In other cases, the FBI would make it clear to local or state government officials that a threat was probably not credible, but they would take action regardless.

"We told California authorities about a threat to the bridges, and what do they do? They made it public. And everybody says, how the hell did this happen?" Cummings says. "We have an obligation to tell the governor of California there's a threat to the bridges, even though the threat was garbage, even though it wasn't vetted."

The tip about the bridges came from a source overseas whose handler was a U.S. Customs agent in the United States.

"The guy e-mailed him and laid out the threat as he knew it," an

FBI official said. "He got it from another source. The customs agent passed on the threat, which then went into the intelligence community for evaluation. This was fairly soon after 9/11. They didn't spend a lot of time massaging these things before they gave them to the entity that was responsible. In this case, it was the State of California."

The customs agent got in touch with his source, who went back to his source, and eventually authorities overseas ran it out, and it turned out to be nothing. In the meantime, the state stationed National Guard troops on the bridges. Traffic became snarled throughout the area. Commuters went into a panic. Many declined to go to work rather than risk a trip across the Golden Gate Bridge and other bridges.

"Obviously, Governor Davis thought that one thing he could do to enhance the security of people using those bridges was to make a public announcement," Homeland Security Director Tom Ridge said at the time. "We did not encourage him to do it."

On the other hand, there was good reason to raise the threat level to high on August 1, 2004. Surveillance plans seized in Pakistan showed that Dhiren Barot, a Muslim convert, was planning to blow up the New York Stock Exchange and a Citigroup Building in New York, the World Bank and International Monetary Fund in Washington, and the Prudential Building in Newark.

Also known as Esa al Hindi, Esa al-Britain, and Abu Esa al-Britani, Barot, thirty-four, was a native of India who grew up in north London. In 1998, Barot served as a lead instructor in a jihad training camp in Afghanistan, where recruits were taught to use weapons and received other paramilitary training.

Barot traveled to Kuala Lumpur around January 2000 with notorious al Qaeda operative Muhammad bin Attash. Also known as Tawfiq bin Attash, he was a fierce, one-legged former Afghan fighter who served as bin Laden's bodyguard. A native of Yemen, Attash later confessed at Guantánamo Bay to organizing the bombing of the naval warship USS *Cole* off the coast of Yemen in October 2000.

A tip from a foreign intelligence agency, combined with good analysis, led to Barot.

"There was a lot of anecdotal reporting about this guy, and he was involved in a bookstore, and he was a serious al Qaeda player," Cummings says. "An analyst put together a lot of common associations and some aliases he used. She was tracking every piece of reporting we could find, people who had worked in different bookstores overseas."

Finally, Barot's plans were found on a laptop computer seized during a raid on a house in Gujrat, Pakistan, in July 2004. British police arrested him the next month.

Eventually, the Justice Department brought an indictment against Barot. In October 2006, he pleaded guilty to charges of conspiring to murder people in terrorist attacks, including by planning to detonate at least one "dirty bomb" in Britain. He was sentenced to life in prison and must serve at least forty years.

Meanwhile, to better coordinate the counterterrorism effort and improve reporting to the White House on possible threats, Bush established the National Counterterrorism Center (NCTC) on August 27, 2004. Later that year, Cummings was named deputy director of the NCTC, which moved into its new building in McLean, Virginia, in January 2005.

To house the complex, the CIA bought an existing office building not far from the agency and stripped it down to the girders. It then rebuilt it as a SCIF. Pronounced skiff, a SCIF is a Secure Compartmentalized Information Facility that shields the inside from electronic eavesdropping.

A tall chain-link fence encircles the six-story stone building. Outside the fence, a grove of tall pines hides everything from the road. Embedded in the roadway to the building is the now familiar red STOP gate with teeth.

The windows of the two-story, crescent-shaped lobby run floor-to-ceiling. For the visitor, there are special red-lettered badges and the

FBI agent Arthur M. "Art" Cummings, who heads the FBI's international counterterrorism operations, says, "You make a mistake, there are dead people."

FBI Director Robert S. Mueller III transformed the Bureau into an effective counterterrorism agency that gathers and uses intelligence to stop plots before they occur.

Michael Heimbach, the FBI agent in charge of operations against al Qaeda, heard horror stories about refusals to share information between the FBI and CIA as recently as 2002.

President Bush created the National Counterterrorism Center (NCTC) to coordinate the U.S. fight against terrorism. Flanking him in the NCTC operations center, from left, are Fran Townsend, assistant to the president for homeland security and counterterrorism; General Michael V. Hayden, director of the CIA; and Vice Admiral John Scott Redd, director of the NCTC.

At the National Counterterrorism Center (NCTC) in McLean, Virginia, FBI and CIA personnel sit side by side around the clock, analyzing threats and parceling out leads.

(NCTC Photo)

(FBI Photo)

As principal deputy director of the National Counterterrorism Center (NCTC), FBI agent Kevin R. Brock presides at the 8:00 A.M. secure video teleconference with the rest of the intelligence community, whose members the media portray as not being on speaking terms.

While FBI Director Louis Freeh drastically downsized the Bureau's headquarters and saddled it with frighteningly primitive computer equipment, beefing up headquarters was a key part of Robert Mueller's transformation of the FBI.

Willie T. Hulon heads the FBI's National Security Branch. He placed Art Cummings in charge of the FBI's response to the British plot to explode nine American airliners in flight from London.

General Michael V. Hayden, director of the CIA, took steps to integrate the agency's operations.

Because of leaks about CIA operations, local agents recruited by American CIA officers have been compromised and killed, and other countries have diminished cooperation.

On one wall of the CIA's Counterterrorism Center (CTC) conference room, a twelve-foot-long sign highlights the agency's mission.

Robert L. Grenier, who headed the CIA's Counterterrorism Center, says media stories on the CIA's so-called secret prisons had a devastating effect, drying up cooperation in the war on terror, even though the stories were mostly wrong.

Because of the work of the CIA—along with the FBI and the military—5,000 terrorists have been rolled up worldwide since 9/11.

As assistant FBI director for public affairs, Cassandra "Cassi" Chandler, a lawyer and former TV anchor, tried to get the media to report honestly on the FBI but found it was a losing battle.

As he drives home at night, Philip Mudd, associate executive assistant director of the FBI's National Security Branch, often pictures the faces of the victims of the 9/11 attack.

Michael Morell, associate deputy director of the CIA, says a big factor in the war on terror is "winning hearts and minds."

usual government building X-ray screenings. Then, to pass through the bank of turnstiles, visitors must scan their badges and enter a code.

While detailed to the NCTC as deputy director, Cummings had access to the CIA's raw intelligence reports. He considered it a way of making sure the "intelligence community operates as a community." The FBI and CIA retained responsibility for their respective operations.

Cummings found that jihadists inspired by bin Laden rather than controlled by him were becoming more common. For example, Ali Al-Timimi, a spiritual leader at a mosque in Northern Virginia, encouraged other individuals at a meeting to go to Pakistan to receive military training from Lashkar-e-Taibi, a designated foreign terrorist organization, in order to fight U.S. troops in Afghanistan. The northern Virginians were from different ethnic backgrounds—Korean Americans, a couple Caucasians, a Jordanian.

"They were just a group of extremists who had a shared kind of way of looking at the world," Cummings says. "They went to a Kashmiri camp, where they learned how to shoot weapons and were given a bunch of extremist Islamic teachings. But they were being taught to kill Indians off in Kashmir. Well, these guys don't want to go kill Indians. They all came running back. They said, 'No, we want to kill the real bad guys, Americans.'"

When they came back, the FBI had them under surveillance.

Yet, as with the Portland and Lackawanna groups, media critics pointed out that none of the suspects had actually engaged in terrorism. But that was the point of Bush's prevention doctrine: He wanted to take down plots before Americans again became victims on their own soil.

"These guys are not as sophisticated as al Qaeda types," Cummings says. "But they're exceedingly dangerous because they're willing to give up their personal safety and personal freedoms to go overseas to a foreign place, with people that are going to teach them how to become a terrorist, essentially. It's this convergence of capability and willingness that cause the person to be unbelievably dangerous. That's our problem. You may have a Marine who's trained to be a Marine. Who cares? He's a Marine, he's a patriot. It's the Marine who's trained to be a Marine and becomes an extremist. Those two converge, and now we've got a significant problem."

The Virginia suspects were talking about becoming suicide bombers.

"I mean, anyone who would marginalize this has got to be out of their minds," Cummings says. "They are our nightmare."

In April 2005, Al-Timimi was convicted of all ten charges brought against him in the Virginia Jihad case. He was sentenced to life in prison.

The month before, Michael Heimbach, forty-eight, took over Cummings's previous job as chief of the FBI's ITOS 1, which focuses on al Qaeda. He was born in Shamokin, Pennsylvania, a coal cracker area, and no one in his family had gone to college. His father was a truck driver and his mother was a stay-at-home mom.

Heimbach started with the FBI in 1988. In 2002, he became an assistant section chief in counterterrorism. When he took over ITOS 1, he heard horror stories about refusals to share information from as recently as 2002.

"People were saying, 'Why does the bureau need to know that?'" Heimbach says. "And people in the bureau were saying, 'Why does the agency need to know that?'"

Some FBI agents were slow to change. But by 2007, 40 percent of FBI agents had come on board since 9/11 and were fully indoctrinated in the new way of thinking.

"We have old-school, they have old-school," he says. "And as the culture changes, we all move forward through attrition. We greet the new agents as soon as they come in the door and tell them, 'Don't worry about building that indictment, you suck them dry for intelligence. What can you get? Why are you getting it? Who are they talking to? Who's directing them, what's their motivation?'"

At the NCTC, "We have two CIA case officers embedded with us, and we have six agents detailed full time in the CIA's counterterrorism center," Heimbach notes. "They have full access to everything the agency does. So we're on the same sheet of music."

To be sure, Heimbach occasionally encounters an obstacle in dealing with the CIA or other agencies. But those instances are rare.

"We always work through them, no big deal," he says. "I can't think of one incident where they would just stonewall us, and we didn't find some middle ground."

According to Heimbach, only about a quarter of terrorism suspects are actually charged with terrorism. Hundreds of others are rolled up on lesser charges. In fiscal 2004 alone, the Justice Department reported 379 convictions related to terrorism. Justice Department Inspector General Glenn A. Fine said the true number was 240, but that was the difference between what the FBI believed and what it could prove or chose to prove in court.

"Sometimes when someone is arrested or indicted, the full nature of what we believe they did is not revealed," Heimbach says. "Because the means and the methods are sometimes so sensitive that we will not disclose them in order to criminally prosecute."

Thus, as portrayed by the media, a case may seem minor because a suspect was deported or was arrested for making false statements, money laundering, or white collar fraud.

"The untold story may be what other intelligence we've collected," Heimbach says.

For example, he says, "You may have a person sitting in the U.S., and you've received intelligence from the entire intelligence community that this person possibly attended a jihadist training camp in the Middle East."

The source may be of unknown reliability, or lack a good track record.

"This still calls for us to draw attention to it, but we never really get any clarity whether indeed the person did or didn't," Heimbach says. "So you've got this smoke. You drill down on the case here in the U.S. You find no connectivity; you find that he's here on a legitimate student visa."

In another example, the FBI may find that a suspect is receiving money from a source tied to terrorism. He may also have ties himself to terrorists. Still, the evidence is not quite solid enough to bring charges. In that case, Heimbach says, the suspect may be charged with money laundering.

"So then we disrupted a group for what appears to the public to be money laundering," he says.

If the suspect is in the United States illegally, the FBI can use deportation as a tool in disrupting a potential plot.

"Sometimes it's great leverage, because they like being in the U.S. and they want to stay here," Heimbach says. "Other times, they're happy to leave."

If a suspect is sent back to his country of origin, "We work closely with our foreign intelligence partners, telling them this person is being deported on a certain date, and they're to receive him when he comes back to his country," Heimbach says.

The FBI gives the other country everything the bureau knows about the individual.

"Some are very interested and will meet the individual at the other port," Heimbach says. "They may use leverage against the person. With some, you're lucky if you get a reply back in a year. We closely work with the CIA in terms of making sure they are in the loop of the information that we're giving back to the foreign intelligence service about the individual."

In investigating terrorists, the FBI's goal is always to penetrate the inner circle.

"That's good for Team America, that's excellent," Heimbach says. "Some of the best cases, whether you make them on the counterterrorism side or the criminal side, usually involve HUMINT penetration [intelligence collection from a source] somehow, some way.

You're getting sometimes even a better assessment of what's going on than you can get from technical collection."

Every time a source provides information, the FBI looks for what's motivating him.

"What's the track record of the source, how much has the source been paid?" Heimbach says. "Has he been polygraphed? What's his reliability? If you have a guy that's got a good track record, then you try to go, 'Okay, where'd you get that information from?' It's a daisy chain, and sometimes it's very unmanageable."

If there is a "hanging chad," Heimbach says, "We've got to come back to him until the matter is resolved. We'll keep getting pinged until something is settled one way or another. Sometimes you just can't get to it."

Usually if a plot is disrupted, that becomes public. Then the media questioning begins.

"We get quizzed constantly: Were they capable of doing it?" Heimbach says. "Well, maybe they weren't being directed by AQ leadership, but one of our big concerns is our home-grown terrorists here in the U.S. Meaning U.S. persons, radicalized, sympathetic to the overreaching cause, and probably not even, I wouldn't even say loosely affiliated with al Qaeda. They probably have no direct link to AQ senior leadership whatsoever. But they are focused and determined to cause harm to America—whether it's to our physical infrastructure or to Americans they want to kill."

Certainly, there was no hint that a gang from the New Folsom State Prison outside Sacramento could be a threat. The gang went back to 1997, when Kevin L. James, a black inmate, started Jam'iyyat Ul-Islam Is-Saheeh, or JIS. James, twenty-nine, preached that JIS members had an obligation to "target for violent attack any enemies of Islam or infidels, including the United States government and Jewish and non-Jewish supporters of Israel."

James recruited fellow inmates who swore that upon their release from prison, they would recruit Muslims, obtain directives from him at least every three months, and attack government officials and support-ers of Israel. So they would not attract suspicion, the group looked for Muslims who had no criminal records and had good credit records.

The group acquired an arsenal of weapons, paid for with the pro-ceeds of stick-ups at gasoline stations. But one member, Gregory V. Patterson, twenty-one, dropped a mobile telephone during a robbery, and the Torrance police picked it up. The police did not know if the phone had any connection with the robbery. Nor did Patterson have any previous criminal record. But when they traced the subscriber and the calls made to and from the phone, they began to ping in on the gang members.

The police brought the phone to the attention of the FBI's Joint Terrorism Task Force in Los Angeles. The task force conducted sur-veillance on an apartment in Los Angeles where the cell phone bills were being sent. They latched onto Patterson and began following him. He would meet with Levar Washington, a former inmate at Fol-som, and a Pakistani at a mosque near the apartment. Finally, they saw Patterson and Washington rob another gasoline station, and the police arrested them on July 5, 2005.

When Patterson's apartment was searched, police and FBI agents found masks, additional guns, money, and jihadist literature. One document said in Arabic, "Modes of Attack." It listed apparent tar-gets, including the Israeli airline El Al, the Israeli consulate, and Army recruiting stations in Los Angeles County.

Hundreds of FBI agents and LAPD officers were then assigned to the case. Eventually, through a series of interrogations and polygraph examination, they learned the full extent of their plans. On September 11, 2005, the group was going to walk into an Army recruiting station and kill everybody in sight with an AR-15 rifle. They were then going to go underground and re-emerge on October 13, which was Yom Kip-pur in 2005, and target a synagogue in Los Angeles. The plan was to massacre as many Jewish men, women, and children as they could find.

Saying they were planning terrorist strikes in southern California,

Mueller announced their indictment on August 31, 2005. The men all faced life in prison without possibility of parole.

"They were very loose but pretty bad eggs that were sitting in jail for takeover armed robberies," Mike Heimbach says. "They formed their own group with a hierarchy, with a leadership chart of who was in charge. We can't afford to ever wait until they're ready to go operational. At some point, you got to pull the trigger."

Predictably, the media and academic critics found fault with this success.

"Although Attorney General Alberto R. Gonzales lavished praise on 'the work of able investigators at all levels of government' in solving this case, law enforcement was as clueless about the JIS gang as was its British counterpart about the July 7 bombers," wrote Daniel Pipes in the *New York Sun*. "If not for the lucky break of a dropped phone, the jihadists probably would have struck. It is extremely disturbing to see law enforcement pat itself on the back for ineptitude."

The criticism reflects a fundamental misunderstanding of how law enforcement works. If it were possible to monitor all potential plots before they took place, there would be no bank robberies, kidnappings, rapes, or murders. Often, crimes are solved because of lucky breaks, just as scientific breakthroughs often begin with a serendipitous observation or an accident.

In unraveling terrorist plots, the question is whether the right observations are made and clues and leads are followed up on. In the case of the California prison gang, they were, and lives were saved. In fact, of all the plots that have been stopped in the United States, that one was closest to actually being carried out. It was taken down with just two months remaining. To say that this kind of success suggests ineptitude is to have a distorted view of the world. It's a viewpoint that FBI agents and CIA officers, putting in long hours at the expense of their families, see every day in the media.

Heimbach comes in at 5:45 A.M. When a big case is brewing, he often doesn't leave until midnight.

"On the outside, there's a wife, there's kids, sick people, sick families, moms and dads," Heimbach says. "If you don't have this phenomenal support structure at home, you can't do it, you just can't do it. What spouse enjoys coming home for two hours, and then you go back in? You missed the vacation, you missed the school play, you show up at the ball game in the fourth quarter, you come at the second half with two minutes left in the soccer match."

Recently, Heimbach's fifteen-year-old son came up to him when Heimbach returned home from work weary at 11:00 P.M. He knew his father was working a big case.

"He was waiting for me," Heimbach says. "And he puts his hand on my shoulder and he says, 'You okay, Dad? And thanks.' Which means a ton."

16

LEAKS

ON DECEMBER 16, 2005, the *New York Times* broke the story that NSA was intercepting calls to hunt down terrorists. The lede used provocative language to suggest government wrongdoing.

"Months after the Sept. 11 attacks, President Bush secretly authorized the National Security Agency to eavesdrop on Americans and others inside the United States to search for evidence of terrorist activity without the court-approved warrants ordinarily required for domestic spying, according to government officials," the story said.

Using the trigger words "eavesdropping" and "domestic spying," the story by James Risen and Eric Lichtblau suggested a massive program with sinister motives. Not until the twenty-second paragraph did the story say that the program only targets calls with an overseas nexus.

Under the journalistic standards that prevailed during the Watergate years, editors at responsible media outlets insisted that any fact that undercuts the lede of a story appear no later than the second paragraph. Giving a complete, honest, and fair picture was expected. Reporters who tried to skew their stories to sensationalize them or distort or suppress the truth found themselves looking for jobs.

All that has changed. Under current journalistic standards, it has become not only acceptable but routine practice to bury mitigating facts near the end of a story to give it greater spin—or to omit the other side entirely. A good example was the flap over Bush's sixteen-word statement in his State of the Union speech that British intelligence believed Saddam had been trying to buy uranium from Niger. To be sure, George Tenet, as director of Central Intelligence, did not believe the information was solid enough to include in Bush's speeches. Tenet had succeeded in cutting a reference to the British report from a presidential speech in October 2002, but the reference slipped into Bush's State of the Union address on January 28, 2003. Yet when Bush said, "The British government has learned that Saddam Hussein recently sought significant quantities of uranium from Africa," the statement was true.

In fact, MI6, the British secret intelligence service, still believed that its intelligence about Niger was correct. Contrary to news reports, its information did not rely on bogus documents. Nor did Colin Powell mention Niger eight days after the State of the Union in his formal presentation to the United Nations. Few news stories mentioned these points. Yet the media pounced on the reference in the State of the Union address as evidence that Bush was purposely fabricating intelligence to support going to war.

For weeks, the White House press corps badgered press spokesmen about the nonissue. Decades ago, reporters understood that press briefings were to convey and clarify news. Questions were asked to elicit information.

Now that briefings are televised, reporters use the opportunity to preen before the cameras and harass the briefer—conduct that years ago editors considered unprofessional. In those days, if reporters wanted to uncover their own facts, they could engage in investigative reporting, as Bob Woodward and Carl Bernstein did during Watergate.

If there was any question about media bias, it was dispelled when the British House of Commons Intelligence and Security Committee reviewed the MI6 intelligence about the Niger claim. It concluded in

September 2003 that, based on the information MI6 gathered, the finding was "reasonable." Moreover, the committee, which is well regarded by members of Parliament, also said MI6 was justified in continuing to claim that the intelligence was credible.

The story reporting the committee's conclusion appeared in the United States as a separate story in only one paper—the *Wall Street Journal*. The *Washington Post* devoted one paragraph to the conclusion near the end of a twenty-two-paragraph story. The *New York Times*, which had run fifty-six stories mentioning Bush's State of the Union address and the Niger claim, had no story on the Parliament report.

As a result of the suppression, it has become part of urban legend that Bush's statement in his State of the Union address was wrong and that he lied in making it. It is as if Soviet-style press censorship has been imposed on the country, except progovernment news rather than antigovernment news is being suppressed.

In the same vein, after years of page one headlines about the alleged White House conspiracy to out Valerie Plame as a covert CIA officer in retribution for her husband Joe Wilson's attacks on the administration, the mystery was finally solved when *Newsweek* came out with a story based on *Hubris*, a book by Michael Isikoff and David Corn. The book said the original leak about Plame to columnist Robert Novak came from Richard L. Armitage, then deputy secretary of State. But not only was Armitage not in the White House, he had been a critic of the Iraq war and the administration. Thus, the facts got in the way of the myth. How to deal with that? The *Washington Post* solved the problem by burying the story that reported Armitage was the original leaker on page A6. The *New York Times* ran a story the next day on page A12.

By portraying the NSA intercept program as a massive "domestic spying" effort, the *New York Times*, in its story disclosing the program, took a similar approach. Bush acknowledged the NSA intercept program and said it was necessary to protect the country. But spurred on by the misleading original story, congressional critics, civil libertarians, and the media went on the attack, depicting the program as "domestic surveillance" against "ordinary Americans."

The intercept program first began two weeks after 9/11 when Bush met with General Michael Hayden, then director of the NSA, and other NSA officials in the Oval Office.

"The president asked, 'What tools do we need to fight the war on terror?'" says Andy Card, who attended the meeting.

Hayden suggested changing NSA guidelines to allow the agency to target calls and intercept e-mails of terrorists if one end of the communication was overseas. Thus, if bin Laden were calling the U.S. to order the detonation of a nuclear device, and the person he called began making overseas calls, NSA could listen in to those calls as well as to bin Laden's original call.

"Bingo. As a result of the president's question, we took a fresh look at what NSA could be doing to protect us," Card says.

Prior to Bush's order, the information from the additional calls would have been lost. Even the emergency provision of the FISA offered no help because each request for an intercept had to be approved by the Justice Department. By the time approval was given, the call had ended. Then, even under the emergency provision, it usually took another two days to compile the information needed to obtain approval of an intercept. Given the number of intercepts needed, the FBI would have had to divert a large portion of its agents to preparing the requests. Moreover, under FISA, NSA could not necessarily listen to any further calls made by someone an al Qaeda operative may have called in the United States because the FBI might not yet have fully established that the person who had been called by al Qaeda was a terrorist operative.

Aside from these impediments, procedures before 9/11 for supplying the FBI with information gleaned from NSA intercepts were inconsistent and burdensome.

"Before 9/11, I used to battle NSA," Cummings says. "If there was an American's name attached to any of it, and he was going over-seas, they wouldn't give it to us."

Depending on where they happened to be based, FBI agents got varying degrees of cooperation from NSA.

"What we got from NSA many times was, 'You should look at these numbers. They may be of interest to the FBI,'" says Kenneth Maxwell, who headed counterterrorism in New York. "Almost every-thing was in code."

On the other hand, Robert Blitzer, who was in charge of coun-terterrorism at headquarters, would be given an entirely different re-sponse by NSA.

"They gave us a summary of the conversation," Blitzer says. "We would go and ask to see it. We would ask for the person's name. That would take four or five days to obtain."

The new procedures ordered by Bush cut through all the mumbo jumbo and allowed NSA to stay on suspicious calls and give tran-scripts to the FBI in real time. The intercept program gave the FBI "a window on al Qaeda activities," according to an FBI agent familiar with the program.

"There are cases out there where it's helped to identify the first point where a case was started and we took a look at somebody," says another agent.

"You can't go back and ask for a FISA for a conversation that's already occurring," Cummings says. "That's the fundamental issue. When they pick up on a U.S. conversation, they can't tell these two guys who are talking: 'Hey, hold on a minute while we go get a FISA.' A conversation is a conversation; it happens, and then it's lost."

The NSA's Hayden subsequently suggested preserving records of calls so that if bin Laden called an operative in New York, the FBI could after the fact trace that person's previous contacts. But a sub-sequent *New York Times* story suggested the program went beyond that.

"Officials in the government and the telecommunications industry who have knowledge of parts of the program say the NSA has sought to analyze communications patterns to glean clues from details like who is calling whom, how long a phone call lasts and what time of day it is made, and the origins and destinations of phone calls and e-mail messages," a December 24 story said.

But contrary to these reports in the *New York Times* and elsewhere, the purpose was not to engage in data mining. It was to follow real leads that would not otherwise be there because the call records had been deleted.

What was true was that switches in the United States handle a great deal of telephone and e-mail Internet traffic between other countries, permitting NSA to intercept those communications easily. The intelligence community considered that disclosure in the *New York Times* stories to be at least as damaging to national security as the stories about the overall NSA intercept program.

"The president has been very careful about what he's done," Card says. "It wasn't that he dictated things and made people do the things that they didn't want to do. I can't think of one time where the president, on his own, came up with something: 'Let's do this!' And everybody said, 'Never thought about that.' And he said, 'Well, let's do it. I don't care what you say, we're going to do it.' That's just not the way it works. Smart, competent people who are trained to help the president and advise the president were involved in these decisions."

To be sure, the fact that Bush bypassed the Foreign Intelligence Surveillance Act, which provides procedures for intercepting communications in terrorist cases, raised legitimate questions. But to the editors of the *New York Times* who spurned Bush's pleas to not publish the NSA intercept story, what should have been of more concern was that al Qaeda and related terrorist organizations were trying to obtain nuclear and biological weapons that could wipe out major cities, kill millions of people, and devastate the American economy. Given the fact that homegrown terrorists in the United States were now trying to reach out to al Qaeda internationally, the need to intercept calls with an overseas nexus became even more urgent.

Bush's argument that he had inherent powers under the Constitution to engage in the program without congressional authorization was the same argument Jimmy Carter's administration made when it proposed FISA to Congress in 1978. Back then, the Carter administration specifically stated that passage of the new law would not necessarily preclude the president from "using his powers granted under the Constitution to carry out foreign policy and intelligence activities," according to Griffin B. Bell, who was Carter's attorney general when the law was drafted and enacted. Thus, there was a "tacit agreement that FISA was not intended to displace the president's authority," said Bell in an interview.

The Bush administration could have asked Congress for a law that would allow NSA to intercept calls and e-mails instantly, then seek retroactive approval after a review. But a quick glance at the history of the USA Patriot Act is instructive. After voting for the act, many in Congress turned it into a symbol of what was wrong with the Bush administration.

According to George Tenet's book *At the Center of the Storm*, the reason Bush did not seek legislation authorizing the NSA program is that congressional leaders, whom the administration secretly briefed on the program, warned that seeking legislation "could not be done without jeopardizing the program."

Rather than invite another fruitless battle with Congress and leaks about the program, the president chose the course of defending the country, as he is sworn to do.

Civil liberties advocates and media critics compared the intercept program to the domestic spying the FBI and the CIA engaged in for political purposes before press exposure and congressional hearings put an end to the practices in the mid-1970s. With the CIA's release in June 2007 of documents detailing the agency's abuses in the 1960s and 1970s, the media pounced, suggesting that those illegalities were similar to the Bush administration's practices.

The truth is quite the opposite. The CIA's past abuses in fact spotlight how legal and properly motivated today's government actions are. In those days, the CIA literally spied on Americans because of their political beliefs, wiretapped reporters to find the source of leaks, broke into homes without a warrant, incarcerated a defector for no legal reason, engaged in foolish and ill-conceived assassination attempts against foreign leaders, and gave harmful drugs like LSD to subjects without their knowledge or consent.

Many of these activities violated criminal laws. They also demonstrated a lack of focus and competence. Some were just silly, such as a plot to get Fidel Castro's beard to fall off in an effort to undermine his authority.

Nearly always ordered or encouraged by Presidents John F. Kennedy, Lyndon B. Johnson, or Richard Nixon, the CIA's actions were not disclosed to Congress. Congressional leaders wanted to remain in the dark about questionable CIA activities, giving them deniability.

In contrast, the Bush White House disclosed its aggressive efforts to combat terrorism to key leaders and committees of Congress and to the courts, which have let them continue.

In the case of the USA Patriot Act, Congress itself enacted the legislation. As for coercive interrogation techniques, Congress recently enacted legislation that still allows the president to order such techniques. Citing the president's constitutional authority, the Bush administration disclosed the NSA intercept program at its inception to the FISA court, to congressional leaders, and to NSA's inspector general.

In addition to these safeguards, in approving the NSA intercept program, Bush set up a Justice Department review process, which retroactively examines the intercepts to ensure that the program is being carried out according to the terms of the president's authorization. Yet after the program was publicly disclosed, Democratic Senator Harry Reid and other congressional leaders who had been briefed on the program early on and did not raise any concerns now hypocritically castigated the president for disregarding the Constitution. None of the reviews found that the NSA program was being used for political purposes, as was the case in the 1970s.

The 9/11 hijackers received instructions from al Qaeda operatives overseas through e-mails at libraries. If the Israelis, for example, had relayed a tip about the e-mails, NSA could have intercepted the communications, and the FBI might have disrupted the 9/11 plot. Waiting for the FISA court to approve an intercept would have meant that a chance to prevent the deaths of almost 3,000 people was lost.

"The intelligence we get from the NSA and the CIA is key," one FBI official says, "because a piece an agent in San Francisco is holding could connect to a piece that's mentioned on an intercept in Pakistan that could be connected to something a cop has in Chicago. The great challenge is making those three pieces find each other within the system."

Bush eventually agreed to let the FISA court oversee the intercept program, preserving the key element, which allows intercepts to proceed without a previous court order. The agreement in effect ratified Bush's view that he had authority to conduct such intercepts without the need for legislation from Congress.

Hayden says there has been confusion about Bush's order on NSA intercepts.

"He's just adjusting what communications you can get access to, in the first place," Hayden says. "At its heart, the president's authorization is about the access to communications, not about how you respect the privacy of the U.S. communicant." Bush's order "simply made it more likely that the NSA would intercept the communications most critical to the defense of the nation—that is, communications we believe to be affiliated with al Qaeda, one end of which is in the U.S."

The disclosure of the NSA program, along with the later disclosure of the SWIFT program to track worldwide financial transactions, created consternation in the intelligence community, which believed revealing the programs undercut American security.

Dean Baquet, then editor of the *Los Angeles Times,* disingenuously compared his decision to run the story on the SWIFT program to monitor money transfers to the *New York Times*'s decision to publish the Pentagon Papers. The *New York Times* ran its story on the forty-seven-volume study and its origins on Sunday, June 13, 1971. The study was commissioned by Robert S. McNamara, secretary of Defense. Essentially, the stories showed that for years, the American government, and particularly the administration of Lyndon B. Johnson, had been lying to the American people about the progress of the war, its goals, and its rationale. But the Pentagon Papers was a retrospective look at the Vietnam War, not a report on current operational capabilities whose efficacy depends on secrecy. Moreover, the SWIFT program entailed no abuses or misleading statements to the public, as clearly occurred during the Vietnam War.

Baquet, like the *New York Times*'s Bill Keller, made much of the fact that they had deliberated for weeks or months about whether to run the stories. That was beside the point. If bank robbers deliberate for weeks about whether to pull off a heist, does that make it right?

The fact is that these editors' decisions, cloaked in sanctimonious arguments about First Amendment rights, harmed American security and made additional attacks more likely. These editors would have Americans believe that they have their interests at heart. If their papers were revealing real abuses, that would be true. But when the papers revealed secrets for the sake of revealing secrets, there was no justification for running the stories other than to glorify themselves and their papers.

Some editors even complained that an FBI investigation into who leaked the information on the NSA intercept program would have a chilling effect on people who might want to leak to the press. By this reasoning, the government should give employees the right to decide on their own whether to declassify government secrets.

The media coverage of columnist Robert Novak's disclosure of Valerie Plame's name as a CIA operative betrayed the same indifference to national security. Novak wanted to know why the CIA sent Plame's husband, former Ambassador Joseph C. Wilson IV, to Niger to look into reports that Saddam Hussein had been trying to buy uranium from that country. For months, Wilson had been using his role in the affair to attack the Bush administration. First without attribution and then publicly, Wilson accused the administration of "misrepresenting the facts on an issue that was a fundamental justification for going to war," as Wilson was quoted in the July 6, 2003, *Washington Post*. The same day, the *New York Times* published an op-ed piece by Wilson with similar charges.

Wilson claimed he had reported to the CIA that it was "highly doubtful" that Hussein had tried to buy uranium from Niger. That was not true. On the one hand, he told the CIA, one former Niger official told him in February 2002 that he was unaware of any contract signed while he was in office to sell uranium to any rogue state. On the other hand, Wilson said the former official told him that in 1999 a businessman approached the official urging him to meet with an Iraqi delegation to discuss "expanding commercial relations" between Iraq and Niger. The former official believed the overture was to discuss uranium sales.

Before going with the story mentioning Wilson's connection to the CIA through his wife, Novak called a CIA official. Novak told him he would be referring in his column to Wilson's wife. The CIA official told Novak that using her name might create "difficulties" if she traveled abroad. He asked him not to name her. Novak did so anyway.

After Plame was outed, Joe Wilson and Bush critics claimed that the White House leaked her name to Novak in retribution for Wilson's attacks on Bush. But the real culprit was Novak. There was no legitimate reason to name Plame, who was in covert status because the CIA wanted to be able to send her back overseas. The CIA had not engaged in any wrongdoing or abuse. Nor did using her name add anything to Novak's piece. Yet no one in the media became outraged over the fact that, while Richard Armitage should not have disclosed her name to Novak in the first place, Novak was the only person who was on notice that identifying Plame would be damaging.

Immediately after the *New York Times*'s disclosure of the SWIFT program, al Qaeda terrorists who had been sending international money transfers stopped the practice, destroying the CIA's ability to track them and pinpoint their contacts around the world, according to a well-informed source.

"They read the papers to find out what to do next," says S. Eugene Poteat, a former CIA officer who is president of the Association of Former Intelligence Officers.

"The targets we focus on read the newspapers, and they look at the Internet, and they will then change their course or their modus operandi based on our capabilities," Heimbach says. "That creates new challenges for us in our ability to collect intelligence."

"The leaks are killing us," Cummings says. "Whatever we receive that helps us better understand how they're motivated, how they're driven, what their current objectives are, how they operate, who they are, is a huge benefit to us. That's how we defeat them. Take that away from us, we're going to be losing again."

Cummings cites a *Washington Post* story revealing that the FBI does radiological surveys, especially when threat levels are high, to detect possible nuclear devices at locations where the FBI has ongoing terrorist cases, including at some mosques.

"Did it not occur to anybody that now the terrorists are going to take countermeasures based on the technology we just rolled out in the newspapers?" Cummings says. "Do we understand that we have this great capability to try to figure out whether or not this material is here in the U.S., and now we just lost that capability? The terrorists are reading the same newspaper, getting on the Internet, seeing the same thing. The minute it's published, the minute there's something that talks substantially about the capabilities of the U.S. government to capture these guys, that is the topic of conversation around the campfire."

17

AN ASSASSINATION ATTEMPT

I N HUNTING DOWN terrorists, Cummings makes use of the FBI's legats, or overseas posts, so that agents could work seamlessly with foreign intelligence and law enforcement services. One of the few positive contributions Louis Freeh made to the bureau was to expand the legat program. Before Freeh took over, the FBI had twenty legats. By the time Freeh left, the FBI had forty-four, from Moscow and Panama City to Nairobi and Islamabad. Mueller increased the number of legats to fifty-eight.

"The bureau overseas has expanded not just to law enforcement, but it's expanded to all security services as well," Cummings says. "Now we work directly with the British Security Service [MI5]."

That kind of cooperation helped when police searched the apartment of Ramzi Yousef in Manila after a fire broke out on January 6, 1995.

"When the fire happened, he was out of the building, and his buddy was in there," says Thomas V. Fuentes, the FBI special agent in charge of international operations. "His buddy gets arrested, he goes back, he gets as close as across the street, he sees the police have gone in, he can't get to his laptop. They get his laptop, that information ends up in U.S. intelligence hands," Fuentes says. "On the laptop were the details of plots to blow up ten airplanes over the Pacific Ocean. That later spawned the idea of planes being used as missiles, full of fuel, flying into a building, and of course they began to circulate that idea."

Eventually, Fuentes says, that created the attack plan that evolved into 9/11.

"But if we don't have good relations with our counterparts over there, they may not want to give it to us," he says. "The aftermath of an attack is not the time to go try making friends."

The reverse of that kind of cooperation occurred when al Qaeda attacked the USS *Cole*.

"Our nearest legal attaché office at the time was in Riyadh," Fuentes says. "Our legat in Riyadh did not have a good day-in and day-out relationship in the territory he covered, which included numerous Middle Eastern countries. Yemen was just one of them. So when Louis Freeh dispatched investigators to Aden to investigate that bombing because seventeen U.S. sailors were killed and a U.S. warship was attacked, they're locked up in hotel rooms. The Yemenis are like, 'What are you doing here? Good time to meet you.' And they were not cooperative initially in helping us begin the work that had to be done."

The FBI team, led by John O'Neill, was getting death threats.

"So they ended up moving to the ship because it was no longer safe to operate on land, and we didn't have an office there," Fuentes says. "Now we have an office there, and we have a direct relationship with the Yemenis and work with them."

Later, Fuentes learned that the Yemenis had sent numerous requests to the FBI for assistance.

"So we're looking through our databases here, and we can't find any evidence or information that the requests were ever received by the FBI here in Washington or a field office," Fuentes says. "We think they were sent through Interpol. And that's the way they packaged it. They didn't actually address it to us. Kind of like sending a letter and not putting an address on it, it just goes out in limbo. The reason they were less than welcoming when we arrived there was that they were mad at us. Because we had never responded to help them, why should they respond to help us now?"

As an example of how the FBI works with foreign countries and develops trust before an incident happens, the bureau's work led to the arrest of a man who threw a hand grenade at Bush when he spoke at a rally on May 10, 2005, in a public square in Tbilisi, Georgia.

"The Georgians had set up the magnetometers all around this area," Fuentes says. "They screened about ten thousand people, and there's about a hundred and fifty thousand that want to get in. They realize they're not going to get them in in time with the president's schedule, so they just shut off the machines and let everybody in. This was unbeknownst to the Secret Service and everybody else. So now this crowd of people's there. The president's up giving his speech. All of a sudden, landing with a thud near the podium, is a hand grenade, wrapped in a scarf."

The grenade did not explode. The Georgians put out a statement saying that it was a training device that had been left over after an earlier exercise in preparation for the president's visit. That was untrue.

"A guy standing off to the side, wearing a head scarf and a black leather jacket, had pulled this military grenade out, pulled the pin out, wrapped a scarf around it, and threw it inside the scarf," Fuentes says. "Because he had the scarf wrapped around it, and he pulled the pin out, there's two spoons that are supposed to disengage, and that allows the chemical interaction that creates the explosion. The spoons don't disengage; they get stuck. So this thing lands, boom, unexploded, live, good to go."

After analyzing the device, the FBI concluded it could have killed the president. The bureau asked the public to turn in any photographs or video that might show the perpetrator.

"None of the pictures actually showed us the guy," Fuentes says. "He was hidden behind other people on the stage. But the pictures showed a guy in the audience up in the bleachers with about a 1,000-meter telephoto lens on his camera."

Figuring the man to be a professional journalist, the FBI sorted through travel documents to pinpoint journalists who had entered the country just before the event.

"We tracked down the photographer, who was from Salt Lake City," Fuentes says.

It turned out he was not a journalist but rather a college professor.

"He gave us access to three thousand pictures that he took that day," Fuentes notes. "And one of the pictures was a beautiful facial portrait of the guy who matched the physical description of the guy who threw the grenade. The Georgians put this photo on national TV, in their newspapers, and in public places."

That led to a call to the police.

"Oh, yeah, that's my neighbor, Vladimir Arutyunov," the caller said.

With an FBI agent, the police went to the suspect's residence on July 19, 2005.

"While they're approaching it, he opens fire on them and actually kills a Georgian police officer," Fuentes says.

Arutyunov confessed, saying he did it because he thought Bush was too soft on Muslims. He was sentenced to life in prison.

18

SADDAM'S FRIEND

A T 5 P.M. on Christmas Eve 2003, George L. Piro was doing his last-minute shopping when his BlackBerry began vibrating. Frank Battle was calling. The head of the counterterrorism response section at the FBI's Counterterrorism Division, Battle said Piro was needed in Iraq for a special mission. The FBI wanted him to try to interview Saddam Hussein, who had been captured eleven days earlier.

Piro, thirty-six, was the perfect man for the job. An Arabic speaker, he was born in Beirut. Just before his thirteenth birthday, Piro had moved with his family to the United States. The young boy could not speak English. The family settled in California, and Piro eventually served in the military and became a police detective. He joined the FBI in 1999.

Piro had already been to Iraq. He was among the first FBI agents sent there earlier in 2003 as part of the bureau's expanding global role. In Iraq, says Art Cummings, "We try to find out who actually issued these orders, who is responsible for a mass killing in a town or other activities that they were engaged in. So we're involved just putting a criminal case together the old-fashioned way, if you will."

As part of his work in Iraq, Piro had dealt with the CIA, which thought highly of him. Ultimately, the agency approved his selection as Saddam's debriefer.

Piro is inscrutably handsome—high cheekbones, chocolate brown eyes under thick black eyebrows, and pearly white piano-key teeth set off by a close-clipped circle beard. His looks are so disarming, his smile so easy, his teeth so even, that it takes a while before you realize you would not want to be sitting across from George Piro at a poker table.

Piro is self-effacing and his build, in this stronghold of toned abs, is almost slight. He probably likes that just fine. He prefers not to bring attention to himself. The job's the thing. Known as a Boy Scout, he is all bureau, all the time. In a holster attached to his belt, his BlackBerry is set on vibrate. Every few minutes or so, Piro draws out his BlackBerry to check it, but doesn't let the text message break his thought. About every fifth call he takes, firing off a terse "This George."

When Piro arrived in Baghdad during the first week of 2004, he had no idea if Saddam would even say hello to him, much less reveal his thinking about the invasion of Iraq, his role in ordering 300,000 people killed, and whether he'd had weapons of mass destruction.

By then, Piro had studied Saddam's life.

"What increases the likelihood of success is subject-matter expertise," Piro says. "It's very difficult to lie to a subject-matter expert. If you come prepared, you're more likely to catch inconsistencies, deception, things like that. So my approach with any interview is to make myself the subject-matter expert before I step into that interview room."

At that point in early January 2004, it was unclear how or where Saddam would be tried. The CIA was calling the shots, and the agency wanted to be able to present prosecutors—whether at the Hague, the United Nations, or in Iraq—with any admissions Saddam might make. Because the FBI is in the business of obtaining statements for use in court, the CIA had asked the FBI to try to debrief Saddam.

Saddam was being kept isolated from other prisoners at an American detention facility at Baghdad International Airport. While Saddam had no particular malady, he was sixty-seven, and the United

States wanted to take no chances with his health. So twice a day, a doctor examined him at the detention facility.

As part of what he called his operational plan, Piro decided he would first get to know Saddam by telling him he would be in charge of all Saddam's needs and would act as an interpreter when the American doctor examined him. The deposed dictator never knew that Piro was with the FBI. Instead, he vaguely understood that he was with the American security services.

"He just came to the conclusion, probably through some of my actions, that I was a senior member of the security service," Piro says. "He didn't realize that I was actually a fairly low-level FBI agent who had taken on this assignment. He would not have responded well if he realized that I was a simple GS-14 from FBI headquarters."

As Piro translated for the doctor, he studied Saddam's interactions.

"I wanted to see what was important to him and what little habits he had," Piro says. "Like he liked to pick lint, because he was a clean freak. He didn't like to shake hands. If he shook your hand, he wanted to wash his hands a lot."

Saddam had a fondness for baby wipes, the disposable moist cloths used when changing a baby's diaper. If Saddam had enough baby wipes, he would use them to clean food such as apples before he ate them. Piro realized that, as a way of manipulating him, he could control how many baby wipes Saddam received.

Piro also noticed that Saddam was an extremely good listener.

"He would prefer you did all the talking, because it allowed him to study you and look at ways to manipulate you," Piro observes. "He was very good at reading people."

Saddam was considered a prisoner of war, and the military gave him a copy of the Geneva Conventions, spelling out in Arabic that he had the right to refuse to be interviewed. While Piro let Saddam know that he would be his debriefer, he waited for a week and a half before starting. With his enormous ego, Saddam had to be wondering why no one was trying to interview him. Finally, on January 13, 2004, Piro formally began the interview process.

Piro arranged the interview room. He wanted it to look simple, with no special fuss. It had a chair for Saddam, a chair for Piro, and a chair for a second FBI agent. In typical FBI fashion, the second agent, Todd Irinaga, would take notes. In addition, the interviews were secretly videotaped.

"I wanted him to realize that, even though he was who he was, to me he was still someone I was over and responsible for," Piro says. "I wanted him to feel that I was not very impressed by who he was."

Piro placed Saddam's chair so his back would be against the wall.

"I was kind of psychologically telling him that his back was against the wall," Piro says. "I arranged my chair so my back was against the door, basically meaning that I was standing between him and the outside."

At the same time, Piro treated Saddam with respect.

"The interviews were designed to develop a rapport between him and me," Piro says. "That is the approach that we use in the FBI. That is most effective, especially in this particular case, because we did have time on our side. We didn't have to rush. I wasn't being told: You have one day, one week, one month with him."

On the first day of interviews, Piro had one goal: to make sure Saddam would want him to come back. That day, Saddam had an upset stomach, so Piro spent more time than usual translating for the doctor who was examining him. Piro figured that military food was the culprit. Piro himself always avoided the chili burgers.

After the exam, Piro schmoozed with Saddam, asking him about the four novels he had written. He focused in particular on the first, *Zabibah and the King,* giving Saddam his take on it. Piro figured that Zabibah, a beautiful Iraqi woman, represented the country of Iraq. Zabibah was married to a man who abused her, and the husband was the United States.

As Saddam answered his questions, Piro studied how he answered.

He wanted to remember those reactions so he could compare them with how Saddam would answer more sensitive questions later.

"Later, if his manner deviated from the way he had responded to questions about the book, then that would be an indicator that he may be deceptive," Piro explains.

Piro knew that Saddam considered himself a great Iraqi leader and reveled in the country's glorious past. Once called Mesopotamia, the country is known as the cradle of civilization, where the Sumerian, Babylonian, and Assyrian cultures flourished. Going back to Nebuchadnezzar I and Hammurabi, Saddam identified with the country's leaders.

Piro happened to be a student of Iraqi history, which impressed Saddam.

"When he recognized that I knew Iraqi history, he said, 'Please come back. I want to talk to you again,'" Piro says. "I knew I had gotten what I wanted out of the first interview."

Over the ensuing seven months, Piro established trust with Saddam. He interviewed him every day. Including informal interactions, he spent five to seven hours a day with him. Piro took no holidays or days off. In addition, he was interviewing other high-value targets like Ali Hassan al-Majid, known as Chemical Ali because of his role in aerial poison-gas attacks on the Kurds.

Piro came to believe that Saddam would not lie to him outright, but he would be dismissive if he did not want to be forthcoming about a particular issue.

"When he was truthful, he was very articulate, very specific and expressive," Piro says. For example, Saddam became animated when talking about a 1959 attempt to assassinate Iraq's military leader, General Abdel-Karim Kassem. During that attack, Saddam was wounded in the leg. Saddam related what he called his "daring escape" from Baghdad on motorcycle and horseback. He swam across the Tigris River with a knife between his teeth.

"When he got to something that he didn't want to be very animated about, he would break eye contact, which in the Arab culture is usually not very common," Piro says. "Or he would start picking on his fingernails, or kind of start picking on his clothes." Saddam wore the traditional Arab *dishdash,* a sort of robe.

Piro's own hand gestures are simple. For emphasis, he makes a light karate chop on the table with the side of his right hand. Relaxing, he clasps his hands in front of him. When pensive, he lightly traces his fingernail along the sternomastoid muscle under his right ear.

Piro asked Saddam about his 1988 use of chemical weapons against the Kurdish town of Halabja in northern Iraq, which killed an estimated 5,000 civilians. The attack was part of the government's campaign to suppress rebellious Kurds across northern Iraq. The campaign left 180,000 Kurds missing and presumed dead.

While Saddam did not want to dwell on the details, he admitted that he issued the orders that led to the killings.

"Saddam said it was a decision he made, but he didn't want to engage in that conversation," Piro says. "He didn't say a hundred thousand people were killed. He said, 'These were my instructions. This is what they needed to do, and that's what they did, and it was because I told them to do it.' "

Saddam told Piro that, if only because he feared they might try to overthrow him, he never used doubles, as was widely believed.

"He told me no one could play him," Piro says with a laugh.

Another misconception was that Saddam dyed his hair black.

"He was very proud of the fact that his hair was black and that he had hair," Piro says.

As their rapport built, Saddam would talk about women. When an American nurse came to draw his blood, Saddam asked Piro to tell her in English that she was cute. Piro demurred. Saddam was never short on advice of the heart.

" 'You have to marry at an early age,' " Saddam told him. " 'American women are very independent.' " Saddam respected that. But, he went on: " 'They can live without you. Whereas if you marry an Arab woman between the ages of twenty and twenty-two, you become her foundation. An American woman, especially an older woman, her bridge is already formed; she can go on without you.' "

While he disagreed with its policies, Saddam admired America, and he especially liked Americans. He disliked President Bush and his father but was not fixated on them. He liked President Clinton and thought Ronald Reagan was a good president.

At one point, Sajida Tulfah, Saddam's wife, sent him a care package. Because Piro did not want to expend capital on sensitive matters not relevant to his mission, he did not ask Saddam about her. Nor did Saddam volunteer anything about her. Piro never wanted to ask a "bad question," one that would impair his credibility and access to Saddam.

But when he thought the moment was right, Piro did ask about Saddam's two sons, Qusay and Uday. Uday, Saddam's eldest son, tortured young girls who would not submit to his sexual demands. He would have them suspended by the backs of their knees from a beam, then club them mercilessly, as many as fifty times. When he saw pretty women on the street or young girls in a school, he would order his bodyguards to deliver them to him so he could rape them.

As for his son Qusay, Saddam mistrusted him. Qusay was to be his successor, but Saddam admitted that he didn't want him to move up too quickly and challenge him.

Piro knew that no one likes to speak negatively about his own kids. But if he could get Saddam to express his true feelings, Piro thought that would help him penetrate Saddam's defenses on other issues.

As Piro pressed him, Saddam finally said, " 'Look. Leave me alone. You don't get to pick your kids. You're stuck with what you're given. And this is what I had.' "

Piro counted that utterance as a win in the cat-and-mouse game he was playing.

Saddam prayed five times a day and read the Koran, but Piro thought that was because of his circumstances.

"Everybody finds a religion in prison," Piro says. "I think even Paris Hilton found God in jail, right?"

The fact that Saddam liked good wine, Johnny Walker Blue Label, and Cuban cigars and loved to talk about women suggested to Piro that he was not a devout Muslim. After women, Saddam's favorite subject was horses.

"His favorite picture is himself on the white horse in the uniform, which is how he started the military parades," Piro says. "It goes back to his childhood, and then his daring escape."

Piro's goal was for Saddam to become emotionally dependent on him. Aside from the English-speaking doctors, no one else had access to Saddam. Nor was Piro's partner with him when he and Saddam had their informal chats.

"He had his own little yard, where he was allowed to go outside and exercise twice a day," Piro notes. "Some of those times I would go to check on him, and we would spend some time in the yard just talking there, or in his cell. Outside of the interview room, we talked about history, politics, art, sports."

Military coffee was never strong enough for Saddam. So, besides supplying Saddam with "tons" of baby wipes, Piro would boil water for him and allow Saddam to brew his own instant cup of coffee, using three or four scoops of Folgers instant.

When Saddam had to be transported by helicopter to a hospital for a checkup, Piro went with him.

"We were flying in the middle of the night," recalls Piro, who was armed except when with Saddam. "You can imagine that transporting Saddam in Iraq during that period was a challenge."

Piro blindfolded Saddam with a soft sleep mask he happened to have picked up in a nice hotel.

"I put that on him, but then I was able to lift it and show him Baghdad in the middle of the night," Piro says. "It looked like any other major city in the world. Later, when we were sitting in the hospital, he said, 'You know, I really wanted to see Baghdad, and it was like you read my mind.'"

Piro gave Saddam a notebook so he could write poems, and Saddam began writing as many as two poems a day. Every day, Saddam would read his latest work to the FBI agent.

"Most of them were love poems," Piro says. "Some of them were okay, but a lot of them weren't that good."

Saddam wrote some of the poems in an old tribal form of Arabic, which Piro didn't understand, so Saddam would try to explain them.

"Saddam was very smart—a lot smarter than we gave him credit for in the West," Piro says. "He knew how to stay in touch with the Iraqi people. He allowed Iraqis to talk to him. And he had an elaborate network of sources. He said that women made the best sources. They can provide you the best information. They collect more information than their male counterparts, and they can articulate it better, and he found them to be a very useful tool."

To help guard against a coup, Saddam would enlist loyal aides to concoct phony efforts to topple him, he told Piro. Anyone who went along with the sham plot was executed. Saddam made certain that his aides and military men knew they could be tested in this way.

Over time, Saddam became more reclusive. By the 1990s, he began losing touch with reality and what was going on in his own country.

"He told me he cared more about what people would think of him in five hundred or a thousand years than they did that day," Piro says. "So he still thought people were going to be talking about him."

As a dose of reality, Piro showed him videos of Iraqis tearing down his statue and riding on his head down the street after American forces entered Baghdad. Piro also read him statements of Iraqis who had been used by Iraqi soldiers as human shields or who had been tortured.

"I understand what you're saying," Piro would tell him. "I'd like to believe you, but here is what is going on. You're telling me people love you, but here's what the Iraqis are doing. I'm a little confused. Maybe you can help me understand. If I'm looking historically at your legacy, your story is not matching what the Iraqis are saying. They're riding on your head, they're slapping your face."

If Piro could erode his confidence, Saddam would become more truthful, Piro thought. When he showed him the videos, Saddam's soft demeanor would turn to anger.

"When he was angered, his eyes completely changed," Piro says. "They became very cold. You could see the power and intensity in them."

Before the invasion, every Iraqi was supposed to hold a celebration on Saddam's birthday on April 28. Any Iraqi caught not complying would be imprisoned or shot. The day after Saddam's birthday, Piro showed him newspaper articles reporting that no one had celebrated his birthday. However, Piro arranged for his own mother to FedEx from California a huge box of her Lebanese cookies and baklava, which Piro gave Saddam for his birthday.

"I came to realize his mother was very important to him," Piro says. "I would focus on his mother, and then my mother. And on his birthday, I took an extra step and had my mom bake me special cookies. So the only person that really cared that it was his birthday was me."

Now that Saddam felt he was dealing with a friend, Piro sensed he could edge him into discussing relations with the United States and the mystery surrounding Iraq's WMD.

"What benefitted him was either being our friend or being our enemy, but not in between," Piro explains. "He had experienced the benefit of being our friend, and then he also was experiencing the benefits of being our enemy. As our enemy, he was viewed in the Arab world as a person who was defiant and a strong Arab man and a leader."

Saddam was especially proud of the fact that, unlike other Arab leaders, he never wavered in his support for the Palestinians. Other Arab leaders would support the Palestinian cause when it served their needs, Saddam told him.

"He claimed to continuously support the Palestinian cause because of his strong Arab beliefs and heritage," Piro says.

On the other hand, Saddam did not consider Israel the threat that his rhetoric suggested. He recognized that Israel was a topic he could exploit to get Arabs to forget some of the other issues they face.

As he proclaimed at the time, Saddam told Piro he invaded Kuwait in 1990 because the country was slant-drilling for oil under Iraqi soil.

"He did not expect us to intervene that quickly and to that level," Piro says. "Saddam told me his goal was to punish the Kuwaiti emir."

When talking about that war, Saddam admitted to having made a tactical error. While he knew U.S. air power was superior, he overestimated Iraq's capability on the ground, so he wanted his ground forces to engage quickly with the Americans. But for weeks, the United States carried out nonstop bombing, cutting off Iraqi supply lines and driving Iraqi troops to the point of surrender.

Seeking to lure the United States into starting a ground war, Saddam attacked a small Marine presence in Khafji. But the Marines held their own, and American air power destroyed retreating Iraqi forces. General Bernard Trainor later called the Battle of Khafji the defining moment of Desert Storm. The outcome undermined the Iraqi army's will to fight and demonstrated to U.S. commanders that "we were really going to kick this guy's tail," as General Norman Schwarzkopf put it. And the U.S. aerial attacks didn't stop.

"That was the first time he acknowledged that he had made a mistake," Piro says. "That was one of the early hurdles."

After Desert Storm, Saddam considered himself to be at war with the United States. But as with the first President Bush, he misjudged the current president. Most important, he failed to take into account the impact the 9/11 attack would have on Bush and the United States.

"Initially, his take was that we weren't going to invade in 2003," Piro says. "He thought we would do another Desert Fox, which was the 1998 four-day aerial bombing that took place when he kicked the inspectors out of Iraq. He expected that would be our response to his defiance. He said he could accept that, and he would not lose control or power."

Saddam confided to Piro why he had no weapons of mass destruction but pretended he did. Saddam said that because of the war of attrition he had with Iran, Iran always remained a threat to him. And if Iran thought he had serious WMD, it would be reluctant to engage him again. On the other hand, if he said he had them, Iran would never listen. But if the U.S. said that he had them, Iran would believe it.

So every time inspectors came, Saddam gave them the runaround, reinforcing for Iran's consumption the notion that he had WMD. And that explains why, if there were no WMD, he acted as if he did have them.

Saddam aspired to develop a nuclear capability in an incremental fashion. Aided by his payoffs to key officials, he thought that sanctions would be lifted within a year or so. He figured he could then re-create Iraq's WMD capability, which had been essentially destroyed in 1991.

"His goal was to have the sanctions lifted," Piro says. "And they likely would have been lifted if it were not for 9/11. Even the United Nations changed after 9/11. So Saddam was on the right track. His plan to have sanctions lifted was working. But he told me he recognized that he miscalculated the long-term effects of 9/11. And he miscalculated President Bush."

Months before the invasion, Saddam came to realize that war was "inevitable," Piro says. As a delaying tactic, he told Piro, he announced in September 2002 that he would allow weapons inspectors to return but stipulated that eight presidential compounds would be off-limits.

When George Tenet, as director of Central Intelligence, told President Bush that a CIA agent in Iraq knew that Saddam Hussein was in a bunker called Dora Farms, Bush gave the order to begin the invasion of Iraq on March 19, 2003. At 9:33 P.M., two satellite-guided one-ton bombs hit the Dora Farms bunker. Warships and submarines in the Persian Gulf and Red Sea fired thirty Tomahawk cruise missiles at the compound as well. Forty-five minutes later, Bush addressed the nation from the Oval Office.

Saddam revealed to Piro that he was in fact at the Dora Farms bunker but had left by the time it was hit. The same thing happened at a second location pinpointed by the CIA—one of Saddam's compounds in Baghdad's Mansur neighborhood.

Did Saddam ever consider coming clean with the United States and demonstrating that he did not have WMD?

"He didn't give me the answer to that," Piro says, "but I can tell you he wouldn't have done that, because that would have weakened him. He was given the opportunity to leave Iraq and go to live in Saudi Arabia and be very wealthy and very happy. The Saudis gave him the option. But what would that have done to his legacy? And if he were to have said 'I'm bluffing,' or 'I'm not as strong as I present myself,' where would he have then fit in the historical scheme of Iraq?"

Looking back, Saddam expressed no remorse or regrets.

"Some of his decisions worked, some of them didn't," Piro says. "If they didn't work, then he moved on and tried to correct them with a different decision."

After every interview, Piro and his FBI partner, Irinaga, sent 302 interview reports to the FBI and CIA. Most are still classified. In his report, Charles A. Duelfer, special advisor to the Director of Central Intelligence on Iraq's WMD, alluded vaguely to debriefings of Saddam. He did not quote exactly what Saddam had said and did not say who had conducted the debriefings or what agency was involved.

Piro credited FBI and CIA intelligence analysts and FBI language specialists, an FBI profiler, and other FBI counterterrorism agents with giving him the knowledge and insights he needed to make the operation a success.

As June 2004 approached and the interim Iraqi government was about to take legal control of Saddam, Piro let him know that he would be leaving. By then, Saddam had taken to calling Piro the director of the security service. Piro prepared Saddam for his first court appearance, giving him a suit. An FBI analyst who was also a hair-stylist gave him a haircut.

"We didn't do that for him. We did that for us," Piro says. "We wanted to show the world how well we had treated Saddam, not because of who he was but because of who we are."

On July 1, 2004, Piro took Saddam to court for his arraignment. Piro prepared a so-called prosecutive memo, which, with exhibits, ran to more than 700 pages. Because the Iraqis wanted the trial of Saddam to be an Iraqi affair, they did not introduce the memo into evidence. However, they used witnesses and evidence cited in the memo that detailed Saddam's atrocities.

Then it was time to say good-bye. In all, Piro had been with Saddam eight months, including seven months of interviews. At a *souq,* for $6 apiece, Piro bought two Cuban Cohiba cigars, Saddam's favorite brand.

"We sat outside, smoked a couple of Cuban cigars, had some coffee, and chatted," Piro says. They said good-bye in the traditional Arab manner: a handshake and then a kiss to the right cheek, a kiss to the left, and a kiss to the right again. That made Piro a little uncomfortable.

Saddam appeared shaken and became teary-eyed.

"When we were saying bye, he started to tear up," Piro remembers.

Piro watched the video shots of Saddam being executed on December 30, 2006. He remembered that Saddam told him why he did not shoot himself—even though he had a pistol—when American soldiers captured him on December 13, 2003.

"He didn't want the spider hole to be the last chapter in his book, the last scene," Piro says. "He saw what had happened to his kids, who were killed in a gun battle with U.S. soldiers. He told me that he knew that he was going to be executed, regardless of whatever defense he would raise, especially once he realized that the trial was going to be in Iraq. It didn't matter to him. He was sixty-seven, he had lived beyond the life expectancy of an Arab man in the Middle East. He had had a good life. Execution would serve his purpose, which was preserving his legacy and his place in history."

As Piro watched the noose being placed around Saddam's neck, he realized that Saddam must have rehearsed for this day.

"He appeared proud, courageous," Piro says. "He refused to wear the mask. He showed no fear. He didn't need any help to walk up to the trapdoor to the gallows. I would say that after that, his stock in the Arab world went back up a little bit. And that's what he wanted."

Piro never forgot what an evil man Saddam was.

"I felt that his conviction and his execution were fair and just," he says. "However, he was charming, he was charismatic, he was polite, he had a great sense of humor, and yeah, he was likable." Comparing Saddam Hussein with Adolf Hitler and other mass murderers, Piro says, "He had certain traits and abilities that let him to get into that position of power, but there have been many before him, and unfortunately, there will be many after him throughout the world."

"You talk about the ability to build rapport, and to work somebody," Art Cummings says. "When Saddam Hussein starts crying because his interrogator's leaving, because that's his only friend, that's George Piro. A lot of personal sacrifice behind it, eight months away from his family, in the middle of a place where mortars are going off."

After Piro returned to Washington, Cummings assigned him to head the international terrorism component of the Joint Terrorism Task Force in Washington. That means Piro is in charge of protecting the nation's capital from an al Qaeda attack.

When Piro had asked his mother to send him her Lebanese cookies and pastries, he had not told her why. After he returned home, he told her in August 2004 that the goodies were for Saddam for his birthday.

Playfully, she gave her son the FBI the agent a hard smack on the back of his head.

"My parents are extremely patriotic and loyal to the United States," Piro says. "We are very, very fortunate to have been given the opportunity to come and live in the United States. I truly feel that we are living the American dream. I moved here when I was twelve. I didn't speak a word of English when I came here, and in a short amount of time I'm working for the premier law enforcement agency in the world, the FBI. I look at what I'm doing as paying my family's debt to the U.S. for allowing us to come here."

19

THREAT MATRIX

EVERY WEEKDAY MORNING at seven o'clock, Vice Admiral John Scott Redd, director of the National Counterterrorism Center (NCTC), picks up the Read Book that lists as many as sixty or seventy potential terrorist threats against the United States.

The white binder is four inches thick, and each copy is specially numbered for the person receiving it. Admiral Redd gets number one. A string of code words across the cover of the Read Book classify it top-secret, compartmented, meaning only a limited number of people can see it.

Inside, a twelve- to sixteen-page document called the threat matrix lists the latest threats. It changes daily. A kind of terrorism spread sheet, the threat matrix notes the type and reliability of the source for each threat, such as: "a new source, unevaluated, first time reporting" or "an established source, generally reliable, has provided reliable information in the past." Besides listing all the threats, the Read Book also contains a situation report produced by the center.

Before 9/11, no one brought together all the intelligence on possible terrorist plots and made sure the appropriate agencies were pursuing leads. Of all the changes since 9/11, the NCTC's role in connecting the dots is most vital.

The 9/11 Commission recommended creation of the NCTC, yet most people are not aware of its existence, and critics still find ways to bash it. In his book, *Preventing Surprise Attacks: Intelligence Reform in the Wake of 9/11*, Richard A. Posner, the U.S. Court of Appeals judge who favors creating an American MI5, called the NCTC a "Rube Goldberg–style organization." According to Posner, "It just made things worse. The CIA already had a counterterrorism center. Why create another one?"

As with his comments about MI5, Posner's criticism reflected a lack of understanding of what the NCTC does. Unlike the CIA's Counterterrorism Center, the NCTC does not run operations. Rather, it pulls together information from all sixteen agencies in the intelligence community, analyzes it, and makes sure the agencies are pursuing every lead.

Since June 2005, when President Bush announced his appointment, Redd has been in charge of the operation. A graduate of the U.S. Naval Academy, Redd's last assignment on active duty was as director of Strategic Plans and Policy for the Joint Chiefs of Staff. After retiring from the Navy, Redd was executive director of the Commission on the Intelligence Capabilities of the United States Regarding Weapons of Mass Destruction.

Redd has a neat, white mustache. His thick white hair is parted low. He is fast-talking and professorial. He sweeps his arms out while he's speaking, in wide, shipboard gestures.

At the NCTC, Redd meets with a small group of analysts at 7:15 A.M. and whittles down the list of threats of greatest concern to twenty-five or thirty. Tossed out are tips from walk-ins who may be looking for money and seem flaky or offer details that don't check out.

Fifteen minutes later, Redd meets with a larger group and cuts the number of threats to be scrutinized to ten or twenty.

Redd regularly goes off for meetings with President Bush, the National Security Council, the Department of Homeland Security, or National Intelligence Director Mike McConnell. Meanwhile, at 8:00 A.M., Kevin R. Brock, an FBI agent who replaced Cummings as the principal deputy director of the NCTC, starts a secure video teleconference with the FBI, CIA, NSA, the White House, and other agencies to review the threats and make sure that the appropriate agencies cover all the leads.

When Kevin speaks, it's with controlled energy. He doesn't open his mouth any wider than he has to, like a cowboy. The word "terrorism" is pronounced "terrism." And except that his days growing up in California and Connecticut deprived him of a Texas drawl, he is an FBI version of the actor Tommy Lee Jones.

Brock doesn't use his hands much when he talks. A major exception is when he's talking about agencies communicating during a threat. He asks "Where's the handshake?" and illustrates it by clasping his own hands in front of his chest and shaking them.

He and his boss, whom everyone calls "The Admiral," share an interesting variation on counting on one hand. "Number one," Brock says, holding up his thumb to catch a ride, "we have seriously degraded al Qaeda's capabilities." Then he continues to count on the rest of his fingers. The admiral sticks out his thumb too, when counting off points he's making. The NCTC acts as a sort of traffic controller, Brock says.

"We want to know, have we thought through the problem?" Brock says. "Are we thinking of everything we could do here? Maybe NSA could help out on this. Maybe the CIA could pursue this angle or this agent. It's more of a collaborative brainstorming on ways that we can enhance the intelligence on this particular problem and get out of it everything that we can. This kind of stuff really wasn't being done before."

In the end, "the vast majority of the threats wash out," he says. "They are not credible or just didn't pan out. But it gives you a sense of what is out there, what does the bad guy community look like. For the one or two threats that are real, we want to move against that threat, to head it off at the pass, interdict it, neutralize it."

"We are better prepared today as a country, in the war on terror, than any time in our history," Redd says. "First reason is our intelligence is a lot better. Terrorists are a tough target. For all the obvious reasons, this is a very small group. They are in the mountains, the out-back border. Secondly, we're sharing that intelligence much more effectively. We give it to the people who need to have it. Third, we are taking the war offensively to the terrorists."

The government now goes after every aspect of the terrorist life cycle, Redd says.

"We go after terrorist travel and terrorist financing," he says. "We work with some expected bedfellows, obviously closely with the Brits, the Canadians, the Australians, the ones you'd expect. We also work with some countries that people might be surprised at. The common enemy takes us there. Bottom line is we have a very effective and very extensive counterterrorism relationship with other countries."

At the same time, security at home has been hardened. The list of changes is endless: Cockpit doors now cannot be opened during flight, security screening at airports has been tightened, cargo from ships is tracked from its origin and inspected on a spot basis, office buildings require visitors to sign in, and balustrades have been erected around government buildings.

"We have made the homeland a hostile place, both to enter and operate in," Redd says. "That's because of the Department of Homeland Security, the FBI, and state and local government."

The public "just knows the tip of the iceberg," Redd says. "There are lots of terrorists out there. You hear about the more famous ones when they get taken down, or something happens to them, but we have really decimated not only al Qaeda but a lot of other ones that most people will never hear about."

Besides integrating intelligence with counterterrorism, the collaboration fostered by the NCTC means different agencies within the intelligence community can hash out their differences in a productive way.

"Let's say that three agencies disagreed on a threat," Redd says. "By bringing people together, we can ask not only what do you know but also what do you *not* know. The CIA may think they've got a

HUMINT [human intelligence] source that they think is really hot, and they're really banking on that. NSA maybe isn't quite so sure because they've got something that's contradictory. Ideally, everybody comes together, but even if they don't, if it goes to a policy maker here, he or she can say, 'Okay. I understand why the intelligence community differs. Here's how and why they differ,' putting it in context."

In the same vein, material presented to Bush every morning in the President's Daily Brief now specifies which agency compiled the report. Included in the PDB are reports from the NCTC.

The heart of the complex is a 10,000-square-foot operations center that looks like a giant television studio. On either end of the operations center are two additional spaces—for the watch centers of the FBI's Counterterrorism Division and the CIA's Counterterrorism Center. There is no wall separating any of the components, so anyone on the floor can walk into another agency's area and discuss the raw intelligence reports available to all of the NCTC's nearly two hundred analysts.

The analysts, men and women in casual dress, look at cables they call up on their flat screens. Each desk has a minimum of three computer screens, and the center has 350 personal computers. During each 24-hour period, 4,000 to 8,000 cables come into the NCTC.

Viewed from a balcony, the operations center has a huge television screen, covering most of a two-story wall. On the large screen, information on the latest threats and incidents, as well as Fox and CNN in segmented sections, are projected. Two junior projection screens, too large for a private home, show other channels. On the many plasma screens throughout the room appear various news channels, including one in Arabic.

When visitors are present, the screen is in unclassified mode, a condition signaled by two red flashing lights on the black ceiling. If a critical incident is occurring, such as the July 7, 2005 London bombings, the transatlantic London plot, or a Cessna flying toward the White House, two flashing blue lights are turned on.

A winding staircase connects the balcony to the lower floor. In the back of the orchestra pit is a large workstation that has four computer screens. At that desk sits a sort of maestro who orchestrates what documents will be displayed on the giant screens in front of all the players, or analysts in the room. The screens can be divided into thirty-two sections.

Besides daytime television, the maestro—actually the senior operations officer—may display on the projector screens whatever is called for by the current situation. That includes geo-spatial pictures, the threat matrix, and military maps showing a ground situation. The analysts at the workstations tell him what documents to show on the screens.

The ergonomic workstations in the Operations Center are kidney-shaped and have light oak veneer. They are generally kept clear of loose paper and personal memorabilia. Instead of the NCTC mugs sold in the coffee shop, there are Styrofoam and Starbucks paper cups, just one stuffed toy chihuahua, and a statuette of a man in a brown suit.

The NCTC's analysts have access to the raw intelligence reports of all the agencies. If they think a sensitive report should be disseminated to the intelligence community at large, the analysts ask the originating agency, which usually provides an edited version. That way, the information becomes available without compromising a sensitive source.

During the design phase of the NCTC operations center, a question arose about how to configure the watch centers of the FBI's Counterterrorism Division and the CIA's Counterterrorism Center. An NCTC official suggested that they be located at either end of the Ops center, with no wall separating them. That was a shocking idea. Even though the NCTC's nearly two hundred analysts are detailed from the FBI, CIA, NSA, and other agencies, and work side by side, having discrete FBI and CIA space open to analysts from other agencies was unheard of.

The two agencies agreed to try the open space idea. After all, too many walls—real and imagined—was one of the 9/11 Commission's major criticisms. The walls have stayed down, with FBI agents and CIA analysts walking back and forth between the two watch centers.

In another wall-busting innovation, the NCTC operates a classified Web site that provides information to five thousand analysts throughout the world. Analysts can search for "Hezbollah" or "John Jones" and pull up anything relating to that person.

"We have created a thing called NCTC online, an elegant but simple solution," Redd says. "It's a classified Web site, top secret compartmented. If the information is available to other agencies, it goes up on that Web site. So more than five thousand analysts around the world can go in there and do a Web search just as you would do on your favorite Web site."

Analysts from each of the sixteen intelligence agencies can discuss the material on secure chatrooms.

"Anybody with the right clearance can get on there and say, 'What do you make of this?' Or, 'How does this compare with that?' " Redd says. "Nothing like that existed prior to 9/11."

The NCTC also operates what Redd calls "the mother of all databases," the Terrorist Information Datamart Environment (TIDE).

"Whether it comes from an operations cable from the CIA or a very sensitive SIGINT [signals intelligence intercept] from NSA, if there's a piece of derogatory information on a known or suspected terrorist, it goes in that database," Redd says.

Each electronic file on an individual includes hyperlinks to the originating information, including raw FBI files and, if available, fingerprint files and photographs. In the future, the files will link to iris scans, facial recognition, and DNA data.

Americans are included only if they have been convicted of terrorist activities or are under investigation by the FBI. The standard is far lower for people overseas.

"What's a terrorist?" asks Russell E. Travers, who is in charge of the NCTC list as deputy director for information sharing and knowledge development. "If you swear allegiance to bin Laden, that's pretty easy. If you went to a training camp and have a history of blowing up U.S. interests, that's pretty easy also. What if you went to a training camp, but then you decided you didn't like this and went home? What if you are the brother of someone who swore loyalty to bin Laden? What if you are a member of an Islamic nongovernmental organization, and some in that organization have clearly funneled money to al Qaeda? So the point is that this can become very gray. And given that we're dealing with information that may be contradictory or it may be partial, this can be a difficult balance for us. We look at all the evidence and try to apply a reasonable standard."

In the case of a foreign individual, "If someone was in a safehouse, and we just have a name that they were in some way associated with a known al Qaeda guy, then even though we may have no other derogatory information beyond that, that would be enough to get them in TIDE and get them on a watch list, so that they won't be able to get a visa to come to the country," Travers says.

From the TIDE database, the NCTC extracts the name, date of birth, and additional basic information to identify each possible terrorist. The NCTC passes those names, each tagged with a TIDE number, to the Terrorist Screening Center maintained by the FBI. Those names then form the basis for the no-fly list and other lists checked by U.S. Customs officers and State Department officers issuing visas. The FBI includes the names on its National Crime Information Center list that police officers check when stopping traffic violators, apprehending fugitives, or identifying stolen property.

If a traffic violator who is stopped in Maine is on the list as a possible terrorist, the officer at the scene can call the Terrorist Screening Center and obtain instructions. If the man is wanted, the officer will arrest him. Or the local Joint Terrorism Task Force may be called into action to conduct surveillance of the individual.

The classified NCTC list has 400,000 names, of which 300,000 are separate individuals. The extra entries are aliases or different spellings of the same name. For example, there are many ways to spell names like Muhammed. Osama bin Laden alone has more than half a dozen names or nicknames, including Mohammad, Usama Bin Muhammad Bin Ladin, Shaykh Usama Bin Ladin, the Prince, the Emir, Abu Abdallah, Mujahid Shaykh, Hajj, and the Director.

The number of names on the no-fly list, maintained by the Transportation Security Administration, is far smaller. Only people who might pose a danger to civil aviation are supposed to be included, but there have been plenty of mix-ups. A deputy assistant director of the FBI once found himself on the list. Massachusetts Democratic Senator Ted Kennedy had a close encounter with the list when trying to take the U.S. Airways shuttle out of Washington to Boston. According to Kennedy, the ticket agent would not let him on the plane. With help from an airport supervisor, Kennedy was able to fly home, but then the same thing happened coming back to Washington.

"This is not an exact science," Travers says. "But it is one of many defenses that the government has for trying to keep prospective bad guys out of the country."

In some cases, the FBI may override the no-fly list because the bureau wants a terrorist to enter the country so agents can arrest him or follow him.

TERROR SUSPECT LIST YIELDS FEW ARRESTS, the lead story in the August 25, 2007, *Washington Post* read.

"The government's terrorist screening database flagged Americans and foreigners as suspected terrorists almost 20,000 times last year," the story by Ellen Nakashima said breathlessly. "But only a small fraction were arrested or denied entry into the United States, raising concerns among critics about privacy and the list's effectiveness."

Besides citing incomplete figures, the story ignored the fact that the purpose of the database is not necessarily to make arrests but rather to enable the FBI and other agencies to track people with suspicious connections and backgrounds so they can try to determine if they might, in fact, be terrorists.

Counterterrorism operatives can't win: If they don't arrest people, the civil libertarians and media are outraged. If they do arrest them, they are equally outraged.

The ACLU and other civil liberties advocates have complained that there is something inherently insidious about the number of names on the lists. Timothy Sparapani, the ACLU's legislative counsel for privacy rights, has called the numbers "shocking but, unfortunately, not surprising."

Back when the watch list had 300,000 names, he said, "We have lists that are having baby lists at this point; they're spawning faster than rabbits. If we have over 300,000 known terrorists who want to do this country harm, we've got a much bigger problem than deciding which names go on which list. But I highly doubt that is the case."

Yet the problem before 9/11 was that there were too few names on the lists. Back then, the government maintained four different classified terrorist identity databases and thirteen independent watch lists. It was in part because the databases were incompatible that two of the 9/11 hijackers managed to slip into the country.

Before 9/11, "The classified databases and the watch lists didn't interact," says Travers. "So the reason that Khalid al-Mihdhar and Nawaf al-Hazmi didn't get watch-listed was because parts of the government knew about them, but that information was not percolated all over the place."

When it was revealed that the government rated travelers who fly in and out of the country by degree of possible threat, critics said the criteria should be revealed and that travelers should have the right to see their ratings and challenge them. Of course, that would only undermine the effectiveness of the risk assessment program.

If a terrorist could find out what criteria were used and how information was rated, he could circumvent the system. Letting travelers know what the criteria are would make as much sense as the Internal

Revenue Service forewarning a taxpayer before he files his tax return which portion of his return the IRS plans to audit. Rather than invading privacy, the risk rating system is a way to narrow scrutiny of millions of travelers and protect them from another attack.

What the ACLU forgets is that people from other countries do not have a right to enter the U.S. Inevitably, some will be listed in error. But the alternative is to limit the list so much that terrorists can enter the country and pull off another 9/11 attack.

The ACLU's opposition to national ID cards illustrates its fuzzy thinking. The organization has no problem with driver's licenses or national Social Security cards which can easily be counterfeited. The 9/11 hijackers had thirty bogus driver's licences among them, allowing them to board planes that killed some three thousand people. When it comes to similar cards that are reliable and allow more intelligent screening of passengers at airports, the ACLU raises the flag of civil liberties concerns. The organization—along with some extreme conservative groups—even opposes uniform state driver's licenses tailored under the federal Real ID Act to prevent counterfeiting.

Ironically, anyone can buy most of the same personal information about an individual on the Web. When the government uses that same information to try to prevent another terrorist attack and minimize intrusive searches of travelers, the critics emerge like vultures swooping down over roadkill.

Besides running the NCTC, Redd is in charge of developing a comprehensive counterterrorism strategy that pinpoints which component of what agency is responsible for every aspect of protecting the country from terrorism. That includes the fighter jets that scramble to possibly shoot down an airplane considered a danger. In that role, Redd reports directly to the president.

"Most agencies do pretty well at what they understand their role in life to be," Redd says. "It's when you come up against a boundary situation—foreign and domestic being a perfect example from

9/11—when people aren't quite sure how to act. We want to make sure they know who is accountable for what."

The admiral's office is stark, with lots of filing cabinets, a stand of nine CPUs (the guts of a computer), two waste baskets, and a secure trash bag. The nine CPUs are a reminder that integration of the intelligence community is not yet complete. While two of the CPUs give Redd access to the computer networks of intelligence services of allied countries, the rest are for the separate networks of the FBI, CIA, NSA, and the Defense Department. All told, the NCTC taps into twenty-eight separate computer networks.

The good news is that NCTC analysts, working in a building protected against electronic intrusions and rarely seen by journalists, have access to all the country's intelligence networks. The bad news is there are still so many systems, each requiring separate access codes and each presenting information differently. Contracts are being awarded to integrate some of them.

"There's this balancing act, which is always going on, in which somebody says you share everything with everybody," Redd says. "That's fine until you have a very sensitive source—a human source or technical source—and the cost of having to replace that source if it becomes blown is maybe a human life. In the case of a technical source, replacing the source may cost millions of dollars." So "there's always this balance between need to know, protecting sensitive sources and methods, and need to share. And that's one of the beautiful things about NCTC. We've got people here from all these agencies who understand what their agencies are trying to do, and they get to see it all coming in here."

20

NEUTRALIZING
BIN LADEN

A	S THE U.S. intelligence community got better at its game, the pace of roll-ups quickened. Most of the stories on the FBI's arrests got very little play, but each one represented a victory that could easily have turned out to be a major disaster.

On February 21, 2006, the FBI arrested three men in West Toledo, Ohio: Mohammad Zaki Amawi, Wassim I. Mazloum, and Marwan Othman El-Hindi. According to the indictment, they planned a holy war to kill Americans who were overseas, including American soldiers in Iraq. One was taking college courses and selling used cars. Another spent time playing in his yard with his children, according to neighbors.

The FBI began watching the suspects eighteen months earlier, when an informant code-named "The Trainer" let the FBI know of his suspicions. He had been approached by El-Hindi to provide security and bodyguard training.

The indictment accused Amawi of twice threatening in conversations to injure or kill President Bush. The three men went as far as identifying a trip Bush was planning to Toledo and talked about ways of trying to get to him, including ramming his motorcade. But they eventually decided that security was too tight.

On June 3, 2006, the RCMP arrested seventeen terror suspects in Toronto. The FBI revealed that Syed Ahmed, twenty-one, and Ehsanul Sadequee, nineteen, from Atlanta, Georgia, met with the terror suspects in Canada in March 2005 to discuss bombing targets.

Several of the men arrested in Canada attended a storefront mosque in Mississauga, a suburb west of Toronto. Three tons of fertilizer, which is highly explosive when mixed with fuel oil, had been delivered to the suspects. Yet the clue that helped the Canadians uncover the plot came from London, where the British MI5 found a surveillance video made by the terrorists on a removable hard drive owned by a terrorist living in London.

The FBI found the two in Atlanta were going on chat rooms with the terrorists in Toronto. Before 9/11, the FBI could not routinely monitor chat rooms even if they were public.

Like many terrorism investigations, this one was successful because of international cooperation.

"The Canadians were monitoring the Canadians," an FBI official says. "We were monitoring the two men in Atlanta. They traveled to New York, they traveled to Canada, and one of them traveled overseas. So it's all starting to link up together, our case and their case," the FBI official says. "They find they're talking to other guys in Bosnia, and police there do a raid. They find suicide bomber vests and more communications between that guy and the guys in Canada and the guy in London. So what's coming into focus is a worldwide network."

At about the same time, the FBI was tracking a plot to blow up PATH train tunnels under the Hudson River between New York and New Jersey. The lead that led to the case came from monitoring a secure chat room, one that is only accessible to members. That lead, in turn, led to individuals in Jordan, where the Jordanian intelligence service pitched in.

On July 7, 2006, a leak to the *Daily News* in New York led to public disclosure of the plot. The ringleader, Assem Hammoud, was arrested in Beirut and confessed. He had been recruited by al Qaeda three years earlier and had been seeking help from the organization for the attack.

Hammoud, thirty-one, was not your typical Muslim terrorist. His mother, Nabila Qotob, said Hammoud drank alcohol, which is forbidden by Islam. He had girlfriends, traveled widely, and lived the life of an international playboy. But Lebanese police who arrested Hammoud said in a statement that the suspect claimed he had been ordered to maintain a fun-loving, secular lifestyle to hide his Islamic militancy.

"He did just that with perfection," the police statement said.

In April 2006, a federal jury convicted Hamid Hayat, twenty-three, of Lodi, California, of plotting to attack targets in the United States, including hospitals and supermarkets, after attending a terrorist training camp near Balakot, Pakistan.

In addition to these successful roll-ups, on June 23, 2006, the FBI announced arrests of seven men in Miami for plotting to blow up the Sears Tower in Chicago, a case that began with a tip from a criminal informant.

Just before the takedown in Toronto, "We had a meeting here at the FBI where they brought in the cops from London and the cops from Canada and the cops from the Netherlands and the cops from Bosnia," an FBI official says. "And they all said, we all have a different strand of this fabric that comes together to make this case, and all the different stages of development of it and all our people are connected to each other. What things do we need to accomplish, who needs to do what before we're comfortable taking down the rest of it? And basically by the end of the meeting, they left with a plan saying, 'Art, you'll take down your piece on this day, we'll do ours on that day.' It's demonstrative of the new shape of terrorism and how it's not so much that al Qaeda is finding the players." Instead, "The players are finding each other, and then they're seeking out the organization," the official says. "It's the original al Qaeda paradigm turned upside down."

During this time, "We had all of these balls up in the air," an FBI official says, "and the guys running these cases face this terrible dilemma: I need to let it go far enough so I don't shut it down too early and miss some bad guys, but I can't let it go so long involving so many people that one of them is able to break off and do some attack that we didn't see coming because we missed an angle somewhere."

Meanwhile, bin Laden was isolated. Those who wondered how bin Laden was able to elude capture for so long need only look at the case of Eric Robert Rudolph, who was the nation's most wanted domestic terrorist for almost six years. After he set off a bomb at Centennial Olympic Park in Atlanta in 1996, Rudolph was able to evade capture by hiding out in remote areas of western North Carolina.

Bin Laden was believed to be in far more remote areas between Afghanistan and Pakistan. While al Qaeda was building more training camps in Pakistan, bin Laden, for all intents and purposes, was no longer a key player.

"Bin Laden has to change his location all the time, constantly," Cummings says. "He can't trust the people around him, no way. He's watched all his ops guys get killed because of pressure from our military and the unbelievable amount of good, productive work the agency's done—getting other countries to work on our behalf and help them and provide them with assistance."

Now, "Anyone who announces that he is a member of al Qaeda becomes an immediate target of the U.S. government," Cummings says. "Boom, done, the military is going to fire him up. So they can't plan very well, and bin Laden can't operate."

When a tip comes in about his location, the CIA, NSA, and military spring into action, along with the NGA. While most people have never heard of it, the National Geospatial-Intelligence Agency (NGA) analyzes and interprets images created by satellites and spy planes.

For years, NSA was known as the No Such Agency because it was so secretive. But now that NSA intercepts have become front page news, the most secret agency is the NGA.

The NGA is a descendant of the National Photographic Interpretation Center (NPIC), which determined that the Soviets were providing Cuba with missiles in 1962, precipitating what was known as the Cuban Missile Crisis.

NPIC was part of the CIA, but in 1996, it became part of the National Imagery and Mapping Agency within the Defense Department. In 2003, it was renamed NGA. For unknown reasons, its founders wanted the agency to have an acronym with three letters like the FBI, CIA, and NSA, so they hyphenated Geospatial and Intelligence. While articles about NGA activities appear regularly in trade publications, the mainstream media rarely mention the supersecret agency.

NGA includes the former Defense Mapping Agency and is located in that agency's building in Bethesda, Maryland. The large complex of red brick government buildings seems out of place in the middle of a leafy suburban neighborhood. Instead of a three-car garage, this neighbor has a guardhouse with military guards armed with assault weapons.

Because NGA's building was originally used for printing maps, it is built like a factory. The low-ceilinged hallways of stucco and tile are deadly dull, the offices anonymous. With the tensile strength to support printing presses, the wide pillars that hold up the building have to be accommodated when planning office space.

Whenever a tip comes in on bin Laden's whereabouts, NGA analysts examine satellite images of his purported location for clues.

While satellites cannot peer into caves even with infrared imaging, they can pinpoint movement in the area. NGA analysts look for tire tracks and campfire smoke. They compare current images with images from the agency's archives. A change might indicate human activity.

Once NGA checks things out, the CIA may send an agent in to try to pick up information. If a military assault is planned, NGA might remotely analyze the soil and terrain to determine where helicopters could land and trucks move in.

"It's not that we hope that bin Laden looks up one day, and we get a picture of him," says Dave Burpee, an NGA officer who gave a partial tour of the complex.

In fact, satellites cannot make out human faces. They can read a license plate, if it is turned upward, intelligence sources say.

Instead, Burpee says, "There are going to be human reports, there are going to be signals reports, there are going to be all these inputs saying, 'We think he's here; we think there's something going on.' Maybe there's a lot of cell phone activity. All right, we're getting a lot of cell phone activity from this location on the earth. What's that look like? And oh, by the way, if we think it's a place on the face of the earth where bin Laden might be, how do we attack it? How do we get a special forces team in there?"

While bin Laden is isolated, he is not out of the picture.

"We think bin Laden and his deputy Ayman al-Zawahiri are still an important part of the chain of command," says Dr. J. D. Crouch, deputy national security advisor. "We don't think they are just symbolic. Obviously, Zawahiri in particular plays an important propaganda role. He's out doing media messages quite frequently, and both remain as symbols of the jihad. But life is harder for them because it's harder for them to communicate. They are hunkered down. In effect, we've sent them back to horse and buggy days. But that doesn't mean they can't communicate, and it doesn't mean they're not communicating."

In January 2005, U.S. intelligence was able to determine that bin Laden tasked Abu Musab al-Zarqawi, his senior operative in Iraq, with forming a terrorist unit to hit targets outside Iraq. Bin Laden specified that the U.S. should be the first target to be hit. Al-Zarqawi welcomed the assignment and reported that he already had some good ideas.

That spring, bin Laden instructed Hamza Rabia, a senior operative, to brief al-Zarqawi on al Qaeda's plans to attack sites outside Iraq, including the United States.

But Crouch says al Qaeda's own mistakes have worked against the organization. The attack on an Islamic wedding party in Amman, Jordan, was one such mistake, says Crouch. The attacks killed fifty-seven people.

"That reverberated across the Muslim world in ways that were really very negative," Crouch says. "And I think al Qaeda has come to understand that they can't afford too many of those."

The fact that al Qaeda now has cells operating semiautonomously can also get the movement into trouble. Crouch cited a letter Zawahiri wrote to Abu Musab al-Zarqawi, the al Qaeda leader in Iraq.

"Zawahiri was saying, 'Don't do things that alienate parts of the Muslim world,'" Crouch notes.

With bin Laden isolated, the FBI focused on obsessively pursuing every lead and tip, no matter how ridiculous they may seem. The bureau also changed the paradigm for declaring that a lead was not valid. Now if a lead turns out to be useless, the FBI concludes that "information has been developed to indicate they're not a threat, as opposed to we couldn't verify the information," Cummings says.

Whenever an agent closes a case, he or she is asked the reason.

"The answer better not be, 'I didn't find anything to show they were a terrorist,'" says Cummings. "Instead, the answer better be, 'I made an informed judgment, based on my collection, that they're not a terrorist. No phone links to terrorists, no finance links, no family links, and I've explained the contacts specifically.'" That is quite different from saying, "I can't find it, so therefore it's not there."

With the new paradigm, "the labor involved goes up by a factor of five or ten," says Cummings. "To have to continue collecting until you make your own judgment that they're not a terrorist? When basically, there's no CIA records, there's no NSA records, there's no FBI records. He doesn't appear to be in a position to be a terrorist. He looks like a regular guy. He's a life insurance salesman; and he's never been out of the country."

If Cummings needs more agents to work a case, "I get more

agents," he says. "We have 12,575 agents in the FBI, and we have 4,000 working terrorism. Before 9/11, at FBI headquarters, we had thirty supervisors working counterterrorism. We're at something like eight hundred now. If I need another thousand working terrorism, then we're going to talk to the director, and something's going to have to give."

In an example of the new approach, when the FBI got a report of a man buying chemicals that could be used for explosives, it was all over the tip. In this case, it would have been easy to dismiss the purchases as innocent, since the man was buying the supplies from a swimming pool company, and his business was shipping pool supplies.

"That explanation wasn't good enough," Cummings says. "It's not okay to say, 'It looks like pool supplies, we're done.' You don't finish there. Who at the pool company, specifically, did he buy them from? What specifically was the transaction, and what happened from there? Is it a friend, is it an associate, is it somebody who wants to do us harm? There was a day we would have said, 'It's a commercial transaction, don't worry about it.' Each and every lead is followed all the way down to the most minute detail."

Taking those extra precautions, which would never have been followed prior to 9/11, frustrates agents.

"They say, 'Come on, it's a pool supply company, the guy ships pool parts,' " Cummings says. "We say, 'Great, go see the company records, find out who bought what, where it was shipped, what was the item exactly, does it have dual use possibilities?'And when you've finished all that, then we can make an informed judgment."

Each of the FBI's field offices now has a threat squad for immediately checking out each lead that is phoned in.

"If someone is buying two hundred pounds of ammonium nitrate, we'll get a phone call," Cummings says. "And every time we go out, and the person who is supposedly a Middle Easterner turns out to be named Garcia or Rodriguez, we're very respectful. We say, 'We're just checking on a report that you bought these chemicals.'

Some of them get very upset, and some of them don't. That's just the way of the world right now. We're not going back to flying by the seat of our pants and saying, 'Well, that's a white guy, his name's O'Reilly, there's no way he's a terrorist.' We did used to do that. Now there is not a stone unturned."

21

PREEMPT, DISRUPT, DEFEAT

O<small>N</small> A<small>UGUST</small> 3, 2006, British MI5 notified U.S. officials that the terrorists they had been monitoring since the previous December appeared ready to move ahead with a plot to blow up ten U.S. airliners as they flew over America from London.

In a second-floor apartment in East London, two young Muslim men had recorded a video justifying a plot to blow up the planes as revenge against the U.S. and its "accomplices," Britain and the Jews. One of the young men added that he hoped Allah would be "pleased with us and accepts our deed." Meanwhile, the men were conducting experiments with chemicals.

Art Cummings was placed in charge of the FBI's response.

That night, CIA Director Michael V. Hayden, his third-in-command Michael Morell, and others from the CIA's Counterterrorism Center met in the office of Hayden's deputy, Steve Kappes, to plan strategy.

The CIA is said to be in Langley, Virginia, but no such town exists. Langley once had its own post office inside a country store. By 1910, the village had been merged into nearby McLean, named for John R. McLean, the then publisher of the *Washington Post* and the principal stockholder in an electric rail line that linked the area with Washington. Because of the rail line, there was no need for a separate village so close to McLean. The Langley post office was closed.

On a map, the CIA's 225.5-acre compound looks like a giant

weather balloon, with its top jutting toward the northeast just below a crook in the Potomac River. The mouth of the balloon forms the entrance to the compound.

As visitors turn off Dolly Madison Boulevard, Route 123, into the lanes leading to the main entrance, an array of signs warns them that they may be searched, and that no photographs are allowed. Anyone who is not an employee is directed to a lane on the right, where visitors must announce their Social Security number over an intercom. If the number matches with a list of visitors cleared to enter that day, they may advance to the next stop, which is the main guard gate, a concrete and glass structure. There, they must show picture identification. If everything matches, the guard provides a visitor's badge and a parking permit with a map of the parking lots. The color of the permit changes daily, and the permit is stamped with that day's date.

If anyone tries to enter the compound without permission, the guard can flip a switch and raise a steel barrier that pivots up from the ground. Just in case, the guards are also armed with nine-millimeter semiautomatic pistols, rifles, and submachine guns.

Once or twice a day, people who do not have appointments show up at the entrances asking to see the director or requesting that the CIA stop the satellite signals in their heads. In those cases, their identity is checked. Often, they are intoxicated, have no driver's licenses, or have outstanding warrants for their arrest. The CIA's police officers arrest them, or the Fairfax County police are called.

In addition to three hundred uniformed CIA security officers, the agency has twelve dogs trained to sniff out explosives or hazardous materials. In one famous incident, Stanley Moskowitz, then the agency's director of congressional affairs, left his car in the CIA parking garage. Later in the day, the Office of Security asked if he would mind coming down to the garage and opening his trunk. Two dogs trained to locate explosives had fingered it for harboring a bomb. Moskowitz opened the trunk. The dogs had detected aromatic tennis clothes.

One evening just before Christmas, a man drove to the entrance at

Route 123. Apparently, he had wound up at the CIA entrance by mistake. As a guard checked his identity, Maggie, a Lab, came over to sniff. The man panicked and jumped out of the car, dropping packets of cocaine. Since Maggie was not trained to uncover drugs, she began eating one of the packets, as any dog would. The man with the cocaine was arrested. Maggie was in intensive care for four days but returned to the force.

The CIA's dogs—mostly German Shepherds and Labs—stay in kennels outside a home on the CIA's property once owned by Margaret Scattergood. Scattergood bought the property in 1933. When the federal government tried to take the property for the CIA, she got a private law passed allowing her to stay there undisturbed until she died. In the meantime, title passed to the government, and she received $54,189 for the property.

The daughter of a wealthy dye manufacturer in Philadelphia, Scattergood was a Quaker and a pacifist. The CIA, in her view, meant war and killing—everything she was against. Scattergood helped civil rights organizations and was corresponding clerk of the Langley Hill Friends Meeting in McLean. But she spent most of her time doling out money from a trust fund set up by her father. She gave to antiwar and other liberal causes and wrote letters to members of Congress urging cuts in the military and intelligence budgets.

Scattergood died on November 7, 1986, at the age of ninety-two, after a stroke. She had lived on the property for twenty-five years adjacent to CIA headquarters—a last show of resistance.

Externally, the CIA has a campus atmosphere—the quiet, the joggers on wooded paths, the blue jays calling in the pines, the fresh country smell, the moss growing at the foundations of the old main CIA building.

The peacefulness is a veneer, of course. They're waging a war inside.

The long room that is General Michael Hayden's seventh-floor office commands a treetop view. Here, the quiet and calm of the agency's campus turns positively genteel—the gold brocade sofas, the regular and decaf coffee served in china with a cobalt and gold trim and a discreet CIA monogram, set out on a low table with chocolate chip and oatmeal cookies. The four-star general pours in his light blue shirt sleeves. His uniform sets him apart here. He wears the standard name tag that reads HAYDEN, not that anyone would have to ask.

The general is a warm, what-you-see-is-what-you-get kind of man, comfortable in his own skin. That skin has the healthy glow that comes from a regimen of running fifteen to twenty miles a week. The command and breadth of Hayden's knowledge is encyclopedic, and he relishes talking about intelligence matters, but not secrets.

When asked about matters that might be classified, he clams up and conveys closed body language—legs crossed and arms folded tightly across his chest. When troubled, he lowers his soft brown eyes and holds a hand to his balding head. He often makes a point by waving an empty water bottle.

Hayden was sworn in as CIA director on May 30, 2006. Before that, he was the first to serve as deputy director of national intelligence. Previously, he had headed NSA. Many in the intelligence community viewed the creation of the position of National Intelligence Director (DNI) over the CIA director and the rest of the intelligence community as a move in the wrong direction, imposing a new layer of bureaucracy and isolating the CIA director from the president. Before the change, the director of Central Intelligence (DCI) briefed Bush every morning, bringing questions back to the CIA. Now the director of national intelligence performs that function.

But Hayden sees advantages to the new setup.

"In many ways, the creation of the DNI actually frees up the director of the CIA to do some stuff," Hayden says. "My workday doesn't start at 10:00 [when the DCI would normally return from briefing the president]. My workday starts at 6:45 when I get in the car. My briefer's there, and I begin to go into the briefing, so that I'm done reading the President's Daily Brief (PDB) and other materials at

8:00. By 8:15, I'm ready to be the director of the Central Intelligence Agency. The national intelligence director's still downtown [briefing the president]."

Unlike previous directors, who had meetings at established times during the day, Hayden's day is flexible.

After 8:15, "I'm in receive mode," Hayden says. "No, that's not totally true, we just had the operations briefing here, when they updated me on ops activity. But I had picked up some things in the PDB, and I said, 'You see that thing there? Here's what I want to do about that.' But in a broad sense, what's scheduled is for staff or others to report to me in the first couple of hours of the day. It's very flexible. And what happens after that depends on the day."

Hayden "sets clear direction, he delegates, he gets out of your way, but he holds you to very high standards," says the CIA's Michael Morell, who is the agency's associate deputy director. "He has a way of getting people to want to do their best. When you talk about an issue with him, he gets to the essence of it. He knows what the issue is, he listens to input, and he makes a decision, even if it's going to make some people in the room unhappy, and then you move on."

Hayden regularly meets with the agency briefers who participate with National Intelligence Director Mike McConnell, a former NSA director, in briefing the president to learn of follow-up questions and concerns Bush may have. Hayden also meets with Bush himself every Thursday.

Porter Goss, the previous director, closeted himself in his office while aides from his days on Capitol Hill communicated his wishes. Goss did not personally run the early-morning staff meeting, leaving that to his executive director. He held his own once-a-week meeting on Wednesdays later in the morning.

Hayden, like former DCI George Tenet, is a schmoozer. At a recent family day event at the agency, Hayden signed autographs, posed for pictures, and proudly introduced his grandchildren to employees. Hayden also likes to chat with employees in the CIA cafeteria.

"I try to show up in the cafeteria on a fairly routine basis," Hayden says. "Grab your tacos and your chips and your Coke and look for a table with an empty chair—not an empty table—sit down and say, 'Hey, what do you guys do around here?' Goes a long way."

At a reception for employees and their spouses on November 16, 2006, Hayden told spouses and partners, "We are sincerely grateful for the encouragement you offer and the sacrifices you make in support of our officers, and by extension, in support of our mission. People outside this organization may not recognize your crucial role, but inside CIA, we never forget it."

As his deputy, Hayden chose Stephen Kappes. A former Moscow and Kuwait Station chief, Kappes played a pivotal role in secret talks that led Muammar el-Qaddafi of Libya to put an end to his program to develop weapons of mass destruction. Kappes resigned from the CIA when Patrick Murray, who was chief of staff to then CIA Director Goss, ordered him to fire his deputy, Michael Sulick, after Sulick criticized Murray over the nasty way he had treated another CIA officer. By bringing Kappes back to the agency and promoting him to deputy director, Hayden made his own statement.

"It's often said that intelligence is the tip of the spear. True enough," Hayden says. "But in today's world, intelligence is even more than that. It is the single most effective weapon in our national security arsenal. Whether you're talking about terrorism, weapons proliferation, regional instability, natural disasters, disease, global crime and corruption—the list goes on—what CIA does makes a decisive difference. The intelligence we collect, analyze and deliver to policymakers, diplomats, law enforcement and military commanders is the basis for decision and action every day."

By way of supporting employees, Hayden pushed Congress for clarity on what tactics CIA interrogators can employ. In an e-mail to employees, he said that language in the law that was eventually passed will give the CIA that clarity and "the support that we need to move forward with a detention and interrogation program that allows us to continue to defend the homeland, attack al Qaeda and protect American and Allied lives."

The CIA has always struggled with the issue of centralization. Originally, the agency's directorates were so compartmentalized and insular that an analyst, without special permission, was not allowed to walk into areas where clandestine officers had their offices.

Now the agency has specialized centers like the Counterterrorism Center where spies and analysts, as well as scientists and engineers from the Directorate of Science and Technology, work together.

The CIA's Counterterrorism Center was started in 1986 after President Reagan instructed William Casey, the director of Central Intelligence, to focus more on catching terrorists. During the previous year, there had been three major terrorist incidents—an attack by the Abu Nidal terrorist group on the El Al ticket counters in Rome and Vienna, the hijacking by Shiite terrorists of TWA Flight 847, and the hijacking of the Italian cruise ship *Achille Lauro* by the Palestine Liberation Front.

The concept of a center cutting across jurisdictional lines represented a sea change for the CIA. Convinced that its job was the most important one in the agency, each directorate, like competing sports teams, vied for attention, funding, and status. Each would put down the other directorates.

Casey promised twenty-five officers for the new center. Six months after he approved the idea, Casey asked to see the new center. Because of internal opposition, beyond a few cramped offices, the center had not been established.

Today the front office of the CIA's Counterterrorism Center (CTC) is on the third floor of the CIA's new headquarters building, an addition completed in 1988 behind the old building. The CTC has office spaces on several floors in both the original headquarters building and the new one.

On one wall of CTC's main conference room is a twelve-foot-long sign that says in red letters, CIA COUNTERTERRORISM CENTER. In black letters below it are the words PREEMPT—DISRUPT—DEFEAT. Framing the four-foot-high sign are the agency seals of all sixteen agencies that form the intelligence community.

Every day, the CTC director holds scheduled and ad hoc meetings in the conference room. Fourteen laptop computers can pop up from the long conference table, and twenty more can pop up from surrounding walls.

The hub for counterterrorism operations is the CTC's Global Response Center. At its entrance is a three-foot by three-foot sign that says, TODAY IS SEPTEMBER 12, 2001. It's a reminder of the urgency required to combat global terrorism. Along the wall are two photos of the World Trade Center and one of the Pentagon after the attacks.

Hayden says that while each specialty within the CIA is rightfully separate, he wants more interaction. As an example of the inconsistencies among different directorates, Hayden says, "When I got here, I was told that it had been decided that the agency was going to reimburse our new hires and other employees who had student loans. That was going to be part of their compensation package. However, the implementation of that decision was left to each of the heads of the directorates. They literally could choose whether they would do it or not. What's the sense of making an agency-wide policy and then devolve it down into the component parts?"

To some degree, it's good that each directorate has its own culture, Hayden says.

"Those clandestine service people, they're like fighter pilots in the Air Force," he says. "And you don't want the fighter pilots thinking that they're just like everyone else. I understand that. But you do want your fighter pilots recognizing they are part of a larger organization. They are airmen, they are part of the Air Force. Well, there's a little bit of that here, in that what we're trying to do is, first of all, establish a more dominant, more pervasive agency identity before our folks assume their more particularized identity within each directorate."

Hayden wants a culture that is "naturally more collaborative," a change that he intends to implement in part by extending the orientation process for new employees.

In Hayden's office, visitors are drawn to the framed American flag at one end of the room. Part of the flag's star field has been burned away. Gold fringe is missing, and there are holes in some of the white stripes. The general explains that the flag was pulled from the rubble of the World Trade Center. A visible reminder during counterterrorist briefings, the flag is displayed in front of his conference table.

When visitors come, there is often a photo op just before they leave.

"We go down to the end of the office," Hayden says. "We take a picture in front of that flag."

22

DR. STRANGELOVE

Three times a day, NCTC holds a secure video teleconference with the rest of the intelligence community—supposedly disorganized, its members not on speaking terms. The conferences are held at 8:00 A.M., 3:00 P.M. and at 1:00 A.M. seven days a week.

The conferences—known as SVTCs (pronounced si-vitz)—take place in a room straight out of *Dr. Strangelove*.

On an oval oak table, which seats at least twenty, there are eight mouses belonging to invisible computers that rise from somewhere in the center of the table at a command on a touch screen. On a wall at the head of the table, the requisite clocks show the time in New York, Paris, Stockholm, Sarajevo, Jerusalem, Teheran, New Delhi, and Shanghai.

At the other end of the table are plasma screens that, during the SVTC, show talking heads of certain high-level, security-cleared members of the intelligence community—at the FBI, CIA, NSA, Pentagon, and Department of Homeland Security, as well as the White House.

The table has another surprise—an open space in the middle. Another command to the touch screen and voilà, the table folds out at one end. This is so that during a video conference, everyone at the table can get into the picture.

One nice Strangelovian touch is the electric glass window for situational awareness. If a big event is taking place, the electronic interface in the glass is switched off so the glass is transparent and the people in the conference room can look directly into the Ops Center next door.

During the conference, which lasts an hour or two, officials discuss the latest threats, get updates, plot strategy, and make sure leads are covered by the appropriate agencies.

Kevin Brock, the FBI agent who is principal deputy director of the NCTC, presides over the 8:00 A.M. conference.

"We review what's happened in the last twenty-four hours," Brock explains. "And the beauty of it is that in real time, we have senior-level executives who can speak to their agencies, hearing what's going on, and being able to ask each other for more clarity and for context."

In the conferences, "We can ask, 'Are you guys acting on this? Can the CIA get more information on that? Can the FBI or NSA? Maybe the Defense Department should consider this?' It's a free-flow exchange of information happening nearly on a real-time basis, something that wasn't happening before."

Each participant has a copy of that day's threat matrix, which describes each current known threat, who reported it, which agencies are aware of it. Threats are listed in the order they are received, with the most recent ones listed first.

"At a glance, you can see, all right, DOD collected this threat out of Iraq, but it pertains to something in Europe, who's been told?" Brock says. "Then it will give the sourcing on it and a little bit of context on the source: Is it a new source? An established source? A walk-in to an embassy? A phone-in, or a write-in to a Web site? That gives some idea of where this is coming from so you can make evaluative judgments."

The listing indicates which threats come from known sources and which ones were called in or were received by letter or e-mail.

The threat matrix will say, "This is a brand-new source, unevaluated, first-time reporting," Brock says. "This is an established source, generally reliable, has provided reliable information in the past. Give the reader some sense or context of what they're dealing with."

Usually, "Close to thirty are listed every day," says Brock. "It'll spike, based on what's going on around the world."

The matrix does not list the status of any investigations.

"The threat matrix is just simply: What's the threat today?" Brock says. "If there's an update on that threat—either it has been washed out as bogus or they got new information that illuminates the original threat—we'll put that in the matrix as well, to modify the original threat listing."

Brock notes that nothing is ever going to be perfect. Institutional pride and concerns sometimes come into play, particularly when it comes to very sensitive sources.

"The FBI runs sensitive sources, the CIA runs sensitive sources, and nobody wants to get anybody killed or have things dry up on them," he says. "But there have been provisions made and agreements reached that now allow a trust environment to exist where that information has to be more widely shared than it ever was before. As that trust builds and builds, and we don't blow it, and some agency just doesn't go sideways and kill the deal, we should see that improve as time goes on."

While occasionally the agencies still trip over themselves, Brock says the kind of "fumbling" that occurred before 9/11 between the FBI and CIA over Khalid al-Mihdhar's and Nawaf al-Hazmi's entry into the United States would not happen now.

"The fact that the U.S. has not been attacked since 9/11 is testimony to the success of the war on terror," he says. That's because, "Number one, we have seriously degraded al Qaeda's capabilities. Two, we have hardened ourselves. It's difficult to pull off the same type of event and conspiracy. Number three, radicalization in this country isn't happening as rapidly as it is around the world, possibly because of our long tradition of assimilation. And there's a lot of luck involved. And because we're on top of our threats, we're exchanging information rapidly, transparently."

When extremely sensitive information is involved, "there'll be a team of analysts from different agencies that will work that problem set," Brock says. "They abide by NCTC rules of the road, which basically say if you work here, you work here. Even though you're still owned by your mother ship, you're not to be reporting back to them all the sensitive stuff that we're working here. That way we build a trust environment, and the agencies are willing to let their information flow in here. They know NCTC analysts are working it, are incorporating it in their own source analysis, but it's not being spread and leaked throughout the whole community."

Since 9/11, al Qaeda has been "diminished," and their core leadership has been "severely damaged," Brock says. Their ability to communicate and issue commands has been "degraded significantly." Mostly, they communicate through notes delivered by courier.

"From that standpoint, it's cumbersome for them to be as operational as they once were," says Brock. "That may be some good news, but the bad news is the degradation of AQ [al Quaeda] has contributed to a vacuum where other radical Sunni terrorist elements, in either direct or philosophical solidarity with AQ, have stepped into the breach in a worrisome way."

Meanwhile, homegrown terrorists who emulate al Qaeda are becoming radicalized in the countries where they grew up.

"They take actions where they actually kill themselves," he says. "This type of threat is out there, it exists, it's very difficult to track, it springs up without a moment's notice. So to gather the intelligence on this is very tricky. It's not a known, concrete enemy like the Soviet Union was—a hard intelligence target that could be studied and strategized against. This is moving fast. And it's changing shape every month. And so from that standpoint, we are still in an intense threat atmosphere."

While al Qaeda is "seriously degraded, and things are significantly harder for them thanks to our government's actions, that doesn't mean they're out of the game. They're still orchestrating plots, but with much greater difficulty than prior to 9/11. We have tense moments almost every day. I don't want to alarm you, but we're dealing with a determined group of individuals. You've got the al Qaeda core, you've got other groups that have been inspired by al Qaeda, you've got people who aren't associated with any known groups who are inspired by al Qaeda and want to carry out similar missions, and you've got a rapid radicalization of young Muslim males, particularly in Europe and in the Middle East, who are now wanting to martyr themselves in this great jihad. Europeans are very concerned about this," Brock says. "They're seeing rapidly accelerating radicalization going on in Europe, by young men who otherwise wouldn't have given a hoot two years ago."

The London plot to crash American airliners flying to the United States was homegrown in the sense that those arrested in Great Britain were born there. That was in contrast to the 9/11 hijackers from the Middle East. But while the London plotters were born in England, they had clear ties to al Qaeda, connections that investigators were still tracking.

As for the possibility of Hezbollah attacking U.S. interests, that does not appear to be likely.

"We know they have the capability, or we assess that they have the capability around the world, less so here in the U.S.," Brock says. "But we do not assess that there's an immediate threat from a Hezbollah terror attack in the U.S."

The disclosures of NSA intercepts and other secret operational methods have hurt the war on terror.

"There is almost a conspiracy mind set that says, 'Well, if the government's got a secret, it's got to be something bad, and it's gonna invade our privacy when I'm talking to Uncle Joe,'" Brock says. "It's a bizarre way of thinking. But the reality is we don't have the staff to listen to everyone's conversations."

Rather than listening to innocuous conversations, the truth is the agencies waging the war on terror let a lot of nefarious conversations slip by because of a lack of linguists. "It is a desperate race to find the most troubling and chilling conversations that exist," Brock says. "We try to single out the ones that are going to inform us about the next plot against us."

Those who say leaks are not harmful because terrorists know they can be listened to have it wrong. It's one thing to know the government has the capability to monitor conversations. It's another to be told by the *New York Times* or the *Washington Post* that a brief conversation between a terrorist overseas and an operative in New York can be listened to without obtaining a warrant beforehand.

The bad guys "get comfortable using a certain way of communicating," Brock says. "If you get access to it, you don't want them to move away from that. And that is the prime reason why we don't want the world to know what we're doing. It's common sense. There is sustained damage when these things come to light. It makes it more difficult for the collectors to get the information from the bad guys. That impairs the public's right to safety."

At the same time, "we're doing a pretty good job, not just the U.S. intelligence community but our allies around the world, of developing the sources that are needed to alert on a lot of potential plots out there," Brock says. "In my experience, we will have a handful of threats in a given time that we're really boring down on. Ones that seem to have some legs, seem to have some credibility. We're worried about the people that are involved in this, they're known bad guys. So they're monitored very closely."

In the case of the London plot, "the cooperation between the intelligence and law enforcement communities in our two countries was fantastic." So Brock says, "There's a lot of good success stories of plots being interdicted. But obviously there are others that are coming to fruition without anybody even knowing about it, until something goes bang."

23

ON THE HUNT

For Art Cummings, the tipping point in the British airliner plot was when MI5 realized that the terrorists were focused on American rather than British targets.

"All of a sudden, it becomes apparent that the focus is flights to the U.S.," Cummings says. "And at that point, it's a scramble."

At the NCTC, Cummings got a briefing on the case from Mike Heimbach.

"They were going to do nine aircraft, an average of two hundred people in each aircraft," Cummings says. "I don't know if they would have succeeded with all of them. But taking nine aircraft out of the sky would have been big."

Once on the case, Cummings began looking for what he calls collection points.

"We started looking at their travel, their associates," he says. "Essentially, you're working a collection operation. The closest thing to traditional FBI investigations is investigating organized crime. Who the heck did this and who's responsible? But what's become more important, who's behind this? Who's coming up behind this to kick us in the butt again?"

In all, 150 agents worked the case. Cummings assigned agents to check on financial connections, communications, associates, travel, and credit cards of the suspects in the United Kingdom.

"In a very short period of time, we had found connections to over ninety people or entities in the U.S.," Cummings says. "Were they in contact with a sister, a brother, a friend? If so, why the contact?"

Because of Bush's order, NSA retained records of calls, so the FBI could check back over calls made by people the suspects called in the United States, going back years. Previously, telephone companies generally destroyed their records of calls after eighteen months. One of those past contacts could conceivably be plotting another 9/11 attack.

"The one thing about intel that is critical: You have to have good records," Cummings says. "Over and over again, you find a guy's name referenced in something years old. Sometimes it gives you the exact context you're looking for, and you can use FISA on it."

When looking at contacts in the United States, "Our first job was to determine whether or not they were witting, whether they knew anything about this plot or were supporting it," Cummings says. "The second was what's the nature of the contact?"

Cummings ordered wiretaps and surveillance of a dozen terrorist suspects who might react to the news of the British arrests, perhaps giving the FBI leads.

"We had surveillance 24/7, wake 'em up, put 'em to bed," he says. "We told all the field offices to get up live on everything, get ready. I wanted to know almost verbatim what this guy's reaction is to this arrest. That tells me that he's either one of two things: He's either unbelievably disciplined if he doesn't react, or he's going to react. And that reaction—and they almost always will react if they're involved—gives us great insight into the level of their involvement. We just want to be sponges, we want to suck it all up so we can make informed judgments about their level of involvement. If there's no reaction, they're either really, really good, or they're not involved. And I'm not buying that they're really good. They're good, but not to the point where they can make no reaction, where they wouldn't go out of the house to a pay phone, wouldn't pick up a cell phone and call somebody and ask what's going on."

The British first learned of the plot when following leads developed from the investigation of the July 2005 plot to bomb London subways and buses.

"They followed leads from all over," Cummings says. "They have a number of different plots going on, a number of different extremist groups and networks involved there," Cummings says.

British MI5 is tracking sixteen hundred individuals who are part of at least two hundred networks that are actively plotting terrorist attacks against British targets, as well as Western targets overseas. At least thirty plots are being followed, many of them linked to al Qaeda in Pakistan using British-born footsoldiers living in the U.K.

Because more than four million video cameras conduct surveillance of streets in Great Britain, tracking terrorists is far easier there than in the United States. The London underground alone has six thousand such cameras, and they helped track the terrorists who detonated bombs there on July 7, 2005.

In America, the ACLU and other civil libertarians have raised privacy concerns, making surveillance cameras far less common. Yet what could be more public than a person walking down a street or entering a subway car? Anyone has the right to take photographs or videotape in such places, just as banks and other businesses watch customers with surveillance cameras. Yet rather than help protect Americans from another attack, the ACLU raises the phony issue of privacy when the government is doing the surveillance.

On the other hand, because their Muslims are not as assimilated as American Muslims, the Brits have a far bigger terrorist problem than does the United States.

"Our Muslim community is at least assimilated," Cummings says. "The Pakistani community in the U.K. is a Pakistani community. They all know each other, they're all related, they know all the tribal relationships. And they claim their opportunity is minimal. Whole villages were relocated to the U.K., and they kept the village culture intact. They live in England, but they hate the English."

To be sure, some believe they will have seventy-two virgins if they blow people up.

"There have actually been suicide bombers in Israel whose genitals are wrapped in oil and paper when they find them blown up," Cummings says. "They're preparing for their deliverance to paradise and the seventy-two virgins that are going to wait for them. But those are the real fanatics. I don't believe the majority of these guys are driven by religious fanaticism at all. I think it's a factor. I've spoken to a lot of these guys and I will tell you that some of them are just young adventure seekers who are influenced by radical Islam, but that's not the driving force. In some ways, it's similar to the gang problems we have in the U.S. They get a sense of belonging, a sense of brotherhood, a sense of mission out of it."

As the FBI and CIA continued to monitor the plot, Cummings met with MI5 officials and CIA officers every day.

"Essentially, we heard and felt the drumbeat of, 'Take this down,'" Cummings says. "People began to get nervous, asking, 'What is it we don't know?' It's high risk, high consequence, which is tough. But you know what? That's the game we're in. But if you just take it down now because we don't know if we know everything, there very well could be someone out there who is going to do this right under our noses. I get nearly violent over it."

When the pressure builds to do an arrest, Cummings will say to cool it.

"You're going to be operating in the blind if you take these guys off the street," he tells colleagues at the FBI and CIA. "They're going to kill an American tomorrow, and that could be avoided if you just have little bit more backbone."

As good as MI5 is in gathering intelligence, Cummings hears all the time from MI5 counterparts how frustrated they are that they don't have the FBI's law enforcement powers. Moreover, the intelligence MI5 gathers cannot be used in a criminal case. New Scotland Yard has to reinvent the wheel by gathering new evidence to present in court.

"We can use our intelligence authorities," Cummings says. "We can conduct an intelligence collection, preserving what we can for evidence where possible. I can go to the court, declassify it, boom. They can't. They've already had to release people who were arrested in the British airline plot because what they found in searches wasn't enough to keep them. Really serious bad guys are back on the street. Right now I know of two. And so now the service has to watch them 24/7."

But to Cummings, the biggest problem with the British system is the lack of ability to negotiate with suspects.

"The British security service is a phenomenal service in terms of their collection," he says. "They have a lot of latitude and great laws in terms of their collection. But the use of that collection against people is not permissible. The police service now has to collect evidence after the fact. We would look at the suspects before we made the arrest and look for the weak link who has the most information. And then we would work that person, in custody and on the street. The British do not have that ability, and that is unbelievable to me. I don't want their model. It just wouldn't work for us."

In closing down the airline plot, the British seized more than four hundred computers, two hundred mobile phones, and eight thousand other items like memory sticks, CDs, and DVDs. The FBI and CIA helped analyze them. In the end, Cummings found no witting accomplices in the United States.

"Nobody was part of it," he says. "But that's a great comfort at the end of the day, after all this massive collection. Okay, what's our call? We got people here or don't we? The answer at the time, for this operation, was we don't have anybody in the U.S. working on behalf of this group."

As that investigation wound down, Cummings began monitoring a new plot, one that led to the arrest on December 6, 2006, of Derrick Shareef near Rockford, Illinois. He was charged with plotting to set off hand grenades in garbage cans at the Cherry Vale Shopping Mall, about ninety miles northwest of Chicago. The idea was to target Christmas shoppers on the Friday before Christmas.

Shareef was a twenty-two-year-old Muslim convert. An acquaintance told the FBI that Shareef was talking about waging violent jihad.

Under Cummings' direction, the FBI taped Shareef discussing his plans. Shareef discussed other targets, including government facilities such as courthouses and City Hall.

"I just want to smoke a judge," he said. "This is a warning to those who disbelieve," he said.

The FBI arrested him after he tried to make an unusual trade with an undercover agent: two stereo speakers for a nine-millimeter pistol and the grenades he would need to pull off the plot.

"He fixed on a day of December 22 on Friday . . . because it was the Friday before Christmas, and he thought that would be the highest concentration of shoppers that he could kill and injure," said Robert Grant, the agent in charge of the Chicago FBI office.

Shareef had been under investigation since September, but Cummings resisted the usual pressures to take him down quickly. Cummings wanted to make sure every bit of intelligence from the case was exploited. In this case, he found no connection to al Qaeda. The British airline plot was a different story.

"Now we find really connected guys who are acting on behalf of al Qaeda," he says. "I don't think any of them is getting to bin Laden with any information about this stuff. But they're still pursuing the airline thing. It's not a successful strategy, at all. You couldn't find a harder industry to penetrate."

Cummings worries about new targets.

"Okay, they did airplanes, they did boats, they did car bombs, what are we missing?" he says. "What's next? Where is it that we're not looking that they are looking?"

Cummings assigns agents to dream up other plots and see what terrorists might do to carry them out.

"To undertake an operation, you have to do certain things," he says. "You have to acquire the precursors for explosives, you have to move bodies, you have to potentially bring stuff into the country, take stuff out of the country. We basically put ourselves in the place of the terrorist and plan a terrorist operation. If they're going to bring nuclear material into the U.S., they're going to need somebody to import it. So, how do you do that? You don't put it in a FedEx pack—especially something for an RDD, a radioactive dispersal device. That is going to require shielding, it's heavy."

So the FBI canvasses companies that might import such materials and might be sympathetic to the cause.

"From there, we build a model of what actually would be undertaken to support that kind of operation," Cummings says.

Those who want to try to understand why some Muslims would become extremists should keep in mind the cultural environment they grow up in, George Piro says. Americans grow up watching *Desperate Housewives* and Britney Spears on television. On the other hand, "You live in the Middle East for a short period of time, and you'll see the values are very different," Piro says. "Neither one is right or wrong. But you look at Al Jazeera and what sells there, it's very different. The coverage that they give to the Iraq war, to Afghanistan, to the occupied territories, and what they promote—it's difficult for us to really understand or grasp that, being here."

On top of that, Palestinians grow up believing that they have lost their homeland.

"Over time, what does that create?" Piro says. "Then you add economic, social, political issues, and does that create a breeding ground for recruitment? Those are all challenges that make it very difficult for us to battle terrorism."

Despite the successes in the war on terror, the FBI and CIA can only do so much to prevent terrorism, Piro observes.

"Some of it has to be done at a very different level," Piro says. "This is only my opinion, but there's a lot of social, economic, and political issues that create at least the opportunity for terrorism to continue to exist."

Yet even within the United States, about a quarter of Muslims ages eighteen through twenty-nine believe that suicide bombings could be justified, a Pew Research Center poll found. Those attitudes, in turn, are generated by imams who preach jihad and hatred in American mosques and in postings on the Internet, according to FBI sources.

One FBI official estimates that imams in as many as one in ten of the 2,000 mosques in the United States preach extremism. Yet that number is far lower than before 9/11.

"Those who actively support extremist causes, saying America is evil and deserves what it gets, and who celebrate the death of soldiers know they may come to our attention," the official says. "So they don't do it as openly now."

Before 9/11, he says, "There was much more of that, because all of it was considered by Justice Department guidelines to be purely protected speech. We do not have incitement laws in America, but once an imam facilitates someone else taking action, he has crossed the line into material support and becomes our business."

An example was Ali Al-Timimi, a spiritual leader at a mosque in Northern Virginia, who preached jihad and provided contact information for those who went over to get training in terrorist camps to murder people. Al-Timimi is serving a life prison term.

The FBI has outreach programs to try to develop sources in the Muslim community and solicit tips, but FBI agents have found little receptivity. They find Muslims are often in denial about the fact that the terrorists who threaten the United States are Muslims.

"I had this discussion with the director of a very prominent Muslim organization here in D.C.," a counterterrorism agent says. "And he said, 'Why are you guys always looking at the Muslim community?'"

The agent began laughing.

"Okay, you know what I'll do?" the agent said. "I'll start an Irish squad, or how about a Japanese squad? You want me to waste my time and your taxpayers' dollars going to look at the Irish? They're not killing Americans. Right now, I'm going to put my money and my people in a place where the threat is."

Then the agent tells Muslim leaders to take a look at the cells that have been rolled up by the FBI in the United States.

"I can name the home grown cells, all of whom are Muslim, all of whom were seeking to murder Americans," the agent tells them. "It's not the Irish, it's not the French, it's not the Catholics, it's not the Protestants, it's the Muslims."

In response, Muslim groups have told him he is rough around the edges.

"I'm not rough around the edges," he tells them. "You're just not used to straight talk."

They respond by getting angry at him.

While Muslims will occasionally condemn al Qaeda, "Rarely do we have them coming to us and saying, 'There are three guys in the community that we're very concerned about,'" one agent says. "They want to fix it inside the community. They're a closed group, a very, very closed group. It's part of their culture that they want to settle the problem within their own communities. They've actually said that to us, which I then go crazy over."

On the one hand, "They don't want anyone to know they have extremists in their community," the agent says. "Well, beautiful. Except, do you read the newspapers? Everyone already knows it. That horse has left the barn. So there's a lot of talk about engagement, but realistically, we've got a long, long way to go."

On top of that, to many Muslims, "The FBI's the enemy," the agent says. "We're equated with security services in countries where security services are equated with oppression and persecution. We've got years of work to do to demystify the FBI to them. They're very suspicious of us, and that's a cultural thing."

At one meeting, a Muslim group suggested having a photo taken of their members with Bob Mueller to show their community isn't a bunch of terrorists and that they are partners in the war on terror. An agent replied, "Let me make a suggestion: When you bring to my attention real extremists who are here to plan and do something, who are here supporting terrorism, and I work that based on your information, then I promise you, I will have the director stand up on the stage with you."

To the agent's amazement, the answer was: "That could never happen. We would lose our constituency. We could never admit to bringing someone to the FBI."

"Well, we've just defined the problem, haven't we?" the agent told them.

To be sure, some individual Muslims have brought leads to the FBI. That led to FBI cases in Lackawanna, New York; Lodi, California; and Atlanta, Georgia.

"But I don't see the community doing that," the agent says. "The individuals who we talk to will approach us individually and say, 'I've got a certain concern.' I talked to a very prominent imam in the U.S. We would have our sweets and our sweet tea. We would talk a lot about Islam. I would say we understand Islam and where they're coming from. We'd tell him about what our mission is, trying to keep people from murdering Americans, or anybody else for that matter."

Months later, the FBI found out that the man's mosque had two extremists who were so radical that they kicked them out. Clearly, those two extremists would have been of interest to the FBI. If they only engaged in anti-American rhetoric, the FBI would leave them alone. More likely, they were planning action to go with their rhetoric.

The agent asked the imam, "What happened?"

"What do you mean?" the imam asked.

"Why didn't you tell me about this?" the agent said.

"Why would I tell you about this?" the imam said. "They're not terrorists. They just hate the U.S. government."

24

COUNTERING SPIN

To try to counter the negative media spin, Mueller named Cassandra M. Chandler assistant director in charge of public affairs in September 2003. A lawyer and former TV news anchor, Chandler was a black woman who went to segregated schools in Louisiana. She enrolled at Loyola University in New Orleans to fulfill her mother's dream that she would become a lawyer.

"She would say, 'You can go to law school. You could be a Supreme Court justice just like Thurgood Marshall,'" says Chandler.

A journalism professor thought she had something special and asked the station manager at Channel 33 (now WVLA) in Baton Rouge to give her an audition. She became an anchorwoman.

One night before she went on the air, a fugitive who had robbed a bank in Washington, D.C., called the station from the French Quarter to say he wanted to turn himself in. He asked if the TV station would televise his arrest so he would not be shot. Chandler's boss said they didn't have time to film the man and told her to call the FBI. An agent who responded encouraged her to join the bureau.

When Chandler applied at the FBI's office in New Orleans, C. Carl Chandler, another agent who met her briefly, made sure he was assigned to do the background check on the gorgeous applicant. Soon, he was helping her prepare for the physical tests. A former Marine, he taught her to do push-ups "the Marine way." Four months later, they married.

When Cassandra Chandler oversaw white collar crime investigations in San Francisco, Mueller, then the U.S. Attorney, worked with her and was impressed. She was sharp, quick on her feet, and aggressive.

At her first meeting with Mueller, Chandler complained that she had ten good white collar crime cases that were languishing because the previous U.S. attorney had not pursued them. Soon, Mueller jumped on the cases and filed charges.

When he became FBI director, Mueller made her assistant director in charge of training at Quantico, then placed her in charge of public affairs.

If they showed any signs of being fair, Chandler tried to woo reporters by giving them access. But she found it was a hopeless cause. Chandler set up interviews with two FBI counterterrorism agents for Eric Lichtblau of the *New York Times*, but on November 23, 2003, the paper ran Lichtblau's story attributing sinister motives to a routine warning that ran in an FBI law enforcement bulletin.

Lichtblau's story in the *New York Times* said ". . . civil rights advocates, relying largely on anecdotal evidence, have complained for months that federal officials have surreptitiously sought to suppress First Amendment rights of antiwar demonstrators. . . . The FBI memorandum [bulletin], however, appears to offer the first evidence of a coordinated, nationwide effort to collect intelligence regarding demonstrations."

A reading of the two-page October 15 bulletin makes it clear that the FBI was saying nothing of the sort. Rather, the bureau was alerting local law enforcement to tactics used by demonstrators who engage in violence, urging them to report "any potentially illegal acts" to the FBI. That was exactly what the FBI was supposed to be doing. If the story had honestly reported what the bulletin had said, the item could not have been run because it was not news.

FBI CHILLS PROTESTERS' SPEECH WITH INTIMIDATION was the headline over a widely distributed column by Nat Hentoff based on Lichtblau's story.

Chandler wrote a letter to the editor, which was published on August 20, 2004. She posted it on the FBI Web site, along with a copy of the FBI bulletin. The letter said the interviews at issue "were conducted as part of a criminal investigation that was predicated on specific information that particular people were planning violent acts to disrupt the Democratic National Convention and additional nonspecific intelligence related to a threat to the Republican National Convention."

Chandler said it would have been "irresponsible" for the FBI and state and local law enforcement officers not to have pursued a "legitimate investigative inquiry into threats to harm people or property."

Nonetheless, civil liberties groups and members of Congress opposed to the Patriot Act jumped on the story as proof that the FBI had returned to the illegal surveillance tactics conducted under J. Edgar Hoover. In liberal circles, it became an article of faith that the FBI was targeting antiwar demonstrators to intimidate them.

"This report suggests that federal law enforcement may now be targeting individuals based on activities that are peaceful, lawful, and protected under the Constitution," said Senator John Edwards, the North Carolina Democrat who was then running for president. "What kind of McCarthyism is that?"

Without tips and cooperation from citizens, the FBI is almost useless. Many of the FBI's terrorism cases began with tips from the public. Misleading stories like Lichtblau's eroded trust in the bureau and diminished that cooperation. Yet when another terrorist attack occurred, FBI agents and CIA officers knew that the *New York Times* editorial page would be the first to castigate the bureau and CIA for failing to protect the country.

After dealing with the press for two and a half years, Chandler could not wait to return to operations. Her goal had always been to run an FBI field office, and Mueller named her special agent in charge of the Norfolk Field Office.

In September 2005, Mueller brought in John Miller as the FBI's assistant director for public affairs. Miller's credentials were impressive. He had been an ABC correspondent and co-host of the magazine show *20/20*. In 1998, Miller interviewed bin Laden. He was one of the few journalists to have done so.

Miller remembers bin Laden's "benign little smile" and "soft, almost effeminate voice." But behind the kind eyes and the fatherly tone, he observes, "He's saying, 'You and your friends need to die.'"

In June 2002, when Miller was a *20/20* anchor, *People* magazine named Miller one of the country's top fifty bachelors. In the accompanying article, Miller admitted that he was sick of being single.

"I've done all the things a guy wants to do," he said. "I always thought you would find the person; there would be angels and music and you would just know."

Within weeks, he did. In November of that same year, Miller, forty-four, wed thirty-six-year-old philanthropist and former teacher Emily Altschul in an offbeat civil service at the Boathouse restaurant in Manhattan's Central Park. Miller had known Emily in high school in Manhattan.

Back in 1993, William J. Bratton named Miller a deputy police commissioner in charge of public affairs at the New York City police department. Miller served in that capacity a little over two years. When Bratton took over as police commissioner in Los Angeles, he named Miller in January 2003 to head counterterrorism there. With a pistol strapped to his ankle, the dapper dresser oversaw any event in Los Angeles that required a massive police response, such as the Academy Awards. A collector of watches, he would show up at hundreds of crime scenes alternately wearing a Rolex, a Patek Philippe, or an Omega.

Miller was drawn to police work. He wanted to be part of the action and help prosecute the war on terror. Miller knew that few journalists wanted to tell the real story of how the war on terror is being prosecuted. Like Cassi Chandler, he wanted to try to change that or at least head off some of the constant negative, misleading stories.

"The media has lost its collective mind," Miller says. Fueled in part by the proliferation of competing media outlets, journalists "feel they have to come back at the end of the day with somebody's head on the end of their stick."

The news cycle used to be fairly basic.

"The event would happen, and then there'd be the six P.M. news, then the eleven P.M. news, then the morning paper," Miller says. "And then a new news cycle began. Now there's twenty-four-hour cable on five different stations, so the news cycle never stops. It's just a news merry-go-round. It goes around and around and around, and sometimes it picks up speed to the point that everybody on it is dizzy. And that's the difficulty. What you now have is this massive beast that gets tangled up in its own wires every day."

The terrorism case in Miami, when the FBI announced arrests of seven men for plotting to blow up the Sears Tower in Chicago, is an example.

"The media see police activity, and they find out it's a terrorist case, and they start eighteen hours of wild speculation and using snippets from sources which they weave together," Miller says. "Then we announce the facts of the case the following day. Then they go crazy on that until they take a breath, and then they say we overhyped it. Because the facts of the case didn't measure up to their hype, how is it that we hyped it?"

As arrests were being made in the case, Mueller appeared on CNN's *Larry King Live* to talk about the FBI. That touched off speculation by the media that it was all a PR stunt. In fact, Mueller hates to draw attention to himself and goes on TV only after being pressured by Miller and previously by Cassi Chandler.

"Mueller was on Larry King after six months of negotiating dates with Larry King, with Mueller cancelling three times prior to that," Miller says. "Finally, we got him to settle on a date when we could actually get him to show up when Larry King was actually in Washington. And during the broadcast, one of the search warrants was being executed. Frank Rich, a columnist in the *New York*

Times who has never covered anything close to real news or law enforcement, went so far as to opine that we had staged the Mueller appearance on Larry King so that we could start to hype the Miami case."

Rich called the "breathless" Miami arrest an "embarrassment." According to Rich: "This amazing feat of derring-do had all the melodramatic trappings of a carefully staged administration P.R. extravaganza. On June 22, the FBI director, Robert Mueller, just happened to be on *Larry King Live* speaking about his concerns about 'homegrown terrorists,' when, by a remarkable coincidence, Larry King announced a 'report just in' from a Miami station on a federal terrorism investigation."

Rich said that the seven men who were accused of trying to take down the Sears Tower in Chicago and collaborating with al Qaeda in a "full ground war" turned out to have neither weapons nor explosives nor links to al Qaeda.

"By Saturday," he said, "the administration's overhyped victory against terrorists was already deflating into a national punch line, a nostalgic remembrance of John Ashcroft orange terror alerts past."

In fact, Miller says, "While we were in the middle of conducting searches, it went against our operational interests to have that revealed."

To Phil Mudd, the CIA officer detailed to the FBI, this sort of belittling of the FBI's efforts because a bomb did not actually go off is foolish and short-sighted.

"I'm somewhat frustrated with characterizations of our take downs of wannabe cells as not serious operations," says Mudd. "Well, Timothy McVeigh and another guy got a truck and blew off the front of a building. I think people confuse wannabe with lack of capability, and that's a dangerous confusion. Some in the media seem to be saying, 'Let the conspiracy keep going, and maybe you'll see it blow up. Then it will get to a more serious conspiracy.' What do they think we should do? Let them go?"

The media gave the same negative spin to the British arrests in the airline plot. "The media were accusing the Brits of overblowing the plot to down the airlines," Miller says. "Then the Brits came forth with their charges, and the media took a second step back and said, 'Well, maybe they really do have things. They found explosives and communications and so on.'"

Meanwhile, Jonathan Alter at *Newsweek* wrote a scathing piece saying that the FBI's "primitive" computers are "frightening."

To be sure, Mueller had stubbed his toe on a contract for a Virtual Case File computer system that was built from scratch and proved unworkable. When it was abandoned, the project had cost the FBI $170 million. Mueller then initiated a new system called Sentinel that uses mainly off-the-shelf software and is expected to cost $425 million.

As a result of the delays, the FBI still does not have a sophisticated system for keeping track of cases. But the FBI has a stopgap system called Investigative Data Warehouse (IDW). The system stores 659 million records culled from more than fifty FBI and other government agency sources. The data includes terrorist watch lists, intelligence cables, financial transactions, suspicious activity reports from the Treasury Department, passport data, driver's license information, immigration data, and pocket litter found in safehouses in Iraq and Afghanistan.

The system was designed largely by Gurvais Grigg, a computer-savvy FBI agent who has a degree in biochemistry and was a former stockbroker. With the data system, an agent can type in "Mohammed Atta" and "flight training" and bring up 250 references. Before 2002, it would have taken 32,222 hours to run 1,000 names and birth dates across fifty databases. Now it takes less than thirty minutes. Agents and analysts make more than a million requests for information from the system each month.

In contrast to the faxes relied on by the FBI on 9/11, an agent on a laptop in Afghanistan can communicate on a classified level to a colleague in Chicago and transmit videos and pictures.

To try to tell the true story, Miller let Sari Horwitz of the *Washington Post* attend the FBI's training classes at Quantico. Instead of fairly portraying the FBI's progress in addressing terrorism and improving analysis, at the prodding of editors, Horwitz wrote a lede that focused on the fact that during a one-hour course on the history of Islam, FBI instructor Rodney Loose said he did not have time to answer a question from a new agent.

"Can you tell us about sleeper cells?" the recruit asked.

"I'm sorry, I don't think we're going to have time to get into this," Loose replied. "I wish I had more time to go through this. But it's just not possible."

Since the course was supposed to focus on such topics as Sunnis and Shiites, the Koran, Mecca and Medina, four-part Arabic names, and the five pillars of Islam, a question about sleeper cells was unrelated to the subject matter. Moreover, training for new agents at Quantico is mainly to give them the basic skills and knowledge to pursue any case. Those agents assigned to counterterrorism receive specialized training throughout their careers. The beauty of the FBI is that agents receive broad training and can be shifted from one program to another as the need arises. Sleeper cells is clearly within the realm of FBI operations, not the history of Islam. But based on an unanswered, irrelevant question in a class on Islam, the *Washington Post* began the story with a lede implying that the FBI had made little progress since 9/11.

OLD-SCHOOL ACADEMY IN POST-9/11 WORLD; NEW FOCUS IS ON TERRORISM, BUT TRAINING IS STRUGGLING TO KEEP UP, read the headline over the story.

As a former journalist, Miller says, "It's hard for me to watch FBI and CIA people stream into these buildings every day, knowing they would probably be making more somewhere else doing something else. They try very hard to protect us—for God, or country, or whatever—or maybe just for the job. And people show up at newspapers and television stations every day saying, 'How can I find one of these guys who trips? How can I find someone who makes a mistake in his judgment? How can I skewer him?'"

Miller says he'd like to challenge "gotcha" journalists to "sit in one of these desks, or to go out in the field and try and run one of these operations one day." Miller found that "the most humbling thing you can ever do as a reporter is get a real job, and bear that responsibility of making those decisions."

Miller had that experience in Los Angeles.

"I would respond to some crisis and under pressure have to call the shots," he says. "It was an awful lot harder than standing behind the yellow tape saying, 'I'm going to judge whether that guy's doing this right or not, even though I have no experience in law enforcement.'"

By refusing to tell the story straight, the media have cut their own throats. While the Internet has played a role in the steady decline in the number of people who buy newspapers or watch the major TV network newscasts, the fact that people cannot trust the news they get clearly is a big factor. Polls show journalists are trusted about as much as used car salesmen and politicians.

25

10,000 THREATS

Every day, Joe Billy, Jr., the chief of counterterrorism at the FBI, receives a scary burgundy binder that contains the threat matrix and other intelligence reports.

On weekends, he still is looking at threats. He gets an update via secure telephone on Saturdays and Sundays between 7:00 and 7:30 A.M. Then Billy advises the FBI director of any significant updates.

On weekdays, Billy arrives at work at 5:30 A.M. and usually leaves at 9:30 or 10:00 P.M. By 7:00 A.M., he is attending Mueller's morning meeting. Besides the threat matrix, Billy reviews a top secret briefing book listing three or four threats the FBI is pursuing. The book is as thick as a college dictionary.

Often threats come in from overseas.

"Someone walks into the U.S. embassy at some location and provides information," he says. That person may say he is aware of people who are involved in a plot and they are planning to enter the U.S. Or the source may be in the U.S. and report that al Qaeda is planning to blow up an airliner on the anniversary of September 11. Another example, Billy says, would be an e-mail to a government Web site.

"An informant who's being operated by another country or by our own intelligence services may have information," Billy says. "He relays that information to his handlers. The handlers, in turn, report it. That makes it part of the threat stream."

Many of the leads are bogus.

"We had an upsurge of people trying to undermine businesses

215

owned by Arabs and Muslims that we picked up on," Billy says. "Occasionally, competitors phone in false allegations. When it can be proven out and shown that it was done in a harmful way, we prosecute these people for false statements."

Often, jilted lovers or ex-spouses phone in bogus tips.

"They might claim a person traveling on this flight coming into JFK at two in the morning has potential connections to al Qaeda," he says. "It turns out the call is from an ex-spouse or something like that who just tries to get them jammed up. You have to sort that out all the time, between the real deal versus just somebody who just happened to get somebody upset, and now they're paying someone back."

In other cases, apparently suspicious activity may turn out to be innocent.

"Today, you don't avoid anything. Everything is looked at," says Billy. "The Joint Terrorism Task Force (JTTF) in Alabama may send a tip back to the local police, saying someone's been moving barrels into their garage at three in the morning over the last two nights, and they looked like they were chemical barrels. Or someone just bought a large quantity of Scotts Fertilizer from a Home Depot in Springfield, Virginia. He paid cash and bought a truckload of stuff. Is that a threat, or is that somebody with a farm? You just don't know."

By and large, most threats turn out to be nothing.

"That's why our country is relatively safe," Billy says. "Most people want nothing to do with this stuff. They come here, for whatever reason, to get away from it, make money legally, send their kids to school, that kind of thing. I think we have that going for us. But in the middle of this, you have pockets of concern, and that's when we have to be as aggressive as we can."

In the case of the man loading barrels into his home at night, the Joint Terrorism Task Force looked into it, and it turned out the man was moving. He worked for a chemical company and was using clean barrels to load his chinaware and other household goods, packing them for the move.

"Completely legitimate, but it had to be at least resolved so there was no concern there," Billy says. "That's what makes us work hard because you don't know what is the bs or what is real."

Billy, who previously headed the National Security Division in New York, has constant tense moments. When a key al Qaeda figure is captured overseas, the FBI has to watch people working for him to see if they will accelerate their plans.

"So, you have the good news situation—somebody was captured—but then on the other side, you have to go to work and really be triple sure that you're not missing something here with regard to one of those individuals," he says.

Because bin Laden has been isolated, al Qaeda has morphed into a sort of franchise operation. Inspired by bin Laden, local groups try to emulate his example. While they try to obtain financing and support from al Qaeda, they generally operate on their own. As examples, Billy cites terrorist arrests in London, Montreal, and Miami.

"The London bombings on July 7, 2005, were a concern in the sense that they were homegrown," he says. "These individuals were not really on the watch of the U.K. authorities. That caused us to really do an introspective look here at this phenomenon of homegrown extremists."

Now nearly all of al Qaeda's original leadership has been rolled up, and its ability to launch an attack has been impaired. Key planners and facilitators of the organization have been captured or killed.

"Obviously, you still have number one and number two who are still about, and they still have influence," says Billy, referring to bin Laden and Ayman al-Zawahiri, bin Laden's deputy and closest advisor. "But their infrastructure and ability to organize and carry out a large-scale attack has been somewhat curtailed. . . . I think we and our partner countries have done well to really hinder al Qaeda's abilities to launch a large-scale, multipronged attack 9/11 style."

The military approach has accounted for some of that.

"Having the military essentially work a good portion of counter-terrorism has changed from our perspective how we do it," he says. "An individual like Khalid Sheikh Mohammed was arrested overseas by the military, and the CIA was working this individual for information, even though he was indictable. Under the old pre-9/11 approach, we would have tried to secure him to bring back to the U.S. to stand trial."

The FBI now has ten thousand terrorism cases under investigation. The FBI counts the number of terrorism-related arrests and convictions in the hundreds. But thousands of others are charged with immigration violations, thefts, or cigarette smuggling. While many of those individuals may have been suspected of being part of a terrorist group, there is no way to know for sure if they have committed a terrorist-related crime.

"They will steal designer-type clothing, which is what they were doing in New York, selling things on Fifth Avenue," Billy says. "They buy blank garments, sew in Tommy Hilfiger or Ralph Lauren labels, and sell them for a fraction of the regular price. It adds up because the tourists buy it. We have had solid convictions in that regard. We can also use the immigration-type laws in a positive way," he says. "To say, 'Look, first of all you're illegal, second of all, you're a member of Hamas.' We have to start looking at it and saying, okay, what can we do to enforce those laws as well?"

Even though al Qaeda is fragmented, it is trying to acquire weapons of mass destruction and could succeed at any moment.

"That's really the race that we're in right now, to prevent the acquisition and use of any kind of type of WMD, to implode a nuclear device or chemical-biological weapon of some type," says Billy. "Hopefully, they're not where they have something like that, but on any given day, someone could acquire something through some rogue state and have the means to bring it into the United States and try to use it."

Like his deputy Art Cummings, Billy worries about what the FBI doesn't know. "The question for us is which ones do we not know about, which groups right now as we sit here are trying actively to put something together to perhaps harm us today or tomorrow? Do we know about all the individuals? I still think it's a small number that have gravitated to this, but nevertheless it doesn't take but one or a small group to wreak havoc on our country and change the dynamics in some way."

Today "you should feel safer in a sense because it's very unlikely that someone's going to slip one by us at this point, with everyone working at it," he says. "I may not catch it, but another agency is going to catch it, or you're going to catch part of it, and then I'll add to it, and we'll figure it out."

The FBI's successful efforts to disrupt the plot against New York tunnels and other plots are examples. At the same time, "the biggest piece for us is this homegrown extremist part where people do not have links to overseas camps or al Qaeda members but yet are sort of self-radicalizing, self-supporting, and sort of build capacity just among themselves," he says. "To me, that's the new domestic terrorism problem that we're going to have to deal with."

Billy cites the case of Mohammed Rez Teheri-azar, an Iranian-born graduate student at the University of North Carolina, who drove an SUV on March 3, 2006, into a crowd at the University of North Carolina at Chapel Hill in retribution for treatment of Muslims throughout the world. He injured nine.

"You can argue about whether this is real serious or not," he says, "but the fact is he mowed some kids down. The purpose was that he just wanted to make a statement. You go back and look at his diary and everything else, and it's full of hate, full of rage against the U.S. But no one picked up on it. His mother said she knew he was a little mad. His friends or people who knew him from school said, 'Yeah, we knew he was kind of anti-U.S. We didn't think he was going to try to kill anybody.'"

Lindsey Jamal, a Muslim convert from Jamaica, was one of the bombers in the July 7 London attacks. He had two children.

"The morning of July seventh, he kisses his wife good-bye, she's sleeping," Billy says. "Kisses his two kids good-bye and leaves to go blow up the subway. His wife afterwards says, 'I knew he was becoming more radical in his thoughts, but I didn't realize how far he was drifting,' clearly shocked over the fact that this young man would then all of a sudden give his life up for a cause."

Billy is amazed that an operation by a lone wolf has not been successful. But he is not amazed that there has not been a large-scale, orchestrated plot.

"I know the effort that's gone into our military operations, our intelligence operations overseas," he says. "And they've been working harder than anybody to disrupt and to keep the al Qaeda organization in a state of not being able to constitute the kind of connectivity and resources they did prior to 9/11.

"You have to work hard to keep a 9/11 style of attack from being uncovered," he says. "Is it possible? Absolutely. If we're struck, it'll probably be a situation where we are completely not aware of it, coming without warning. We'll start to go back and say, how did we miss this? But I think our chances of potentially getting a piece of something are much greater than before 9/11."

26

PULLING OFF
A NUCLEAR ATTACK

SOMETIMES, ROBERT MUELLER wakes up in the middle of the night worrying about the possibility of a nuclear strike by al Qaeda. That is al Qaeda's paramount goal, he says. In contrast to homegrown terrorists, al Qaeda is far more likely to be able to pull off such an attack.

"I think it would be very difficult to wipe out the United States, but you'd have hundreds of thousands of casualties from a nuclear device, depending on the size of that device," he tells me.

Al Qaeda could obtain such a device in one of two ways.

"One is to obtain a device that's already been constructed from one of the former Iron Curtain countries, and the other way is to put together the fissile material and the expertise and do an improvised device," Mueller says. "And there's no doubt that al Qaeda, if it had the capability, would go down either route to get a nuclear device."

Nor is there any doubt in his mind what the target would be: "It would be someplace in the United States, in most likely Washington and/or New York, depending on how many devices they have. Or both cities."

In 1993, bin Laden attempted to buy uranium from a source in the Sudan. He has stated that it is al Qaeda's duty to acquire weapons of mass destruction. And he has made repeated recruiting pitches for experts in chemistry, physics, and explosives.

Because the United States has not been attacked in more than six years, "we are in danger of becoming complacent," Mueller observes. "Al Qaeda is tremendously patient and thinks nothing about taking years to infiltrate persons in and finding the right personnel and opportunity to undertake an attack. And we cannot become complacent, because you look around the world, and whether it's London or Madrid or Bali or recently Casablanca or Algiers, attacks are taking place."

In the conference room adjoining his seventh-floor office at FBI headquarters, Mueller conducts an interview in his shirtsleeves, a G-man white oxford cloth with a subdued Brooks Brothers tie. While he is handsome, with silvery hair that he smooths down thoughtfully as he speaks, what impresses most is his commanding presence. He has the demeanor of an FBI agent combined with a prosecutor, which he once was.

While he doesn't feel he's fighting terrorists singlehandedly, he shows signs of tension. Even more than the CIA director, Mueller is responsible for keeping America safe. There are dark circles under his heavy-lidded brown eyes. When he utters the words "nuclear device," he knits his brow and clenches his teeth. At one point when he is discussing the possibility of a nuclear threat from terrorists, an anxious thought lifts his left eyebrow like an arrow poised in midflight.

However, Mueller is far more relaxed now than when I interviewed him a few months after 9/11, when he was trying to prevent a feared "second wave" of attacks on the West Coast. Back then, Mueller declined to describe why, when he was in the Marines during the Vietnam War, he was awarded the Bronze Star and the Purple Heart. A man who hates to talk about himself or use the word "I," he said only that he "got into some firefights," adding, "You never get the medals for what you probably deserve them for. You always get the medals for that which you don't even think about doing."

Obtained recently from the Marine Corps, the citation that went with the Bronze Star says that on December 11, 1968, the platoon that Mueller commanded came under a heavy volume of small arms, automatic weapons, and grenade launcher fire from a North Vietnamese Army company.

"Quietly establishing a defensive perimeter, Second Lieutenant Mueller fearlessly moved from one position to another, directing the accurate counterfire of his men and shouting words of encouragement to them," the citation says.

Disregarding his own safety, Mueller then "skillfully supervised the evacuation of casualties from the hazardous area and, on one occasion, personally led a fire team across the fire-swept terrain to recover a mortally wounded Marine who had fallen in a position forward of the friendly lines," the citation adds.

Sitting in his conference room, Mueller commands the head of a long conference table. With apparently nowhere else for it to go, a standing wooden sign has been relegated to a place against a wall of the meeting room. The gold lettering reads DIRECTOR, FEDERAL BUREAU OF INVESTIGATION. The sign used to stand outside the director's office when the bureau was located in the Department of Justice across the street on Pennsylvania Avenue.

That was a more innocent time, when anyone could walk into the building without a security check. Now the director's office is in a secure wing, sealed off behind electronic doors with security cam and a keypad with a code. Even most bureau execs—who must have a top secret clearance to enter the building in the first place—don't have access.

The FBI is changing the way it looks at terrorism, Mueller tells me. Instead of categorizing the problem by individual cases, it is focusing on threats. Using Jamaat al Islamiya or Hezbollah as examples, Mueller explains, "In the past, when you asked what's the presence of these groups in the United States, analysts would come in and say, 'Okay, we've got cases open down here and up in Detroit and in Chicago and the like, and that is the picture of Hezbollah.'"

That response does not take account of gaps in information.

"What's most important is not what we know but what we don't know. What is the presence of Jamaat al Islamiya? What is the presence of Hamas or Hezbollah? And if you don't know the presence, what are the gaps? And then fill those gaps with collectors, which are basically agents. It's an analytical approach, and it's a threat-driven approach, an intelligence-driven approach."

Those who advocate creating a new domestic counterterrorism agency similar to Britain's MI5 don't recognize the value of having a law enforcement agency combined with one that uses intelligence to uncover threats, he says.

"A critical difference I think people don't focus on between ourselves and the U.K. is the fact that the criminal justice system here disseminates intelligence by reason of its plea bargaining capability. If you look at what's happened in the U.K. over the last three or four years, it has arrested probably a hundred individuals in various terrorist operations, and of those hundred, maybe one or two have cooperated. And in almost every case that we've had in the United States, one or more have cooperated and given us the full picture of the cell. And that's intelligence."

Mueller now briefs President Bush every Tuesday.

"He's interested in the same issue that he was interested in on September 12, 2001," Mueller says. "What's the FBI and the rest of the law enforcement community doing in the United States to make certain that there will not be another September 11? And he is briefed on ongoing cases. He asks penetrating questions, the types of questions that one would hope that I and others would ask of our own people: not only how a particular case is developing, but what have we learned from a particular case."

Mueller kept Bush informed, for example, on the FBI's sixteen-month investigation of a group allegedly plotting to attack Fort Dix and kill U.S. soldiers. After the arrests in May 2007, Bush wanted to know what has been done to assure that such military targets are protected and whether the FBI has focused on the possibility of similar groups attacking other targets.

In the Fort Dix case, five of the men who were arrested were born in Jordan, Turkey, and the former Yugoslavia. They were radical Islamists training at a shooting range to kill "as many soldiers as possible" at the Army base twenty-five miles east of Philadelphia, according to the charges against them. A sixth man was charged with helping them obtain illegal weapons.

The investigation began with a tip from a store clerk who told police that one of the men brought in a videotape that he wanted copied to a DVD. The video showed the men firing assault weapons, calling for jihad, and yelling "God is great" in Arabic. The FBI then infiltrated two paid informants into the group.

"Before September 11th, we would have been probably inclined to disrupt them earlier than we did," Mueller says. "We wanted to play it out to determine what ties they may have had to other individuals in the U.S. or overseas."

In this case, the group began looking to buy weapons from sources other than the FBI informants, and that led the FBI to move in.

"The fear being that if they purchased weapons from others and we did not know about it from our sources inside, they could undertake the terrorist attack without us knowing about it," Mueller says. "So when we started to lose control of their weapons purchases, a determination was made that now's the time to make the arrest. And it's that kind of thinking that goes into every terrorist case that we have at this juncture."

Without knowing such inside details, critics routinely knock the FBI for either making terrorist arrests too soon or too late. Last June, for example, after the FBI arrested seven men in Miami for plotting to blow up the Sears Tower in Chicago, some critics said the FBI rolled up the plot too early. Other critics said the men never could have pulled off the plot and the FBI arrests were a publicity stunt.

In the Miami case, "we exhausted every possibility for intelligence there, and it's a substantial commitment involving thousands and thousands and thousands of dollars and man hours to conduct surveillance and make sure that there is not a terrorist attack," Mueller says.

"And so while people can second guess, what do we do, let 'em walk? And if we let 'em walk, who is to say that two or three months down the road they don't go to somebody who actually will provide the weapons or the explosives or what have you and you've got a terrorist attack that we've walked away from? Can't do that. I have no apologies whatsoever on the Miami case."

The FBI is constantly being accused of abuses, but does Mueller consider any actions by the FBI to have been abuses?

"In the wake of September 11th, every individual who was detained was detained on valid charges," he says. "But those who were detained on immigration charges waited longer because we had to clear them of other charges. And in the future, I'd want to focus on more swiftly making that determination for those who are detained on immigration charges."

Mueller's biggest frustration is that, despite the calls for the FBI to act more like an intelligence organization, when it comes to its budget, the bureau is still considered a law enforcement organization. For fiscal 2007, the budget is $6.1 billion, equal to the cost of a few Stealth bombers.

"The Congress and the administration have been generous, but they don't think of us as a separate entity that is trying to be built utilizing a firm foundation," he says. "The country wants us to build a domestic intelligence capacity, but it costs money. And we are still perceived as being in the law enforcement community and not necessarily in the intelligence community."

He says he has told National Intelligence Director Mike McConnell, "Just give me the rounding errors off of the intelligence budget, and I would be very happy."

Mueller doesn't smile often, mostly a pleasant half-smile for emphasis. He does laugh, however, when he mentions his fantasy budget.

27

THE CEO OF THE WAR
ON TERROR

B EHIND THE SCENES, the person responsible for the sea
change in the way the United States fights terror is George W.
Bush. Much maligned by the media, he operates as the CEO of
the war on terror, pushing countries to cooperate, keeping track of
terrorists, asking tough questions, changing the structure of the intelligence community, and guiding the agencies responsible for combat-
ing terrorism.

Bush "fundamentally transformed" the way the country fights the
war on terror, says Fran Townsend, assistant to the president for homeland security and counterterrorism. On the morning of an interview
with Townsend in her West Wing office, Bush was briefed on a particular piece of intelligence, says Townsend, a former federal prosecutor.

"Isn't that the guy that you told me about six months ago?" he
asked and cited a related fact.

"It was just extraordinary to everybody in the room," Townsend
says. "With as much as the president manages and hears and gets
facts and information on, he remembers detail like that. He's good
with names, he's good with facts, and oftentimes, I think people would
be surprised when he is being briefed on something, he will ask operational questions: Are agencies doing particular things to follow
up? And so he takes his responsibilities in the terrorism area very
personally."

In the days before the British took down the terrorist plot to blow up airliners over the Atlantic, Bush was following the developments while on vacation at his ranch in Crawford.

"The challenge there was you didn't want to let it go too far," Townsend says. "You can imagine that if something had gone wrong, there's no question that people would have second-guessed the decisions that were being made."

After the arrests, some in the media criticized Bush for being at the ranch on vacation.

"I will tell you that, even if no one else had talked to him but me, we occupied a good amount of his time on this U.K. plot by video conference," Townsend says. "He was very, very involved in terms of knowing what the details were, knowing what the progress was, what actions we were taking. He was talking to Prime Minister Blair. So this was very much a partnership with our British colleagues to disrupt the plot."

The plot was "intended by our enemies to be a second 9/11," she says. "It was going to be multiple, simultaneous attacks aimed at killing thousands. It's just chilling to me that, five years later, their determination to kill us is undiminished."

Bush's efforts to enlist the cooperation of countries like Saudi Arabia and Pakistan have paid off.

"Prior to 9/11, it would have been unthinkable to most people that you could make an ally out of Pakistan and Saudi Arabia," Townsend says. "They have become actually critical players in the fight. They have enabled us to be successful in terms of gathering intelligence on real threats. We never would have had that intelligence absent their cooperation."

As Bush's counterterrorism chief, the five-foot-tall former organized-crime prosecutor meets with the president every morning. Townsend is known to utter expletives when she encounters foot dragging and will cut people off in midsentence if she thinks they are not giving her the straight scoop.

At the same time, says an FBI counterterrorism official, "She understands our business and is completely supportive of the intelligence community."

The daughter of a Greek American father who was a roofer, and an Irish American mother who was an office manager for a construction company, Townsend was raised in Wantagh, Long Island.

At age eleven, Townsend wrote letters to her priest, bishop, cardinal, and finally the Vatican asking to be an altar boy. Turned down, she tried to sneak into Mass in a borrowed robe, before her priest caught her.

Townsend was the first in her family to finish high school. Because money was tight, she took an accelerated course load in college and worked as a waitress. She graduated cum laude from American University in 1982 and received a law degree from the University of San Diego School of Law in 1984.

A frightening incident at her college dorm room, where she was physically threatened by a man who was let off with little more than a warning, led to her interest in becoming a prosecutor.

After law school, she prosecuted Gambino crime-family members for the U.S. Attorney's office in New York City under Rudolph Giuliani. She went on to take a high-level position at the Justice Department.

As someone who was involved in the U.S. Attorney's office in Manhattan and at the Justice Department in the investigation of the East Africa embassy bombings, the USS *Cole*, and the 1993 bombing of the World Trade Center, Townsend has seen changes that she calls remarkable.

"The most important thing has been an overall strengthening of the intelligence community," she says. "It's intelligence reform, it's greater resources in human intelligence, it's the transformation of the FBI, it's the Patriot Act, and the technical tools like the NSA terrorism surveillance program and the financial program. The sum of these changes is greater than the parts."

Now, the United States is on the offense.

"It's so much more effective than waiting until something blows up and then coming in afterwards to try and piece together, from what you find, what happened historically," she says. "Almost every single one of our major disruptions has resulted from some under-standing or lead information, intelligence that we got from some-body inside the organization. It's really classic, going back, getting somebody who can basically explain to you what's going on behind enemy lines. And in that regard, this war isn't different from sort of traditional wars. It's a different kind of fight, but in that regard, that concept of getting into the enemy's mind and understanding their ob-jectives is the same."

Though Bush goes over constant threats that come in every day, Townsend says she has never seen him get ruffled. Nor does he waver in the face of criticism of his often controversial decisions.

"The president, not just by his words but by his actions and his decisions, has made perfectly clear that first and foremost in his mind is personal commitment to protecting the American people—even if it results in criticism of him personally, that doesn't get factored in as far as he's concerned," she says. "He is of single mind and single focus about preventing the next attack and never letting that happen again."

As Bush's approval ratings started to plunge over the Iraq war, the media depicted the White House as distraught and distracted. But they never got what Bush is all about. In many ways, Bush is an anti-politician. Like Harry Truman, he has an aversion to the acting and pretense of politics.

"He dislikes snobs, hypocrites, the glitterati, and the so-called intelligentsia," says Collister "Terry" Johnson, Jr., one of his room-mates at Yale. "He dislikes all that stuff because he thinks it's phony."

Bush's aversion to pretense means he refuses to schmooze with members of Congress or even conservative supporters for the sake of advancing his agenda. Somewhat naively, he assumes members of Con-gress will do the right thing for their country regardless of whether he bonds with them over dinner at the White House or smokes cigars with them on the Truman Balcony.

Bush is no hermit. He maintains a wide circle of close friends going back to high school and college days. He is loyal to them and invites them to dinner at the White House and to Camp David. But he draws a clear line between those friends and the rest of Washington. He considers socializing in order to gain support to be artificial and a waste of time. If there is anything he hates, it is pretense.

Bush the CEO views the press the same way. While there has been improvement of late, the White House attitude toward the press has been, "When we need you, we'll call you." In part, that is because, as a good CEO, Bush hates leaks. He thinks reporters should concentrate on what he says at press conferences and speeches. Thus, even friendly reporters are not given access and may not get their phone calls returned. Dissed, reporters take out their frustration on those who make their jobs tough. On the other hand, if they were being fed inside tidbits as innocuous as what kind of TV Bush plans to watch the Super Bowl on, even unfriendly reporters would find it harder to write slanted stories.

Lately, Bush has invited members of Congress to the residence for drinks, but that is too little, too late. Previous presidents have wooed legislators with invitations to Camp David. Bush will have none of that.

"My perception is a lot of those people want to say, 'I was at the White House this morning,'" one top aide to Bush told me. "They get to trade on that and have cachet. We're not here to puff up the reputations of people who want to trade on their access."

Because of that attitude, the personal relationships that are necessary to succeed in any job often are missing, and the media are more hostile to Bush than they otherwise would be. Yet Bush will one day be recognized for transforming the way the war on terror is fought and making the country safer.

Like Warren Buffett, Bush keeps his eyes on the horizon. Buffett invests in companies he believes have long-term growth potential and holds on to those stocks regardless of short-term price fluctuations, negative media coverage, and downgrades by stock analysts. Today, Buffett is the second richest American, with $52 billion in assets.

Nor is Bush particularly interested in his place in history. Like any CEO, he simply wants results, and he views challenges as opportunities. But he is also aware of how transitory opinion polls can be. When Harry Truman left office, his approval rating stood at 25 percent. Yet today, because of his firm approach to national security, Truman—whom the press portrayed as a simpleton—is viewed as one of the great presidents.

Similarly, the media portray Bush as a buffoon, a religious fanatic, or a monster with the temerity to topple a man who had killed 300,000 people, not to mention the fact that Bush liberated fifty million people.

In similar fashion, Democratic papers and critics disparaged Abraham Lincoln as a "dictator, ridiculed him as a baboon, damned him as stupid and incompetent," according to Stephen B. Oates's book *With Malice Toward None*.

The media portrayed Ronald Reagan as a bellicose fool. When Reagan appealed to Soviet leader Mikhail Gorbachev to "tear down this wall," the media went ballistic. Yet Reagan's policy of dramatically increasing defense spending eventually convinced the Soviets essentially to give up.

Ultimately, the distortions in the media rub off on voters. But despite the criticism, these leaders stayed the course. They understood, as country music singer Toby Keith sang in "American Soldier," that "freedom don't come free."

Thus, when it comes to national security, Bush is not about to stop listening to calls between al Qaeda and U.S. operatives as they order the next 9/11 attack. He is not about to cave on the USA Patriot Act, which, among other things, allowed FBI agents on the same case to talk to each other and allowed the CIA to pass along intelligence to the FBI. Bush is not about to cut and run in Iraq, confirming Osama bin Laden's portrayal of the United States as a "paper tiger" and inviting more attacks.

Given the fact that Iraqi generals thought before the U.S. invasion that they had chemical weapons that they were supposed to use, it would have been impossible for anyone to have reliably found out otherwise. After the war, the Defense Department debriefed Iraqi military officers and presented the findings to the CIA.

"They came up and did a briefing for George Tenet and a number of us," says Robert Grenier, who was then the CIA's mission manager for Iraq. "And one of the findings was that basically nobody whom you might have expected to be in a position to know one way or another whether there was WMD really knew. They were all convinced that there were WMD, particularly chemical munitions. Each of them of course knew that he didn't know where they were. But they all assumed that others did, and that they were supposed to use them."

To be sure, the postinvasion planning was abysmal. In a paper published a month before the invasion, two Army War College professors, Dr. W. Andrew Terrill and Dr. Conrad C. Crane, laid out in remarkable detail every problem that has since arisen in Iraq and outlined exactly what postinvasion planning was needed to avert the current difficulties. In the months before the invasion, they communicated their concerns to Pentagon leaders. They were ignored.

It's also true that the war in Iraq has given jihadists a perfect propaganda and recruiting tool. On the other hand, when bin Laden unleashed the attacks on American embassies in Africa and on the World Trade Center, the United States had not invaded Iraq.

As for the proposition that going after terrorists and perceived threats creates more terrorists, the CIA's Michael Morell says, "I don't know how you don't take them on, when they want to kill you."

Regardless of the merits of going into Iraq, the fact is that a quick withdrawal could lead to devastating casualties within the United States from al Qaeda attacks, Fran Townsend, the White House's chief of counterterrorism, says.

"I think there is an attraction and a very sincere commitment by everybody, Republicans or Democrats, to bringing the boys and girls home," Townsend says. "Nobody wants our men and women in the military to be there one day longer than they need to be."

But, she adds, "What you don't hear is the same people talk about the consequences of bringing them home. The consequences could very well be dead Americans inside the United States if Iraq becomes a safe haven. I've never heard a good explanation of, Okay, if your plan is you want to bring the men and women in our military home, what is your plan to deny them safe haven in Iraq? Frankly, that's the right next question, and I haven't heard a good answer to that."

When Bush says that Iraq is the "central front" in the war on terrorism, he means that Iraq harbors the greatest number of al Qaeda fighters, Townsend says. Confirming Bush's point, Ayman al-Zawahiri, al Qaeda's ideological leader, has called Iraq "the place for the greatest battle of Islam in this era."

Intercepted communications show that al Qaeda central considers al Qaeda in Iraq to be a subsidiary of the terrorist organization. And while he is isolated, Osama bin Laden communicates orders through couriers, Townsend says.

If the United States pulls out before Iraqi forces can take over, al Qaeda will use Iraq as a safe haven to train, plot, recruit, and generate propaganda.

"Al Qaeda's vision is to establish a caliphate," Townsend observes. "Nobody should make any mistake: These smaller groups, these affiliates, are not separate entities with a separate agenda. There is a strategic—if you will, corporate—vision of al Qaeda, and they are all pieces in that puzzle."

In an example of the shortsightedness of some, Democratic presidential candidate John Edwards claimed, in a major foreign policy speech, that the war on terror is not a strategy to make America safer. Rather, it's a political slogan or "bumper sticker" used by the Bush administration to cover up its mistakes.

"It has damaged our alliances and weakened our standing in the world," Edwards said. "The 'war' metaphor has also failed because it exaggerates the role of only one instrument of American power—the military. . . . [W]e must move beyond the idea of a war on terror."

"Remember that old Edmund Burke quote," Republican candidate Mitt Romney responded. " 'The only thing necessary for the triumph of evil is for good men to do nothing.' And that, I am afraid, is the boiled-down version of what John Edwards said—that good men should do nothing. Put their head in the sand and hope it all goes away."

"When you go so far as to suggest that the global war on terror is a bumper sticker or slogan," Rudy Giuliani said, "it kind of makes the point that I've been making over and over again that the Democrats or at least some of them are in denial."

Nothing could demonstrate that more than votes in August 2007 by presidential candidates Hillary Clinton and Barack Obama—as well as by House Speaker Nancy Pelosi and Senate Majority Leader Harry Reid—against updating FISA. Going back to the founding of NSA in 1952, the agency could intercept the communications of people outside the United States without obtaining a warrant, because overseas communications were usually intercepted abroad through the atmosphere.

Now, because of technological advances, 90 percent of communications between countries are routed through switches within the United States over fiber-optic lines. Because the phone calls, e-mails, and faxes pass through hard wires in the United States and thus require physical interception, FISA court judges in early 2007 began challenging the interceptions. They said that even though the calls are between foreign countries, FISA requires a warrant before the communications can be monitored. That brought the system to a standstill: The FBI and CIA could not obtain the content of calls that might have been critically important to stopping a terrorist plot.

The fix that Clinton, Obama, Pelosi, and Reid opposed was

meant to return the situation to the status quo, so that calls between foreign countries could be intercepted without a warrant, as Congress intended when it passed FISA.

Civil liberties should not have been an issue. Because the targets are on foreign soil, they are not subject to the probable cause and warrant requirements of the Fourth Amendment. Under the revision, if the surveillance of an overseas call targets a person who is in the United States, a warrant still must be obtained. And incorporating President Bush's original NSA intercept program, the revision provides that the FISA court retroactively review intercepts of calls between an overseas al Qaeda operative and an American on U.S. soil. What was at issue was the two presidential candidates' effort to appeal to the left and their disregard for the safety of Americans. Indeed, at the annual left-wing Kos Convention, Clinton drew praise and applause for her vote.

Fortunately, Republicans and a minority of moderate Democrats passed the new legislation, although it would have to be renewed in six months. Had Clinton and Obama prevailed, if Osama bin Laden placed a call to an al Qaeda member in London to arrange a nuclear hit on Manhattan, a warrant would first have to be obtained. By the time that happened, the call would have been over. Even using FISA's emergency provision, it takes at least two days to prepare the paperwork and obtain all the necessary approvals. Because a call was not intercepted in time, millions of Americans could have been killed.

Contrary to John Edwards's take, the lesson of the 1990s, when terrorists first attacked the World Trade Center and attacked American embassies in Africa and the USS *Cole,* is, "We just didn't take it seriously enough," Senator Joe Lieberman, also a Democrat, tells me.

Asked how he feels about Democrats' attacks on measures like the Patriot Act and programs like the NSA intercepts to help track and apprehend terrorists, Lieberman says he is "disappointed" because "my colleagues for various reasons—some ideological, some political—are missing this threat to us."

The first responsibility of government, Lieberman says, is to "provide for the security of the country, the common defense. This is our constitutional responsibility. And without it we enjoy none of the other blessings of liberty that the country provides and that all of us, including most Democrats, want to help deliver."

While much derided by the left, the war on terror has worked so well that Americans have become complacent. Because of Bush's policies, the FBI and CIA, often with the help of foreign partners, have rolled up some five thousand terrorists since 9/11. That success story, in turn, is the reason the country has not been attacked since 9/11. But you will never see the headline 5,000 TERRORISTS ROLLED UP SINCE 9/11 in the *New York Times* or the *Washington Post*.

Instead, the media, with the help of politicians, continue to hammer the intelligence community, pretending that little has changed since September 2001 and insisting that the FBI and CIA don't talk to each other. Instead of hailing the efforts to connect the dots, the media portray them as sinister invasions of privacy. When a plot is successfully rolled up, the media minimize it.

With no independent source of information, Americans are at the mercy of the media's slant. In a poll, 66 percent of Americans said they thought the FBI and other federal agencies are intruding on privacy rights during terrorism investigations, although a solid majority thought investigating threats is more important than protecting those rights.

The negative spin is echoed by politicians who often know better. In talking with FBI or CIA officials, they privately acknowledge the progress. But in front of TV cameras, they excoriate the agencies for imagined failings. Thus, the former 9/11 Commission gave the government mediocre to failing grades for improving since the attacks. The group said there has been little progress in forcing federal agencies to share intelligence and terrorism information. In private, many of those same commission members praise the efforts that have been made since 9/11.

Meanwhile, the media ignore the real story. In the fifteenth paragraph of a December 6, 2005, *Washington Post* story reporting on the former 9/11 Commission's "report card," the paper said the White House had distributed a lengthy list of changes since 9/11. Anyone who looked at that list would have to wonder what the 9/11 Commission members were talking about when they claimed little progress had been made. But the *Washington Post* story listed none of the changes cited by the White House.

Similarly, the story in the *New York Times* quoted White House press secretary Scott McLellan as saying, "We have taken significant steps to better protect the American people at home." Again, the story cited none of the changes.

When the FBI, with the help of the Joint Terrorism Task Force in New York, foiled a plot to blow up fuel tanks, terminal buildings, and the web of fuel lines running beneath John F. Kennedy International Airport in June 2007, the *New York Times* buried the story on page A37 of its final edition. Four men, including a former airport employee and a former member of the Parliament of Guyana, were charged in the plot. The men had violent fundamentalist beliefs but were not tied to al Qaeda.

"Anytime you hit Kennedy, it is the most hurtful thing to the United States," said Russell Defreitas, a Brooklyn resident who was born in Guyana and formerly was a cargo handler at the airport, in one of dozens of conversations secretly recorded during the eighteen-month investigation.

"They love John F. Kennedy," he said. "If you hit that, this whole country will be in mourning. It's like you kill the man twice."

Defreitas boasted that the explosions "can destroy the economy of America for some time."

While the plotters put a great deal of time and travel into their plan, they never managed to obtain any explosives before authorities arrested them and foiled the JFK scheme. The plot could have resulted in damage and fires but not on the scale that the defendants had envisioned.

Yet the fact that the FBI stopped the plotters before they killed innocent people not only merited burying the story inside the paper, it was the inspiration for a second *New York Times* story the following day pooh-poohing the plot. Six days after the first story ran, the paper played a story about Paris Hilton going back to jail on page one.

In the dream world of the editors of the *New York Times*, such threats to America are far less important than the fact that seventy-five-year-old Andrea Mosconi has a job playing violins in a museum in Italy to keep them in shape, a feature played on page one on the same day the editors of the *Times* buried the JFK plot inside the paper.

While the media minimize the threats and mischaracterize the progress in the war on terror, they undermine it by revealing secrets of how the FBI and CIA are trying to stop the next attack.

Al Qaeda in Pakistan has a counterintelligence arm that specifically looks for leaks in the American media so the organization can adjust its tactics and ways of communicating, a CIA official says. Because of leaks, local CIA agents recruited by American CIA officers have been compromised and killed, the official says.

"The leaks have led to some of our sources [agents] being arrested in some places and being executed, because information that gets published in the media can be traced back to a specific individual who then is compromised."

Leaks also lead foreign intelligence services to hold back from sharing information.

"That is one of the big implications of stuff showing up in the media," the CIA official explains, "because when they get us this stuff, they do it on the expectation that we can protect it. And when they see their stuff showing up in the papers, in the media, they have a natural inclination to hold back."

"It never fails, when we see an unauthorized disclosure, that we suffer from it," Fran Townsend says. "You know people often say the terrorists assume we're tracking them. But it's different when you have government sources coming out and either confirming it or you have the details of it and how we do it published. We find that after these disclosures, the enemy shifts their tactics around based on what they learn we are doing."

Calling the leaks "devastating," Townsend says, "It's not just a question of [whether] you're putting individuals at risk. The real risk is to the lives of Americans who may suffer an attack because we couldn't stop it, because the source was taken out. When a technical program is compromised, literally hundreds of millions of dollars are lost because a technique that's been invested in over many years is no longer productive."

The disclosures impair the morale of FBI and CIA personnel who are trying to protect the country from another attack.

"My responsibility is to help the president make good decisions to protect the American people," Townsend says. "The leaks make my job that much harder, and they make me not only frustrated but angry, because leaking classified material when no abuse is involved puts us all at risk."

"I would say that they follow our media as closely as we follow their media," says J. D. Crouch, the deputy national security advisor. "We have seen them adapt to things that were revealed, in terms of their own operational security, in terms of their own communications."

"Even though al Qaeda is diabolical, they're smart, and they're students who watch us and listen to try to understand our capabilities," says FBI agent James Bernazzani Jr.

After 9/11, Bernazzani worked with Art Cummings in SIOC to ferret out a possible second wave of attacks. He went on become deputy director of the CIA's Counterterrorism Center.

"Communication is huge, and once we understand how they communicate, we can put ourselves in a position to understand what they're trying to do," he says. "But once terrorists understand our capabilities, they're going to launch an offensive to defeat it. When you get the *New York Times* running stories about finite techniques, they are handicapping our ability to stop these guys. It never ceases to amaze me some of the things that come out that play right into the hands of the bad guys. And they're licking their chops."

When people ask Bernazzani, "Who's our greatest enemy?" his answer is, "It's not any terrorist group. It's us. We as a society have a very short attention span. And with the success of the FBI and the U.S. forces and the intelligence community in preventing any attack in this country, there's a tendency to feel that the threat is back overseas, and the threat here has abated. And it has not. Our greatest enemy is our own societal apathy. When we begin to forget, we're going to get bit in the ass again."

Indeed, another attack could occur at any time.

"Despite the successful disruption that we've done, the organization remains capable of attacking us, because they're constantly evolving, and they're constantly trying to get back on track," says Michael Morell, the CIA's associate deputy director. "And their command and control to some extent remains in place, and their ambition in no way has been diminished. They want nothing more than to have a success here in the homeland. The U.K. plotting is another example of that. So their capabilities, although diminished, remain."

Al Qaeda has established a safe haven in the ungoverned spaces of Pakistan, making it stronger than a year or two ago but still weaker than just before the 9/11 attacks—a point the *Washington Post* buried in the eighteenth paragraph of a story about an NCTC threat assessment. Yet comparing this country's ability to uncover and thwart attacks since 9/11 is like comparing the original IBM personal computer with today's latest desktop. Underscoring that point, a National Intelligence Estimate released in July 2007 said terrorist groups "perceive the homeland as a harder target to strike than on 9/11."

While the *New York Times* ran that finding as part of the text of the NIE, the paper ignored the point in its story about the resurgence of al Qaeda in Pakistan. Only three other newspapers—the *Virginian-Pilot,* the *Mobile Register,* and the *Cincinnati Post*—referred to the finding. And no television networks mentioned it at all.

For all the successes, counterterrorism operatives marvel at the fact that the United States has gone so long without a successful attack. Sometimes, luck plays a part in thwarting a plot, as when an ambulance crew responding to an emergency noticed smoke from a parked Mercedes at 1:30 A.M. on June 29 in central London's crowded theater district. Authorities were able to defuse bombs fashioned from gasoline, gas cylinders, and nails hidden inside the Mercedes. After news of the first bomb filled the airwaves, workers at an underground garage in Hyde Park notified police that another Mercedes reeked of gasoline. The car had been towed to the garage after British police ticketed it.

"We get to be lucky every once in a while," says Art Cummings.

Beyond killing or capturing terrorists, the United States needs to focus on ways to diminish recruitment of terrorists.

"People become terrorists for all sorts of reasons," says a senior CIA official. "Because you're a true believer. Because you're unemployed and have nothing else to do. Because your friends are into it, and you get drawn into it, not because you particularly believe, but because they're your friends."

Typically, "you have a young Muslim male who is alienated. He could be alienated in the sense of feeling that Muslims don't get a fair shake in the world. Or, in his particular county, he can't get a job or doesn't fit in socially."

Terrorists buy into certain beliefs: that the West is trying to undermine Islam everywhere, and so it is the responsibility of Muslims everywhere to attack the West. And a belief in a utopian idea of a single caliphate, a single Islamic ruler running the Muslim world.

One way to attack these beliefs is by "demonstrating the contradictions that exist in their arguments and by getting the message out in the media," the official observes. For example, he says, al Qaeda attacks actually kill more Muslims than non-Muslims.

"Their argument is they're protecting Islam, yet they're killing more Muslims than anybody else."

In fact, most jihadists have "a very poor understanding of Islam," the official notes. "In other words, the recruiters are taking advantage of their lack of knowledge of Islam by making arguments about what their religion says they should be doing that aren't true. And so helping to educate folks about the reality of Islam, which is a peaceful religion, is very important, and getting Islamic countries to help us do that is very important."

The final way to impinge on recruitment is to try to attack the sense of alienation. This can be done by offering economic opportunities and social opportunities and by trying to get a message out that "you can change the world, you can change your circumstances, with non-violent approaches," the official says.

"You have to get at what makes a terrorist," says J. D. Crouch, deputy national security advisor. "You've got to attack the full spectrum, going after their recruitment, going after their training, going after their financing, going after their supplies, going after the ideological source of all this. All those are links in a chain."

That means, for example, supporting moderate groups and encouraging moderate governments in the Middle East to support religious figures who are inclined to denounce taking innocent lives, he says.

Humanitarian aid has an effect as well.

"In a part of the world where we're not particularly popular, taking the actions we took to help earthquake victims in Pakistan really had an impact on the Muslim population," Crouch says. "U.S. helicopters are now a symbol of good in the world there."

"The war in part is about winning hearts and minds," the CIA's Michael Morell says. "The war is about stopping the production of terrorists. And that's how you ultimately win this war, and that takes a whole government. We're headed in the right direction on that, I think. But that is not going to be easy."

Vice Admiral Redd, NCTC director, says, "My grandchildren, I hope, will be around when the war on terror is finally over with.

There'll be a lot of battles out there. It's a long war, and we may well lose a battle or two. It's just strict laws of probability that something's going to happen at some point. But by and large, we are better prepared than we've ever been."

"Our success in this war is often measured by the things that did not happen," Bush said in his 2007 State of the Union address. "We cannot know the full extent of the attacks that we and our allies have prevented, but here is some of what we do know: We stopped an al Qaeda plot to fly a hijacked airplane into the tallest building on the West Coast. We broke up a Southeast Asian terror cell grooming operatives for attacks inside the United States. We uncovered an al Qaeda cell developing anthrax to be used in attacks against America."

For each life saved, he said, "We owe a debt of gratitude to the brave public servants who devote their lives to finding the terrorists and stopping them."

That line got a standing ovation. But it was theatrics. Many of those same members of Congress, along with members of the media, have made careers for themselves by belittling and undercutting the efforts of the men and women who are trying to protect us.

Instead of being grateful to them, politicians like John Edwards dismiss their efforts as a political gimmick, and papers like the *New York Times* bury their successes on page A37.

In their quest to undermine the war on terror, the media have used the propaganda and censorship techniques of the old Soviet Union to misinform the public. Without winning the war being waged by the media against our own government, we are going to lose the war on terror because the tools that are needed will be taken away by a Congress swayed by a misinformed public and by other countries unwilling to cooperate with the CIA or FBI because they fear mindless exposure by the press.

"The leaks have gratuitously harmed our ability to prosecute the war on terror," says Robert Grenier, the former chief of the CIA's Counterterrorism Center.

While legitimate criticism should be welcome, the critics appear to think that the enemy is our own government, not Islamic murderers. With so many people—especially those in the media—saying America is on the wrong course and the government cannot be trusted, one wonders why Americans are so gloomy. Did too many of us watch too much television when we were very young, altering the brain's structure and causing a short attention span? How about not enough fat in our diets, reducing serotonin levels? Or did some Americans smoke too much marijuana, causing depression?

All or none of the above may be the culprit, but one thing is certain: Americans are spoiled.

Craig R. Smith, a conservative columnist, makes the case by asking what Americans are so unhappy about. Is it that we have electricity and running water twenty-four hours a day? Could it be because more than 95 percent of us have a job? That we have freedom of speech, press, and religion enjoyed by few other countries in the world? Or that we see more food in any supermarket than Darfur has seen in a year?

"Fact is, we are the largest group of ungrateful, spoiled brats the world has ever seen," writes Smith. "No wonder the world loves the U.S. yet has a great disdain for its citizens. They see us for what we are—the most blessed people in the world who do nothing but complain about what we don't have and what we hate about the country instead of thanking the good Lord we live here."

What the critics do not appreciate is that America is in a war for its survival. As KSM made clear in his confession, bin Laden and his followers declared "war" on the United States in his fatwa of 1998.

KSM professed no regret for the deaths. He called such indiscriminate killing "the language of any war" that was justified by his religious design. Proudly taking credit for decapitating *Wall Street Journal* reporter Danny Pearl, KSM said, "For those who would like to confirm, there are pictures of me on the Internet holding his head."

In his broken English, KSM said: "For sure, I'm American enemies."

Too many Americans have forgotten that fact. Too many are intent on demonizing those who are trying to protect us. Too many are in a state of denial about the horrific deaths that we face if we underestimate the threat of radical Islam. Too many fail to recognize that al Qaeda's long-term goal is to send the United States the way of the Roman Empire. And too many in the press are willing to take the chance of compromising the lives of innocent Americans by running stories that gratuitously disclose operational secrets.

Those who are fighting the silent battle against terrorism have produced an American success story. They are unsung heroes who have indeed made us safer. But only if Americans recognize that fact and pull together will we win this war for the country's survival.

ACKNOWLEDGMENTS

I AM LUCKY to have my wife, Pamela Kessler, as my partner both in life and in writing. A former *Washington Post* reporter who wrote *Undercover Washington*, about Washington's spy sites, she accompanied me on key interviews and contributed vivid descriptions to the book. She also pre-edited the manuscript. I benefitted throughout from her good judgment.

My grown children, Greg and Rachel Kessler, round out the picture with their love and support. My stepson Mike Whitehead is a loyal and endearing part of that team.

This book arose from a discussion with Jed Donahue, executive editor of Crown Forum. I am grateful for Jed's enthusiasm and brilliant guidance.

Since 1991, my agent, Robert Gottlieb, chairman of Trident Media, has guided my book writing career and has been a source of unswerving support. I am fortunate to have him on my side.

At times, I used material gleaned from interviews for NewsMax. com, where I am chief Washington correspondent. Chris Ruddy, editor in chief and CEO of NewsMax Media, has my appreciation and admiration for his dedication to the truth.

From the start, John Miller, assistant director for public affairs at the FBI, was a strong supporter of this book. He went out of his way to provide an unprecedented look at the war on terror.

Those who were interviewed or helped in other ways include:

James Bernazzani Jr., Joseph Billy Jr., Brad Blakeman, Robert M. Blitzer, Lane Bonner, W. Allen Bostdorff, John O. Brennan, Kevin R. Brock, Dave Burpee, William D. Carter, Cassandra M. Chandler, J. D. Crouch, Arthur M. "Art" Cummings, Pasquale J. D'Amuro,

Thomas V. Fuentes, Robert L. Grenier, Bill Harlow, General Michael V. Hayden, Michael Heimbach, Leslie Pessagno Jewell, Weldon L. Kennedy, Chad Kolton, Mike Kortan, John L. Martin, Barry Mawn, Ken Maxwell, T. McCreary, Susan T. McKee, John Miller, Michael Morell, Philip Mudd, Robert S. Mueller III, George L Piro, Ernest J. Porter, S. Eugene Poteat, Vice Admiral John Scott Redd, Oliver B. "Buck" Revell, Mark T. Rossini, Stephen Solomon, George Tenet, Rex Tomb, Fran Fragos Townsend, Russell E. Travers, Dale L. Watson, and Debra Weierman.

INDEX